grow fruit

US Consultants Lori Spencer, Fern Marshall Bradley
Project Editor Anna Kruger
Project Art Editor Alison Gardner
Senior Editor Helen Fewster
US Editor Kate Johnsen
US Senior Editor Shannon Beatty
Managing Editor Esther Ripley
Managing Art Editor Alison Donovan
Associate Publisher Liz Wheeler
Production Editor Joanna Byrne
Production Controller Sophie Argyris
Picture Researcher Ria Jones
Jacket Designer Mark Cavanagh
Publisher Jonathan Metcalf
Art Director Bryn Walls

**Special photography at West Dean Gardens,
West Sussex**

First American Edition, 2010
This edition published in the United States in 2016 by
DK Publishing, 345 Hudson Street, New York, New York 10014

Copyright © 2010, 2016 Dorling Kindersley Limited
DK, a Division of Penguin Random House LLC

Text copyright © 2010, 2016 Alan Buckingham

16 17 18 19 10 9 8 7 6 5 4 3 2 1

002–288668–Feb/2016

A catalog record for this book is available from the Library of
Congress.
ISBN 978-1-4654-4485-1

DK books are available at special discounts when purchased in bulk
for sales promotions, premiums, fund-raising, or educational use.
For details, contact: DK Publishing Special
Markets, 345 Hudson Street, New York, New York 10014
SpecialSales@dk.com

Printed and bound in China

A WORLD OF IDEAS:
SEE ALL THERE IS TO KNOW

www.dk.com

grow fruit

ALAN BUCKINGHAM

Specialist consultant FERN MARSHALL BRADLEY

CONTENTS

Why grow your own?

There are many, many reasons why it's worth growing your own fruit. Freshness, flavor, good health, and choice are all part of the equation, but so too are concerns about the industrialization of commercial food production and the feeling that we want to know more about where our food comes from, how it is grown, and what is done to it before it reaches us. That, and the fact that many are rediscovering a very simple truth: it is not only delicious but also extraordinarily satisfying to eat food we have grown ourselves.

Perfectly ripe, perfectly fresh

All fruit reaches a peak of perfection, a moment when it is perfectly ripe. Usually—though not always—it is still on the tree, bush, or vine and the trick is to harvest it and enjoy it as close to that moment as possible. If you grow your own, you'll have a good chance of anticipating and then tasting this perfect ripeness. If you buy fruit from the grocery store, you'll certainly miss out. Commercially grown fruit is almost always picked before it is ripe so that it can be transported without damage, and it may then be stored in climate-controlled warehouses to halt the ripening process. The idea is that the fruit ripens either when it reaches the supermarket shelf or when you get it home. In any case, it never tastes as good as fruit that is left on the plant to ripen naturally.

Seasonal and local

Blueberries in February. Melons at Christmas. Apples and pears in May. How does that work? The answer is obvious: these are fruits grown on the other side of the world that have traveled thousands of miles before they reach us. But at what cost to quality and flavor? And what about their carbon footprint? We're so accustomed to everything we want being available all year that we've lost touch with how much better fruit tastes if it is grown locally and eaten in season.

A perfectly ripe peach: meltingly soft, sweet, aromatic, and juicy, picked and eaten straight from the tree. Can you imagine a better reason for growing your own?

Choice and variety

An aisle of well-stocked supermarket shelves may give the impression of choice, but what you are looking at is a mere drop in the ocean compared to the real choice you have if you decide to grow your own. Even modest garden centers and plant nurseries offer a surprising range of fruit varieties, and a specialty supplier may have literally hundreds. Some will be modern cultivars, bred for particular attributes such as size, color, flavor, or resistance to various pests and diseases. Others are likely to be heirloom varieties, often unusual, and sometimes rediscovered after being forgotten for decades or more. You'll also find unusual fruits that you will probably never see at the grocery store because they are simply impossible and too expensive to transport—mulberries, for example.

The organic option

Using chemicals in the garden is a sensitive issue, because most of us would rather eat food that is as natural and unadulterated as possible. Fruit is prone to numerous pests and diseases, however, and sometimes action is called for to save a crop. Keep in mind that a few blemishes on fruit usually don't affect overall flavor and quality, and that more and more organic options for pest and disease control are becoming available for home gardeners. Whatever methods and products you decide to use, always follow safety precautions and read and follow label instructions.

(below, left to right) **Spring blossoms** can be so spectacular that they're almost reason enough to plant fruit trees. Apple blossoms are irresistible to bees and other pollinating insects. **Clusters of young grapes** begin to form in May or June once flowering is over. Then, slowly, over the course of the next few months, they swell and the bunches become denser. (opposite) **Picking cherries** and eating them straight from the tree, sun-warmed and ripe, is one of the high points of summer.

The Fruit Gardener

How difficult is it to grow your own fruit? How much know-how do you really need? How much time and effort are involved? These are difficult questions to answer, because it all depends on where you live, what sort of yard you have, and what fruit you want to grow. Some fruits are certainly easier than others. Gardeners in almost any part of the U.S. and Canada can grow strawberries. Apples and pears grow well everywhere except regions where winters are too warm to meet their need for a cold dormant period. On the flip side, only gardeners in Florida and a few other warm-winter areas can grow citrus in the ground; elsewhere, citrus is a container crop. Peaches, apricots, and melons do best in areas with long, warm summers.

The bottom line is that none of the fruits in this book are hard to grow, but you are likely to have much more success if you read up on what they like, choose the right varieties for the growing conditions you can offer, look after them attentively, and gently coax them into producing a good crop of fruit.

Picking developing fruitlets in early summer and throwing them away may seem wasteful, but thinning is vital. The remaining apples will grow larger and tastier if the tree is not overburdened.

What fruit can I grow?

To answer this question meaningfully, you need to start with your climate. That, of course, will depend on where you live. At what latitude? At what altitude? Is your yard exposed or sheltered, inland or near a large body of water, north- or south-facing? These elements all help to determine the climatic conditions in which your plants grow. The composition of your soil is important, too. So are fertilizing, mulching, watering, training, pruning, and so on. But the climate—or, to be specific, the microclimate—is almost certainly the most important factor.

Regional differences

Climate in the United States and Canada varies from semi-tropical to alpine. But those are the extremes, and in most areas, a wide range of fruit will grow well if you choose the right types and varieties. Tree fruits that are native to cool climates, such as apples, pears, plums, and cherries, along with soft fruits such as raspberries, blackberries, gooseberries, and currants, can be grown in most regions. They are all likely to flower earlier, and fruit will ripen and be ready to pick sooner, in the warm South than in the cool North. Fruits whose natural habitat is a warm temperate or Mediterranean climate, such as peaches, nectarines, apricots, citrus fruit, melons, and grapes, will thrive best in the South and along the West Coast. But with the right choice of variety, microclimate, and growing method, home gardeners in the Midwest, New England, and parts of southern Canada can also succeed with peaches, melons, and grapes.

Fruit varieties and cultivars

A quick look at the catalog of a specialty plant nursery—or, indeed, at a few of the pages that follow in this book—will give you an immediate idea of just how many different varieties or cultivars there are of each major type of fruit. There are literally thousands of different apples, and dozens if not hundreds of pears, plums, cherries, grapes, strawberries, melons, and so on. Choosing a variety is not merely about size, shape, color, and flavor. It's also about suitability for your climate. Many of the

Must-grow fruit

1 Strawberries
Difficulty *Easy to grow*
Protect fruit against birds and slugs, and replace plants after two or three years.
■ See p.183.

2 Grapes
Difficulty *Tricky to grow well*
Grapes can be challenging because of pest and disease problems and the need to train and prune them for best production.
■ See p.264.

3 Plums
Difficulty *Easy to grow*
Plums are notorious for having good years and bad years. A lot depends on whether blossoms are fertilized in spring.
■ See p.103.

4 Cherries
Difficulty *Easy to grow*
Nets to protect fruit against birds are an absolute must.
■ See p.121.

5 Quinces
Difficulty *Very easy to grow*
Almost maintenance-free and a good choice if you want to try something unusual.
■ See p.158.

6 Blackberries
Difficulty *Very easy to grow*
Cultivated varieties produce better fruits than wild brambles. Try some of the hybrid bramble fruits, too.
■ See p.209.

7 Blueberries
Difficulty *Easy to grow*
Given the right sort of acidic soil, blueberries are fairly easy to grow.
■ See p.247.

8 Red currants
Difficulty *Very easy to grow*
These cold-hardy shrubs are very productive. Try the slightly sweeter white currants, too.
■ See p.231.

9 Apples
Difficulty *Easy to grow*
Teach yourself how to prune. You'll get better fruit and heavier crops if you do.
■ See p.41.

named cultivars have been bred—and many of the traditional ones are still grown—because they to do well in particular regions. Sometimes there's a clue in the name: 'Empire', 'Roxbury Russet', or 'Wolf River 1881', for example. These are all local apples attuned to their local climates. Even if you are growing fruit that's from farther afield, it's best to choose varieties that share similar requirements. So, if you are attempting to grow wine grapes in New York or Ohio, go for a variety from Germany or northern France, not one from Italy or Spain.

Microclimates

Most gardens contain microclimates. Usually, they're a good thing: a patio that acts as a late-afternoon sun trap, a warm sheltered corner, or a south-facing fence or wall can make all the difference to what you're able to grow. They may offer just the right site for, say, a container-grown fig, a dwarf peach, or a wall-trained apricot, all of which might survive but not produce ripe fruit elsewhere.

Unfortunately, the corollary is true, too. Gardens sometimes have the kind of microclimates that you'd prefer not to have: a low-lying spot at the foot of a slope that acts as a frost pocket, for example, or a patch of soil that's in what's called a "rain shadow," overhung by a nearby wall or fence and therefore prone to drying out even when the rest of the yard is damp.

Growing fruit under cover

You can exploit greenhouses, conservatories, hoophouses, and even cold frames to extend the range of fruit you can grow. They allow you to create microclimates over which you are in complete control. If you live in a mild-winter region, they provide a warm, frost-free environment for sheltering tender, container-grown fruit such as citrus during the worst of the winter months. And a heated greenhouse or hoophouse is really the only means of growing subtropical and tropical fruit.

There is a long tradition, at least in Europe, of growing fruit in large, custom-built greenhouses, so that tender and exotic fruit such as grapes, oranges, peaches, apricots, melons, figs, and even pineapple could be served almost year-round. Orangeries were designed with tall glass doors that opened directly onto wide terraces, so that heavy container-grown citrus trees could be wheeled outside in summer and back inside in winter, where they continued to receive plenty of light from the huge windows. In the 19th-century, greenhouses were heated not just by coal furnaces that fired hot-water systems but also by the warmth that emanated naturally from decomposing farmyard manure, sometimes piled in special "pineapple pits."

10 **Peaches and nectarine**
Difficulty *Moderate*
These stone fruits need a warm, sheltered site and plenty of sun in order to ripen.
■ See p.145.

11 **Citrus fruit**
Difficulty *Moderate*
In cool climates, grow citrus trees in containers and bring them indoors in winter.
■ See p.285.

12 **Gooseberries**
Difficulty *Very easy to grow*
Given the right conditions, and barring attack by mildew, plants are almost indestructible. Pruning and netting are all that's required.
■ See p.219.

13 **Raspberries**
Difficulty *Easy to moderate*
Choosing the right variety for your climate and providing proper support is key to success with raspberries.
■ See p.197.

14 **Figs**
Difficulty *Easy to moderate*
Trees are not hard to grow, but figs need sun and warmth, so the amount of fruit you get may be variable.
■ See p.167.

15 **Apricots**
Difficulty *Easy to moderate*
In cool climates, choose an appropriate variety and grow in a sheltered, sunny spot.
■ See p.137.

16 **Black currants**
Difficulty *Very easy to grow*
These soft fruits are easy to grow as long as you prune them annually to encourage continued growth and production.
■ See p.239.

17 **Pears**
Difficulty *Easy to grow*
Pears are slightly fussier than apples, but easier to prune. The hardest thing is knowing the best moment to harvest them.
■ See p.81.

18 **Melons**
Difficulty *Easy to moderate*
In warm climates, melons are easy to grow. In cool climates, special methods can provide the heat melons need to grow well.
■ See p.295.

Growing fruit in small yards

A small yard should not prevent you from growing your own fruit. Admittedly, if space is limited, you're hardly going to be planting an orchard of full-sized fruit trees. And a large walk-in fruit cage is also likely to be off the agenda. But with a little ingenuity and careful thought about how to make the best use of the space you have, there are plenty of other crops you can grow.

Dwarfing and compact fruit trees

One of the achievements of specialty fruit breeders during the last few decades has been the production of smaller trees. It's something we now take for granted, but not so long ago, cherries and pears, in particular, grew into very large trees. Apples and plums, too. They were hard to prune and care for, and difficult to harvest. Everything had to be done using ladders. It was, therefore, very much in the interests of commercial growers to develop smaller trees that could be planted more closely, fruited more heavily, and were easier to pick. Their success has led to the development of a wide range of modern varieties grown on dwarfing rootstocks to restrict their size (see p.52). Home growers have benefited, too. There's now a good choice of fruit trees ideally suited to the small yard.

Space-saving tree forms

The way you train and prune your fruit trees plays a big part in controlling how large they grow. For a small yard, you may want to experiment with formal training methods such as a short row of vertical or oblique cordons. These take up very little space and allow you to grow several different varieties. Or, you may want to try growing single-stem or columnar apple trees, which grow only about 8 ft (2.5 m) tall. Miniature horizontal stepovers make good edgings for flower borders. And walls and fences can be used to train espaliers and fans against. If they are south-facing, even better; they may allow you to

(clockwise, from top left) **A row of dwarf pear cordons** not only makes a fruitful use of space but will grow into a fashionable designer hedge. **A red currant** grown as a standard frees up planting space at ground level for a short-term crop of salad leaves and onions. **Grape vines** climb naturally over arbors and arches, though they will crop better if pruned regularly. **Apple stepovers** are single cordons bent over horizontally at about knee or waist height. A real space-saver, they are the most compact of all the tree forms. (right) **A hanging basket** for strawberries saves on valuable ground space and should protect the fruit from all but the most athletic of slugs.

grow tender fruit such as peaches, apricots, figs, and citrus, which would struggle in an open, unsheltered spot in the garden.

If you have room to plant only one tree of each sort of fruit, buy a self-fertile variety that will pollinate itself without a partner. A multi-variety tree, which has more than one cultivar grafted onto a single rootstock, is a way of broadening the range of fruit you grow (see p.53). If it's an apple, for example, it may give you both eating apples and cooking apples, some for harvesting early in the season and some for later on.

Growing fruit in containers

All but the largest, most vigorous fruit can be grown in pots. In a few cases, it may even be better to grow them in containers than in the open ground. Figs positively thrive and will produce more fruit and less foliage if their roots are constrained (see p.171). Blueberries will grow only in acidic soil, so if your garden soil is neutral or alkaline, a large pot filled with special acidic potting mix is the perfect solution (see p.252). Tender fruits that won't tolerate frosts become portable when grown in containers: they can be carried or wheeled indoors or under cover in winter and out into a spot in full sun in the summer.

There are a few simple rules to follow if you are growing fruit in containers. In the case of trees, choose dwarfing varieties that won't grow too large. However, don't overdo the size of the pot to start with; it's better to begin with a small or medium one and pot on into incrementally larger ones every couple of years. Use the right soil: usually a mix of all-purpose loam-based potting medium mixed with sand or gravel to ensure that it drains freely. Thereafter, water regularly, much more often in the summer than in the winter, and fertilize as needed.

(left) **Container-grown plants** are the ultimate in mobile fruit gardening. They are perfect for making the best use of a restricted space and, provided they do not become too large and heavy, they can be moved from one microclimate to another. You can give them a sheltered, frost-free corner over winter, then move them out into full sun to ripen their fruit in summer.

Traditional kitchen gardens

Historically, a separate area of the garden was reserved for growing vegetables, fruit, and herbs. It was quite distinct from lawns, flowerbeds, and other ornamental areas. The reasons were largely practical. The first was to provide shelter and to create a warm microclimate by enclosing the whole kitchen garden within walls or tall hedges. The second was to conceal the sheds, storerooms, greenhouses, bins for compost and manure, and other working outbuildings that were deemed better kept out of sight. Fewer people have yards large enough for such a luxury nowadays, but there are still benefits to be gained from dedicating an area to growing your own.

Kitchen garden layouts

Because most fruits are long-lived plants, and most vegetables are grown as annuals, fruit trees and bushes have always tended to form the main structural components or "bones" of the kitchen garden. Cordons planted on either side of main paths can be trained up and over to form arches and fruit tunnels, and rows of espaliered fruit trees can

(below) **A formal grid** of beds planted with fruit, vegetables, flowers, and herbs, all hedged with clipped boxwood, and neat paths arched with fruit cordons— all hallmarks of a traditional potager.

form a series of living fences or screens. These help divide up the garden into beds in which vegetable crops can be grown in rotation from one year to the next.

Potager gardens took this idea to a highly stylized level. The word is French and the literal translation is "a vegetable stew or soup," although potagers are much more formal than that implies. They divide the kitchen garden into strict geometric units, usually squares, rectangles, or triangles. Each of these is planted with different vegetables, fruit, herbs, and even flowers, and the neat paths separating the beds are bordered by low hedges, espaliers, or stepover fruit trees. The effect is wonderful, but there's no getting away from the fact that they involve a lot of painstaking work.

The art of espalier

The technique of training fruit trees into espalier forms dates back centuries, certainly to medieval Europe, and perhaps even to the Romans or ancient Egyptians. The variety of forms is astonishing, as is the terminology—from elaborate candelabras to palmettes, and from curvilinear fans to three-dimensional spiral vases or goblets. It's true that espaliered trees are sometimes dismissed as the fruit grower's version of topiary, but they serve a practical purpose as well as an ornamental one. First, espalier trees are space-saving. They can be grown where there would not otherwise be room. Second, they are more productive. The way they are pruned and trained is designed to get them to produce the maximum yield of fruit. Third, they are healthier, because they are, quite simply, nurtured and fussed over. Fourth, they are easier to harvest. And lastly, when northern gardeners grow espaliered peaches, nectarines, and other tender fruits against a warm, sunny, sheltered wall, they may be as successful with these fruits as they are with apples and pears.

It's quite possible to train your own espaliers, starting from scratch with young maiden whips or branched whips. You'll find instructions on how to do so in the following pages, or you may be able to find pretrained young trees for sale even in regular garden centers.

(right, top to bottom) **A fruit tunnel** is created by training two parallel rows of pear cordons up and over a pathway to form a series of arches. **An apple espalier** in full blossom brings welcome color to the kitchen garden early in the year. **Three-dimensional shapes** require a high level of expertise. Here, a pear has been trained on a wire frame into a "vase" or "goblet" form.

(left) **A multiple cordon** apple tree has been skillfully trained against an old brick wall in a garden.

Large gardens and orchards

If you're lucky enough to have a large parcel of land you can devote to a fruit garden or even a small orchard, then your growing options are wide open. Be wary of large fruit trees, though. It's far better to grow small trees on modern dwarfing rootstocks; they're easier to care for and you can plant more of them in the space, while at the same time trying lots of different varieties. For soft fruit, a fruit cage can't be recommended too strongly. It will certainly mean you eat much more of your fruit, instead of sharing it with the birds. And if you have the space for a good-sized greenhouse or hoophouse, you can grow even more.

Planning an orchard

The secret to designing and planting an orchard lies in choosing the right mix of trees. Let's assume you want apples, pears, plums, and cherries. Perhaps you want some more unusual fruits, too: quinces, medlars, mulberries, crab apples, and peaches and apricots as well. The first thing to consider is whether the trees are self-fertile or not. If not, they will need pollinating partners nearby. Then think about whether they will flower at the same time. Pollination charts elsewhere in this book will give you the information you need. Next, find out when the fruit will be ready to harvest. Ideally, you want a mix of early, midseason, and late harvest fruit, to extend the season for as long as possible. Finally, try to select a good balance of dessert and culinary varieties, including some that are best eaten soon after picking and others that will store well.

The fruit cage

There are few things more satisfying than stepping inside a large, walk-in fruit cage. If you've ever experienced the loss of a whole year's crop of strawberries, summer raspberries, cherries, or plums to a flock of voracious, hungry birds, then you'll think you've died and gone to heaven. Unlike scarecrows, wires, strings, windmills, and all manner of other less-than-useful bird-scaring devices, the fruit cage offers total protection—and total peace of mind. Just remember to remove the nets in late fall. Winter is when you actually want the birds inside the cage, so that they pick off and eat any lurking insects as well as their eggs.

(left) **A newly planted** apple orchard. (right, clockwise from top) **A fruit cage** strong enough to withstand a hurricane, let alone birds. **Harvest time** in an established orchard. **Wire frames** support young trees being trained into formal pyramids.

The fruit grower's year

The gardening year has its own rhythm. In fact, one of the pleasures of growing your own produce, especially for desk-bound city-dwellers, is that it gets you back in tune with the changing seasons. It's partly about knowing what tasks need to be done at different times of the year, but it's just as much about heightened sensibility, about being more aware of what is happening around you outdoors as the seasons change, and of how your plants are growing, flowering, fruiting, and ripening.

Winter

Winter is the dormant season. Apart from certain tropical and subtropical species, most fruit trees and bushes enter a period of shutdown. Deciduous plants drop their leaves, and their metabolism slows to a crawl. In fact, temperate fruit trees and bushes actually need this period of winter chill—not just to rest but also because a certain length of time at a low temperature produces a hormonal trigger that jump-starts dormant winter buds into growth again, and results in better-quality fruit the following year. Most apples, for example, are thought to need 1,000–1,400 hours below 45°F (7°C) each winter. The figures vary according to variety, however; apples bred to grow in warm regions such as the Southeast may need as few as 300–500 hours of chilling per year. Other fruits differ. Cool-climate raspberries, currants, and gooseberries are happy with longer, colder winters and don't require particularly hot summers for fruits to ripen; in fact, they don't do well in warm climates at all.

(below, left to right) **Truly hardy plants** such as this black currant can withstand most hard winters. They are tougher than you think, and once completely dormant are able to survive sub-freezing temperatures. **The symmetrical form** of an expertly pruned pear espalier is clearly revealed in winter. **Prune most fruit** trees and bushes in winter when they are dormant. Grapes, however, require pruning in both winter and summer.

Spring

Spring is a crucial time, and if you live in an area prone to frost, it can be
an anxious one, too. It's exciting to see buds burst, new leaves start to unfurl,
and blossoms begin to open, but plants are at their most vulnerable now.
Frost can strike at almost any time. The first trees to flower are usually
apricots, peaches, and nectarines—and they are the ones most likely to need
some kind of protection. They are closely followed by pears and plums, then
cherries and apples, and all the soft fruits as well.

Spring is also a critical time for pollination. Successful fertilization and fruit
set depend on compatible flowers being open at the same time and also on the
weather being warm enough for pollinating insects such as bees to be out and
about, doing their job. It's often said that the deciding moments governing
whether or not the year will produce a successful fall crop take place during
the course of just a few days in spring.

(clockwise, from right) **An apple bud**
bursts into leaf as spring temperatures
rise and days begin to lengthen. **Red
currant blossoms** don't last for long
but the tresses of pale yellow-green
flowers are unexpectedly beautiful.
A bee collects pollen from a cluster
of blueberry flowers. **Sowing melon
seeds** indoors early in spring ensures
that young seedlings will be ready to
plant as soon as the weather is warm
enough. **Spring blossoms open** on
a row of apple cordons.

Summer

The first ripe fruit of the year is always eagerly, impatiently awaited. To walk in from the garden with a dish of fragile, freshly picked strawberries and raspberries, a full bowl of gooseberries and currants, or a handful of early-season cherries is confirmation that summer has arrived.

The summer months are not a time for idleness, however. Certain tasks still need to be done. Watering is the most important of all. Don't let your plants dry out, especially young, recently planted ones, those growing in containers, and any that are close to fences and walls in potential rain shadows. Fertilize plants that need it, thin fruit so plants are not overburdened, and keep a watchful eye out for insect pests, for scavenging birds, and for any early warning signs of disease.

(clockwise, from right) **Thinning plums** from June onward stops the tree from being too heavily laden and produces better-quality fruit. **A bowl** of freshly picked strawberries perfectly captures the taste of summer. **White currants** are naturally sweeter than the better known red varieties. **Modern black currant varieties** are being bred so that when ripe they are sweet enough to be eaten raw. **All container-grown fruits** need regular watering in the summer months, as fruits swell and ripen.

Fall

If all has gone according to plan, late summer and early fall should overlap in one long continuous harvest, as summer berries and tender fruits such as peaches, apricots, and melons give way to plums, apples, and pears. To grapes, too, of course—as well as more unusual fruits such as quinces, damsons, mulberries, medlars, kiwifruit, and Cape gooseberries.

Before the year comes to an end, it's time to start thinking about the next one. If you live in an area with mild winters, you can plant new fruit trees and bushes while the soil is still slightly warm. Gardeners in cold-winter areas will have to wait for early spring to plant, but fall is still a good time to clean up and tidy the garden, and to begin winter pruning.

(clockwise, from right) **Fall** is a good time for planting in mild areas. Here, new raspberry canes are bundled up ready to go. **The apple harvest** can last for three months or more, depending on the varieties you grow. Early apples are for eating immediately, while later ones can be stored. **Late-season grapes** may still be ripening on outdoor vines until well into October if the weather is mild. **Quinces** are the perfect example of why you should grow your own: slightly out of the ordinary, they are rarely available in stores. **'Conference' pears** are one of the most popular homegrown varieties: easy, reliable, and delicious.

Tree Fruit

At the risk of stating the obvious, tree fruits are fruits that grow on trees. They're also known as "top fruits," to distinguish them from those that grow lower down, on bushes, canes, or vines. Apples, pears, plums, and cherries grow successfully in most temperate climates, though certain varieties are better suited to long, hot, dry summers and others to short, cool, damp ones. Peaches, nectarines, apricots, and figs are hardy enough to withstand cold winters (figs may need protection), but they do need some hot summer weather in order for their fruit to ripen reliably. In cool northern regions, they can be coaxed into fruiting by being grown in sunny, sheltered spots, usually trained against a wall or fence, in containers, or in a greenhouse.

In addition, there are a few more unusual tree fruits—quinces, medlars, mulberries, damsons, mirabelles, and so on—most of which have a long history. They are all worth trying if you have the space for them. Nuts such as almonds, walnuts, pecans, chestnuts, and hazelnuts are all, strictly speaking, tree fruits too, but they are beyond the scope of this book.

Apples for storing must be picked and handled carefully, as any bruising or splits in the skin will cause them to rot. Gather windfalls and use them right away—for cooking if they are no longer appetizing enough to eat raw.

Growing tree fruit

In truth, most fruit trees pretty much take care of themselves. As long as they're planted somewhere broadly suitable, and provided they receive the essentials they need to keep them alive—light, air, warmth, water, and nutrients from the soil—they should get along just fine, with the minimum amount of intervention. That said, the more care you do give them, the better they will grow. If you feed, water, weed, mulch, prune, and protect them against pests and diseases, then they will repay you with more reliable, more generous crops of better-looking, better-tasting fruit.

Buying fruit trees

The first decision to make when buying a new fruit tree is whether to go for one that has bare roots or one that is potted up in a container. Young trees for sale in garden centers are usually sold container-grown and can be bought throughout the growing season. Specialty nurseries usually sell their trees bare-root. They are dug when dormant, so they are available in late fall and again in the spring. After being uprooted from the nursery bed, most of the loose soil is shaken from their roots, and the trees are bagged up, usually in plastic. It's important that

the roots are kept moist and that a bare-root tree is planted as soon as you get it home or, if you bought it online or via mail-order, as soon as it is delivered.

The advantages of buying a bare-root tree are that you will have a much wider choice of varieties and the tree you choose is likely to be in better condition, since it will have been removed from the ground only very recently. The disadvantage is that you can plant only when the stock is available. Container-grown trees are easier to obtain and can, in theory, be planted at any time of the year, regardless of whether or not they are dormant. However, it's always wise to avoid hot, dry periods.

Whenever or wherever you buy fruit trees, always obtain them from a source that can guarantee the plants are officially certified disease-free.

How young trees develop

Most young trees are sold as one- or two-year-olds. One-year-old trees that have just a single stem without any sideshoots are called maiden whips. One- or two-year-old trees that have had time to develop sideshoots are called branched whips. Both are suitable for home gardens, although a whip will take a little longer to establish itself and start bearing fruit.

It's also possible to buy pretrained trees. These are usually three years old, and will have already been pruned and trained by the nursery. They are a good choice if you want to get off to a quick start or try a formal espalier project.

(opposite, left to right) **Container-grown trees** are available year-round, and are therefore often bought when in leaf. **A maiden whip** is a one-year-old tree. At this age, it is nothing more than a single stem or leader growing from the point where it was originally grafted on to the rootstock. **A branched whip** may be one or two years old. By now, a few sideshoots will have appeared. It's likely that some of these will grow on to form the main branches.

BUYER'S CHECKLIST

Bare-root trees
▨ Look for a strong stem that has been trained vertically, without excessive kinks.
▨ If the tree is branched, it should have up to half a dozen strong, well-spaced laterals forming wide V-shaped angles with the main stem. They should be capable of eventually forming the main framework branches.
▨ Be wary of trees with too long, spindly growth.
▨ Roots should be healthy and vigorous, radiating evenly all around the base of the tree.
▨ The union should be strong and undamaged.

Container-grown trees
▨ Choose a tree with a straight main stem or central leader, clean of sideshoots at the base.
▨ Look for a healthy root system, with a balance of strong main roots and plenty of thinner, white feeder roots. Avoid plants that are potbound with roots that coil around the sides or grow out of the bottom of the container.
▨ Potting medium should be moist, not dried out, and should have no weeds or moss growing on the surface.
▨ If the tree is in leaf, look for discolored or distorted foliage, any signs of dieback or weak growth, and infestations of aphids, mites, or other insect pests.
▨ Check the union, where the scion has been grafted onto the rootstock (see p.32). It should be strong and clean, with no signs of splitting or other damage.

When choosing container-grown trees, always examine the rootball. The tree on the left has a healthy root system whereas the roots of the tree on the right are congested and will struggle to spread out into the planting hole.

Rootstocks

Most fruit trees are propagated by grafting a bud or shoot (called the "scion") from the original tree onto the roots from a different one (called the "rootstock"). Sometimes, the best rootstocks aren't even from the same species. Pears, for example, are usually grafted onto quince rootstocks, and apricots are often grown on plum or peach rootstocks.

(right, far right) **The "union"** is the seam where the scion from one tree was grafted onto the rootstock of another. It's visible as a knobby joint. Keep it above soil level or the scion may start to root. **Evidence of grafting** can still be seen on mature trees—even on the trunk of this thirty-five-year-old apple.

FRUIT TREE FORMS

Fruit trees can be grown in a wide variety of different shapes and sizes. Free-standing, free-growing forms are the most natural, though they all involve a certain amount of pruning and shaping. They include dwarf, semidwarf, and standard trees pruned to open center, central leader, or modified central leader forms. Wall- or wire-trained trees are much more strictly trained and pruned. They include cordons, espaliers, and fans.

Genetic dwarf trees are naturally compact, growing about 7 feet tall at maturity. They are not as hardy as standard trees, and are best for mild-winter areas. This dwarf tree has been pruned to an open-center form.

Grafted semidwarf trees vary in size depending on the variety and the particular rootstock, but overall they will be smaller and easier to manage than standard trees.

Standard fruit trees grow to 30 feet or even taller. They are long-lived, but it is hard to pick fruit from large trees. Standard stone fruit trees can be trained to control their size more easily than apples or pears can.

Stepovers are single cordons that have been bent over at a right angle close to the ground to form a low, horizontal tree. They are ideal for small gardens and can make a decorative border edging.

Cordons comprise a single central leader with short fruiting spurs along its length. It may be upright (vertical) or oblique (trained at an angle). All cordons need regular summer and winter pruning.

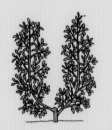

Double ("U") cordons are formed by cutting back the central leader and then training two laterals upward as vertical arms. They are economical on space and best grown against a fence or wall.

Multiple cordons have three or four vertical arms. Sometimes, each of these arms is divided or "bifurcated" yet again, slightly higher up, to create ever more complex trained forms.

It's the rootstock that largely determines how big the tree will eventually grow. Today, there is a much wider choice of rootstocks than previously, as well as many more that produce small, more manageable trees, better suited to smaller yards and even to container growing. These are called dwarfing or semidwarfing rootstocks.

Pollination

All trees need to be pollinated in order for fruit to be produced. The process involves pollen from the male parts of a flower (the stamen) being transferred to the female parts (the stigma)— sometimes by insects such as bees, sometimes by the wind. With luck, fertilization then takes place and fruits start to form. Most flowers contain both male and female parts, but in some cases separate male and female flowers exist on the same tree, and in one or two instances (kiwifruits, for example) a single tree has either male or female flowers, not both. Figs are an exception; they do not produce flowers in the normal way at all.

Some fruit trees can fertilize themselves with their own pollen. They are called self-fertile. Others need pollen from nearby trees. Indeed, as a general rule, it's always better if trees are cross-pollinated,

Spindlebush training is used by some commercial growers. The branches are relatively few in number and radiate out from the central leader to form a low, conical shape.

Central leader training results in a roughly pyramid-shaped tree. The arrangement of the branches allows sunlight to reach most parts of the tree.

Dwarf central leader trees are pruned in the same way as larger central leader trees. In modified central leader training, the top of the central leader is removed when main scaffold branches are established.

Columnar trees are specially developed apple trees of a limited range of varieties. The trees grow about 8 feet tall, and the side spur branches remain short and are easy to maintain. These are good for container growing.

Espalier trees have tiers of evenly spaced horizontal arms, which radiate outward to the left and right from a main stem or central leader. On a perfectly trained espalier, the arms are all of the same length, and the tree is completely symmetrical.

Fans usually have a short trunk from which two main ribs radiate. Each of these ribs then produces sublaterals, which are spread out evenly and tied in to wire supports. This creates the classic fan shape, one of the most attractive trained forms.

Palmettes are a cross between an espalier and a fan—a combination of two very decorative tree forms. Like an espalier, they retain a main stem or central leader. Like a fan, the lateral arms are trained at an angle rather than horizontally.

whether they are self-fertile or not. However, not all trees will pollinate each other. Some are simply incompatible. The whole issue of cross-pollination and compatibility can get complex, especially with pears and cherries, but specialty nurseries will be able to advise you if necessary.

With pollination, timing is everything. Not all fruit trees flower at the same time, and of course no insect on earth is able to transfer pollen from a blossom that's open to a blossom that's not. For this reason, fruit trees are often put into pollination groups to help you choose trees that flower simultaneously.

There are further potential problems with trees that flower very early in the year—apricots, peaches, and nectarines, for example. When the blossoms open, it may be too early for pollinating insects to be around. If so, hand pollination may be required (see p.148).

Even if pollination does take place, it doesn't guarantee fertilization. A certain minimum temperature is required, because fruit just won't form if it's not warm enough.

Most fruit growers are used to crops varying from one year to the next. In some years there's a bumper yield, while in others a tree may produce next to no fruit at all. Often, the cause goes right back to that crucial week or two in the spring, when the weather will have determined whether pollination was successful and whether or not there was a good fruit set.

Planting fruit trees

Arguably the most important thing that happens to a fruit tree during its lifetime is the way it's planted. If you plant it properly and get it off to a good start, there's a strong chance that it will be trouble-free.

Tree stakes can be wood or metal. If you use wood, choose a rot-resistant type such as cedar.

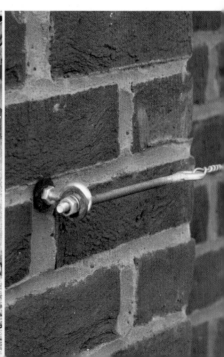

Choosing the right site is crucial, of course. But preparing the ground is important, too. A few weeks beforehand, weed the whole area very thoroughly. Perennial weeds such as bindweed and couch grass are hard to remove once trees are established. Dig over the soil and incorporate plenty of well-rotted manure or garden compost. You may also want to add some general fertilizer, and balance the pH of the soil if necessary. Don't dig the actual hole for the tree until just before you are ready to plant.

When is the best time to plant a new tree? That depends on where you live. In areas with mild winters, November or thereabouts is a good time. Gardeners in cold-winter areas can plant in the fall too, but need to work earlier in the season (using container-grown stock) so that plants will have time to establish roots before the soil temperature drops too low. Spring planting is fine too. Many mail-order nurseries can hold bare-root stock in refrigerated storage and ship it to you at the ideal time for planting in your area. Midsummer planting is not a good idea in most regions.

Staking and supporting fruit trees

New, young, stand-alone trees need to be staked after planting, until their roots have a strong enough hold to secure them in strong winds. For vigorous freestanding semidwarf or standard trees, use a short stake 4 ft (1.2 m) long driven vertically into the ground to a depth of about 2 ft (60 cm) if it is bare-root or a stake 5 ft (1.5 m) long driven in at an angle if it is container-grown and you want to avoid damaging the rootball. The stakes can be removed after four or five years. For dwarf and some semidwarf trees, use longer 8-ft (2.5-m) stakes and be prepared to leave them in place permanently. Put the stake on the side of the prevailing wind.

(opposite, left to right) **Special tree ties** are available for securing the tree to its stake. All allow for adjustment so that they do not become too tight as the trunk grows. **If rabbits, deer,** or other animals are a problem, protect young trees by encircling the trunk and stake with a mesh tree guard. **Fix wire supports** to walls, fences, or posts with eye bolts. Leave a space of at least 2–3 in (5–8 cm) between the wire and the wall or fence, to allow air to circulate freely. Use 12-gauge wire for cordons and espaliers, and 14-gauge for fans.

Oblique pear cordons take up relatively little space and can be trained on galvanized wires held taut between sturdy wooden posts. Mesh tree guards protect the stems from grazing animals.

Trees that are trained as cordons, espaliers, or fans all need to be supported on wires strung between vertical posts or attached to a wall or fence. Use wooden or metal posts that are 3 in (8 cm) or 4 in (10 cm) in diameter. Sink them into the ground to a depth of at least 2 ft (60 cm) and brace them with diagonal supports at each end. Use heavy-gauge, galvanized wire strong enough to support the branches of the tree when fully grown and laden with fruit. Attach horizontal lengths of wire with eye bolts and tension them with straining bolts to keep them taut.

Pruning and training fruit trees

In terms of pruning, there are two stages in a tree's life. In the first few years, the aim is to train the tree into the desired shape or form. This stage is called formative pruning. Thereafter, the aim is to keep the tree tidy and healthy, and to encourage it to produce fruit as reliably and generously as possible. Depending on the tree, this stage may be referred to as regulative or renewal pruning. If a tree has been neglected and left unpruned for several years, it's likely to need renovation pruning to get it back into shape (see p.76).

When to prune

The best time to prune apple and pear trees is in late winter, when they are dormant. However, for stone-fruit trees such as plums, cherries, apricots, peaches, and nectarines, wait until after buds start to open, in order to reduce the risk of infection by canker diseases.

Wire-trained or "restricted" trees such as cordons, espaliers, and fans are an exception to this rule. They need to be controlled and shaped much more strictly, so they all require pruning during spring and summer, either to encourage the new growth that you do want or to remove the growth you don't.

What to prune

Let's start with what's easy. At least once a year, inspect your trees carefully and prune out any stems or branches that are dead, damaged, or diseased—sometimes known as "the three Ds." Once you've done that, look for areas that are crowded and congested or where branches are touching or crossing. Thin those out so that light can get in and air can circulate freely. Cut back any branches that are hanging too low or touching the ground. Check the overall height, spread, and form of the tree and adjust it to keep it balanced and well-shaped.

Next, turn your attention to the pruning that will ensure your trees produce as much fruit as possible. For this you first need to understand that trees bear fruit in different ways. Most, though not all, apples and pears fruit on wood that is two years old or older. Peaches, nectarines, and sour cherries fruit on shoots that are younger—those that grew the previous year. And plums, apricots, and sweet cherries fruit on a mixture of wood that is one and two years old. Fruit is sometimes borne on

(left, top to bottom) **Diseased** branches should be cut out before infection can spread. **Damaged** branches allow bacteria and fungal growths to take hold. **Crossing,** touching, or crowded spurs and branches must be removed. If they rub against each other, wounds open up and can become infected.

clusters of stubby spurs, sometimes along the length of branches, and sometimes mostly at the tips (see p.83). The aim of pruning is to remove old wood that is no longer fruitful and to stimulate new growth that is.

Beware of over-pruning. Removing too much wood at one time tends to spur the tree into rapid growth, but it will produce mostly foliage at the expense of fruit.

How to prune
There's an art to knowing where and how to cut. It's hard to generalize about what you should and shouldn't remove because everything depends on the type of tree, its age and size, and the form in which it is being grown. But here are a few simple guidelines to follow.

Cutting back to a bud
If possible, identify a healthy growth bud and cut back to that. Select one that is pointing in the direction you want the new growth to go, usually outward from the tree, not into the center.

Cutting back to a shoot
If you are removing overly long stems or old wood that no longer produces much fruit, cut back to a younger sublateral or sideshoot—one that is strong and healthy, and already growing in the right direction.

Cutting back to a branch or trunk
Use loppers or a pruning saw to cut substantial lateral or sublateral branches. Cut at a very slightly sloping angle to the main branch or

(top to bottom) **Prune close** to a healthy growth bud. **Make clean,** angled cuts parallel with the shoot to which you are cutting back.

REMOVING A HEAVY BRANCH
Heavy branches have a tendency to tear under their own weight if you try to remove them with a single cut. It is safer to prune them in stages.

The first cut is made on the underside, about 12 in (30 cm) from the trunk. Saw only a quarter of the way through.

Make a top cut straight down and about ¾ in (2 cm) farther along the branch from the undercut.

The branch should now fall to the ground safely. It shouldn't tear but if it does it won't damage the trunk.

Cut away the branch stump from the top, sawing just beyond the collar, where the branch meets the trunk.

The correct cut is sloping and parallel with the bud so that rainwater drains away from it. Cut close but not too close.

Cut too close and you will slice through the base of the bud, leaving a large surface area that will be slow to heal.

Cut too far away and the stub left above the bud will die back and may become infected with disease.

A torn and jagged cut made with a blunt tool produces a large, ragged wound that won't heal well.

Cut at the wrong angle and you will leave an unnecessary stub. Water will drain toward the bud instead of away.

(clockwise from top) **Loppers** are ideal for cutting out old or damaged stems, and for those that are hard to reach. **Pruning saws** must be kept sharp. To avoid rust and maintain sharpness, wipe them with an oily rag after use. **Clean pruners** by removing any dried-on debris with steel wool, and always disinfect them if you've been pruning diseased material.

trunk, leaving the collar encircling the joint intact so that the wound will heal cleanly.

Good cuts and bad cuts

Always use a sharp, clean pair of pruners and ensure that the thinner of the two blades is the one closest to the bud, even if this means coming in at a different angle or turning the pruners upside down. That way you'll be able to make a more precise cut.

Pruning tools

The most important tools are a pair of pruners, loppers, and a pruning saw.

Use pruners to cut pencil-thick stems—up to ½ in (1.5 cm) in diameter. Bypass pruners are the best kind. Their blades cross over when they cut, like scissors. Anvil pruners have a sharp cutting blade that presses down onto the flat metal edge of the lower blade, like a knife on a chopping board.

For stems or branches up to about 1½ in (4 cm) thick, use loppers. And for anything thicker, use a pruning saw. For tall trees, long-armed loppers and saws are available. A sharp garden pocket knife is also useful—not for pruning as such but for neatening and smoothing the edges of pruning cuts.

All pruning tools should be kept sharp. Otherwise cuts will be ragged, and wounds will take longer to heal. They must be kept clean, too. To reduce the risk of spreading infection, sterilize them.

FRUIT TREE ANATOMY

The vocabulary for the different parts of a tree can be confusing. Trunks, branches, and twigs we're all familiar with, of course. But professional fruit growers talk of leaders, laterals, sublaterals, and spurs. Here's a guide to what the jargon means.

(far left) **The central leader** is the main trunk or stem. It can be left to grow to full height—central leader form—or cut back once the tree has established several branch leaders—modified central leader form.
(left) **Laterals** are shoots or stems coming off the main trunk or off branch leaders. (above) **Sublaterals** are sideshoots that come off laterals. They are secondary branches.

Spurs are knobby clusters of fruit buds that grow each year on short, stubby lengths of wood. In time, they may become so overcrowded that they need thinning.

Fruit buds are fatter than growth buds because they contain the embryo flower. If this flower is successfully pollinated and fertilized, it will grow and develop into a fruit.

Growth buds, sometimes called vegetative buds, are usually thinner and more pointed than fruit buds. They produce new shoots that carry leaves but not fruit.

Apples

Apples are believed to have originated in Central Asia, in the mountains of what is now Kazakhstan. From there they spread, and there are written accounts of Roman apple growers propagating new varieties using grafting techniques. Settlers then took the apple to North and South America and to Australasia, where extensive cross-breeding took place. Indeed, 'Golden Delicious' and 'Granny Smith' originated in the US and Australia, respectively.

There are literally thousands of named cultivars, and new apple varieties are continually being introduced. From time to time, long-lost traditional varieties are also rediscovered. Choose your varieties wisely and you'll not only get to experience a much wider range of wonderful flavors than any supermarket will ever offer, but you could well be eating your own homegrown fruit for six months of the year or more—from the first early-season apples of late summer through to fruit you've stored over winter to eat in spring the following year.

When choosing a dessert apple, decide whether you want a variety for early picking and eating or one to store. 'Court Pendu Plat' (shown here), a late-harvest variety with a wonderful flavor, has been in cultivation since the 17th century.

Which forms to grow

- **Dwarf and semidwarf trees** These small trees are easier to care for than standard trees and produce fruit within a few years.
- **Central leader training** Apple trees usually respond best to this type of training.
- **Multi-leader training** If one leader becomes diseased, you can prune it out and still have other leaders to work with.
- **Cordon** Wire-trained single or multiple stems that produce fruits on short sideshoots.
- **Columnar** A short, vertical stem—good for small spaces.
- **Espalier and fan** A wire-trained form with arms growing on either side of a central stem or radiating from a short trunk.
- **Stepover** A knee-high, horizontal cordon.

Must-grow dessert apples

1 **'James Grieve'**
Pollination group B
A Scottish variety that flowers early but is hardy and frost-resistant. Good yield and good flavor. Does not grow well in humid conditions, which can encourage canker and scab. Spur-bearer.
■ **Harvest** September
■ **Eat** September–October

2 Improved versions of the classic 'McIntosh', such as 'Cortland' and 'Empire', have excellent flavor and will last well in storage. 'Empire' is very crisp and has a touch of tartness. 'Cortland' is very juicy and has dark red skin. Both ripen in late September.

3 **'Ashmead's Kernel'**
Pollination group C
Reputed to have been bred by a Dr. Ashmead in England in about 1700— and still rightly popular. A late-harvest, russet eating apple with a wonderful flavor—though it can be unreliable and prone to frost damage. Spur-bearer.
■ **Harvest** October
■ **Eat** December–March

4 **'Court Pendu Plat'**
Pollination group D
Written records of this apple go back to 1613, although it is rumored to have been grown in Roman times or even earlier. Late flowering, medium-sized, sweet, and aromatic, with a slight pineapple flavor. Spur-bearer.
■ **Harvest** October
■ **Eat** December–April

5 **'Laxton's Superb'**
Pollination group C
Traditional, 19th-century English variety still grown for its flavor, frost resistance, and keeping qualities. Sometimes biennial, spur-bearer.
■ **Harvest** October
■ **Eat** November–January

6 'Mother'
Pollination group D
Sometimes known as 'American Mother' owing to its 19th-century US origin. Sweet, juicy apples with a distinctive, aromatic flavor. Spur-bearer.
■ **Harvest** October
■ **Eat** November–March

7 'Ellison's Orange'
Pollination group C
Sometimes know as 'Red Ellison'. Juicy, slightly soft flesh with a rich taste that has a hint of anise when fully ripe. Sometimes biennial, spur-bearer.
■ **Harvest** September
■ **Eat** September–October

8 'Cox's Orange Pippin'
Pollination group B
Grow this one for its outstanding, justly famous flavor—it is one of the very best. But be warned: it's not easy to grow. Easily damaged by frost, it is prone to disease, and needs optimum growing conditions. Spur-bearer.
■ **Harvest** October
■ **Eat** October–January

9 'Golden Delicious'
Pollination group C
Contrary to most preconceptions, this is not a modern apple but one that dates back to around 1890 and comes from Virginia. A favorite of commercial growers—it is heavy-fruiting, reliable, and stores well. In warm climates, it ripens to a honeyed sweetness; in cooler regions it may disappoint. Spur-bearer.
■ **Harvest** October
■ **Eat** November–February

10 'Elstar'
Pollination group B
A mid-20th-century Dutch variety bred from 'Golden Delicious'. Generous crops of sweet, juicy, well-flavored apples. Sometimes biennial, spur-bearer.
■ **Harvest** October
■ **Eat** October–January

11 'Jonagold'
Pollination group B

Derived from 'Jonathan', and now grown all over the world. Crisp, juicy, with a rich, sweet-acidic flavor. Triploid, spur-bearer.
- ■ **Harvest** October
- ■ **Eat** November–March

12 'Greensleeves'
Pollination group C

A cross between 'James Grieve' and 'Golden Delicious'. It has similar qualities: heavy-fruiting, hardy, reliable, good balance of sweetness and acidity. Tip- and spur-bearer.
- ■ **Harvest** September
- ■ **Eat** September–November

13 'Gala'
Pollination group C

From New Zealand, this cross-breed of 'Golden Delicious' and 'Kidd's Orange Red' is crisp and juicy. Best eaten soon after picking, even though it will keep into the new year. Spur-bearer.
- ■ **Harvest** October
- ■ **Eat** October–January

14 'Adams's Pearmain'
Pollination group A

Traditional variety that dates back to the early 19th century. Aromatic fruits with a nutty flavor. Biennial, tip- and spur-bearer.
- ■ **Harvest** October
- ■ **Eat** November–March

15

Bright red apples such as 'Honeycrisp', a popular new variety, and 'Enterprise' have great appeal. 'Honeycrisp' ripens in September, with exquisite texture and flavor. It grows best in cooler climates. 'Enterprise' ripens in mid- to late fall and is tart and full-flavored. Plus, it is resistant to many common apple diseases. Both varieties last well in storage.

16

Although they don't keep well in storage, apples like 'Gravenstein' and 'Spigold' are worth growing for their flavor and texture picked right off the tree. 'Gravenstein' grows best in the West or New England, ripens in late summer, and has crisp, fine flesh. 'Spigold' is a good choice for the South and Midwest, has rich flavor, and ripens in mid-fall.

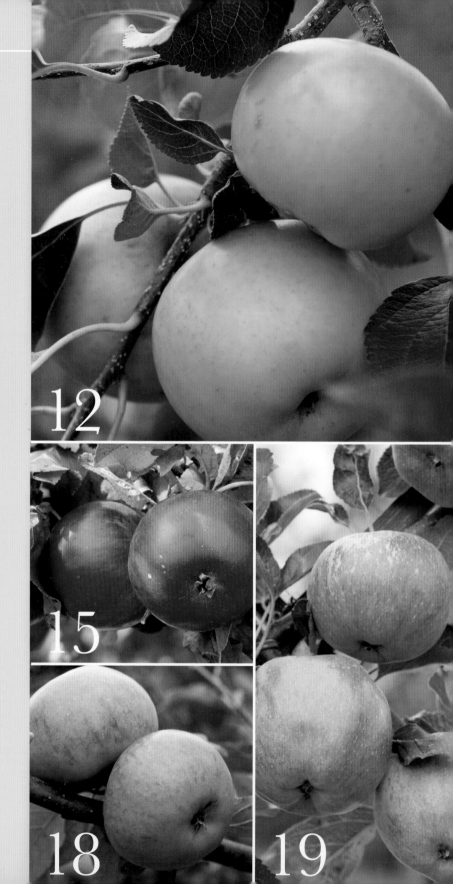

11

13

14

16

17

20

17 'Worcester Pearmain'
Pollination group B

Traditional English apple with a distinctive, strawberrylike flavor. Best left to ripen fully before picking and then eaten promptly. Tip-bearer.

■ **Harvest** September
■ **Eat** September–October

18

Apples don't have to be red. Try apples of other colors too, such as 'Tompkins King' or 'Esopus Spitzenberg'. Yellow-green 'Tompkins King' has red stripes, is a tip-bearer, and ripens in September. Mottled orange 'Esopus Spitzenberg' is well suited to the Pacific Northwest and ripens in late October.

19 'Kidd's Orange Red'
Pollination group B

Not the easiest apple to grow, as it is prone to disease, needs sunshine, and requires careful thinning, but it has outstanding flavor. Originally bred in New Zealand as a cross between 'Cox's Orange Pippin' and 'Red Delicious'. Spur-bearer.

■ **Harvest** October
■ **Eat** November–January

20

'Fuji' and 'Melrose' are both great dessert apples, but consider your climate before you decide which one to grow. 'Melrose', with a flavor that combines tartness and sweetness, is popular in the Pacific Northwest, but since it can tolerate humid conditions, it will grow well in many areas. However 'Fuji', a classic sweet dessert apple, needs warm days and cool nights when it ripens. It does well in the South and southern half of the Midwest. 'Melrose' ripens in mid-fall, 'Fuji' in mid- to late fall.

21 'Queen Cox'
Pollination group B
A self-fertile strain of 'Cox's Orange Pippin'. Crisper, tastier, more colorful, and heavier-fruiting. Spur-bearer.
■ **Harvest** October
■ **Eat** October–December

22
Adding a disease-resistant dessert apple such as 'Redfree' or 'Sundance' is good insurance. Mildly tart 'Redfree' is resistant to scab, cedar-apple rust, and fire blight. 'Sundance' is both sweet and tart and it's resistant to scab and cedar-apple rust. 'Redfree' ripens mid-August; 'Sundance' ripens in early fall.

23 'Ribston Pippin'
Pollination group A
A traditional apple that, in Europe, dates back to at least the 17th century. Not the easiest apple to grow but worth trying for its sweet, aromatic, old-fashioned flavor. Triploid, spur-bearer.
■ **Harvest** September
■ **Eat** October–January

24 'Egremont Russet'
Pollination group A
Very firm with a sweet, nutty flavor. It flowers very early, so it may need frost protection. Spur-bearer.
■ **Harvest** September
■ **Eat** October–December

25 'Braeburn'
Pollination group C
A relatively modern variety that originates from New Zealand. Needs a warm, sunny climate to ripen successfully. Crisp, juicy, aromatic, with good acidity. Spur-bearer.
■ **Harvest** October
■ **Eat** December–March

26 'Tydeman's Late Orange'
Pollination group C
A crossbreed of 'Laxton's Superb' and 'Cox's Orange Pippin'. Needs thinning or the fruits will be small. Only moderate yields, but flavor is outstanding and apples will keep into spring. Spur-bearer.
■ **Harvest** October
■ **Eat** December–April

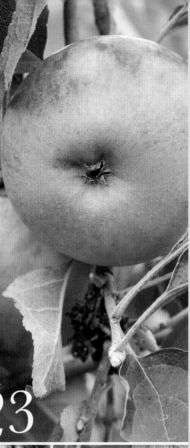

27 **'Fiesta'**
Pollination group B
Also known as 'Red Pippin'. Bred from 'Cox's Orange Pippin', it has inherited some of its flavor but is much easier to grow. Spur-bearer.
- ■ **Harvest** September
- ■ **Eat** October–January

'Gold Rush' (not illustrated)
This apple looks like 'Golden Delicious' but is much more disease-resistant. It is very long-keeping, with a wonderful spicy flavor. Best suited to areas with moderate summers.
- ■ **Harvest** mid-fall
- ■ **Eat** late fall to late spring

'Hudson's Golden Gem' (not illustrated)
This apple has a mild, sweet flavor that is sometimes called pearlike. Resistant to scab and other diseases and suited to a range of climates. Fruit can be used for cooking too.
- ■ **Harvest** mid-October
- ■ **Eat** mid-October to February

'Limelight' (not illustrated)
Pollination group B
A modern English apple, the result of a cross between 'Greensleeves' and 'Discovery'. It has almost luminous, bright yellow-green fruits. Compact, heavy-fruiting, and disease-resistant. Perfect for a small yard.
Tip- and spur-bearer.
- ■ **Harvest** September
- ■ **Eat** September–November

Must-grow culinary apples

'Liberty' (not illustrated)
Pollination group A
Really an all-purpose apple, 'Liberty' makes excellent pies, sauces, and cider. Highly disease-resistant; good for New England gardeners.
- ■ **Harvest** early October
- ■ **Eat** October–December

'Rome Beauty' (not illustrated)
With fabulous flavor but tough skin, this is a top-notch cooking and baking apple. Grown almost everywhere apple trees are found.
- ■ **Harvest** mid- to late fall
- ■ **Eat** mid-fall to midwinter

'Stayman Winesap' (not illustrated)
Although this apple can be eaten fresh, it's best-known as a great pie and sauce apple with its full flavor. It grows well in the South and Midwest.
- ■ **Harvest** mid-fall
- ■ **Eat** mid-fall to mid-spring

Must-grow culinary apples

1 **'Edward VII'**
Pollination group D
Late-flowering so good for northern regions or frost-prone sites. Fruit will store all through winter until spring. Spur-bearer.
- **Harvest** October
- **Eat** December–April

2 Long-keeping apples such as 'Criterion' and 'Granny Smith' guarantee a supply of apples for cooking until spring. 'Criterion' is sweet; 'Granny Smith' is tart. 'Granny Smith' ripens in mid-fall; 'Criterion' ripens in early October.

3 **'Bramley's Seedling'**
Pollination group B
Traditional cooker with excellent flavor and fluffy texture. Very vigorous but can be grown on dwarfing rootstocks. Triploid, tip- and spur-bearer.
- **Harvest** October
- **Eat** November–March

4 Pie apples such as 'Golden Russet' and 'Rhode Island Greening' have a long storage life. 'Golden Russet' has high sugar but is still tart and highly flavorful. It ripens from early to mid-fall depending on location. 'Rhode Island Greening' develops best tart flavor in storage, ripening in late summer.

5 Some old-time varieties such as 'Duchess of Oldenberg' and 'Sheepnose' make excellent pie and sauce apples. The tart 'Duchess' ripens in late summer; sweet 'Sheepnose' ripens in the fall.

6 **'Golden Noble'**
Pollination group C
Yellow-green 19th-century English apple. Excellent flavor and texture. Hardy and heavy-fruiting. Tip- and spur-bearer.
- **Harvest** October
- **Eat** October–December

Must-grow, dual-purpose apples

1 All-purpose apples like 'Macoun' and 'Grimes Golden' are well worth growing even if they're not well known. Very good all-around apples for dessert, baking, and sauce. 'Macoun' is ready for harvest in early October; it has pure white flesh and grows well in the Northeast. 'Grimes Golden' is ready to harvest in mid- to late September and does well in all apple-growing areas.

2 **'Idared'**
Pollination group A
Originating from Idaho, 'Idared' is crisp, juicy, and sweet, if rather bland. Useful as a dual-purpose cooking and eating apple. It stores exceedingly well. Spur-bearer.
■ **Harvest** October
■ **Eat** November–May

3 Time has proven that antique varieties like 'Smokehouse' and 'Roxbury Russet' are worth growing for both fresh eating and cooking. 'Smokehouse' has firm, juicy flesh and ripens in September. 'Roxbury Russet' is both sweet and tart and ripens in mid-October.

4 **'Blenheim Orange'**
Pollination group B
An 18th-century apple worth searching out for its distinctive, nutty flavor. Triploid, sometimes biennial, tip- and spur-bearer.
■ **Harvest** October
■ **Eat** November–January

'Baldwin' (not illustrated)
Pollination group C
A large apple with high sugar content. Triploid, sometimes biennial; resistant to cedar-apple rust. Excellent for New England and mountainous parts of the Mid-Atlantic and North Carolina.
■ **Harvest** September
■ **Eat** September–February

Choosing and buying apple trees

Before buying an apple tree of any kind, there are four things to consider. First, what form of tree do you want? The answer will probably depend on how much room you have. Planting a freestanding semidwarf or dwarf tree and training it to a central leader form is the most common way to grow apples, but if space is limited, consider a columnar tree, or a wire-trained form such as a cordon, fan, or espalier. The size to which the tree will grow is determined by the second factor: the rootstock. Certain rootstocks produce dwarf trees; others are much more vigorous and can end up very tall. The third factor to consider is the cultivar or variety you'd like to grow, and the fourth is when the flowers appear—which is crucial for pollination.

Choosing a tree form

Freestanding trees normally have a central leader. Open-centered trees, which are uncommon in the U.S., have had their central leader cut out, in order to create a shape rather like a cupped hand, palm upward with the fingers outspread. Central-leader trees are usually smaller and more conical in shape.

Trees trained against walls, fences, or wire supports are called restricted forms. They can vary in size from large-scale arches and espaliers to tiny, knee-high stepovers, and their shape can be as simple as single columns or as complex as traditional zigzag and diamond cordons. It's possible to train apples as fans, but it's perhaps less common in practice.

(left) **Many garden centers** will stock a range of container-grown trees, but specialty nurseries will offer a much wider choice. Buying bare-root trees from nurseries in fall or spring is the cheapest option.

(opposite clockwise from top) **A mature espalier** takes several years to reach its full potential and is a beautiful sight in bloom. **Modern dwarfing** rootstocks ensure small trees that may produce fruit just a year or two after planting. **A row of cordons** is ideal for a small garden and is an efficient way to use space.

CHOOSING A ROOTSTOCK

Apples are never grown on their own roots. Instead, they are always grafted onto a special rootstock by the fruit nursery where they are raised. In most cases, grafting restricts their size to manageable proportions, and it encourages them to start fruiting relatively early. It also makes them less prone to disease.

Traditional apple rootstocks are classified according to a system of alphanumeric codes. The "M" stands for Malling—the East Malling Research Station in England, where much of the early work on developing dwarfing rootstocks was done. "MM" stands for Malling-Merton.

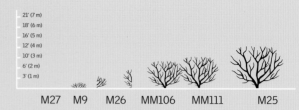

21' (7 m)
18' (6 m)
16' (5 m)
12' (4 m)
10' (3 m)
6' (2 m)
3' (1 m)

M27   M9   M26   MM106   MM111   M25

Research at Cornell University has produced a new line of Geneva (G) rootstocks, and BUD rootstocks from the former Soviet Union are also available. The list below describes some traditional M and MM rootstocks. Ask your supplier for the best rootstock for your conditions.

M27
- VIGOR Very dwarfing
- CHARACTERISTICS Very small trees ideal for urban gardens and patios. Even after 15 years, they may not be much more than head-high. M27 rootstocks suit vigorous, strong-growing apple varieties and need rich, fertile soil. Keep them free of weeds and surrounding grass.
- FIRST CROP At 2–3 years old.
- SUPPORT Stake permanently.
- HEIGHT 5–6 ft (1.5–2 m).

M9
- VIGOR Dwarfing
- CHARACTERISTICS The best choice for a small yard. Will grow best in good soil. Weed, water, and feed regularly, and keep grass away from the trunk.
- FIRST CROP At 3–4 years old.
- SUPPORT Stake permanently.
- HEIGHT 6–10 ft (2–3 m).

M26
- VIGOR Semidwarfing
- CHARACTERISTICS A slightly larger, stronger tree than M9, producing heavier crops and larger apples. Less demanding in terms of growing conditions, though it will establish quicker in good, fertile soil.
- FIRST CROP At 3–4 years old.
- SUPPORT Stake for first 3–4 years.
- HEIGHT 8–12 ft (2.5–4 m).

MM106
- VIGOR Semivigorous
- CHARACTERISTICS A good all-around choice. Will grow well on most sites and in most soils—although the better the soil and the more vigorous the variety, the larger the tree.
- FIRST CROP At 4–5 years old.
- SUPPORT Stake for first 4–5 years.
- HEIGHT 12–17 ft (4–5.5 m).

MM111
- VIGOR Vigorous
- CHARACTERISTICS Unless grown in poor soil conditions, will produce a tree too large for all but the biggest yards. Takes several years before fruiting begins, and then pruning and harvesting require ladders.
- FIRST CROP At 6–7 years old.
- SUPPORT Stake for first 4–5 years.
- HEIGHT 17–21 ft (5.5–6.5 m).

M25
- VIGOR Very vigorous
- CHARACTERISTICS Uncommon nowadays, even in orchards, since trees are so large that pruning and harvesting are extremely difficult.
- FIRST CROP At 6–7 years old.
- SUPPORT Stake for first 4–5 years.
- HEIGHT 21–25 ft (6.5–8 m).

Choosing a variety

The choice of varieties or cultivars is bewildering. Even your local garden center will probably offer a reasonable selection, and specialty nurseries may have a catalog listing hundreds of different apples. Some of the names you will recognize—'Granny Smith', 'Golden Delicious', 'McIntosh', and so on. Others may be less familiar—'Cox's Orange Pippin', 'Jonagold', or 'Braeburn', perhaps. How to choose? Here are some criteria to bear in mind when making your selection.

■ Do you want the apples for eating fresh or for cooking? Varieties are classified according to sweetness/acidity, and are described as either dessert or culinary. There are a few hybrids, too, which can be used for either purpose.

■ Do you want the apples for eating right away or for storing through the winter? Apples that are ready to pick early in the summer don't keep well and should be eaten within a few days of picking. In contrast, apples that ripen later in the season may actually need to be stored for a while before they are ready to eat.

■ What sort of climate do you have? Apples don't all flower at the same time. In early-flowering varieties, the blossoms can appear by mid-spring. So, if your area is prone to severe frosts in spring, choose a late-flowering or frost-resistant variety instead. And if you suffer from cold, damp winters, avoid varieties such as 'Cox's Orange Pippin', which need more favorable growing conditions.

■ What other apples are you growing or do you plan to grow? Apples are not usually self-fertile. For pollination to be successful, they need to be grown close to compatible trees that flower at the same time. Choosing varieties from the same flowering or pollination group should help ensure this.

Insect pollinators can only transfer pollen from tree to tree when flowers are open, so ensure that neighboring trees are from the same pollination group and therefore in blossom at the same time. Cross-pollination won't take place between an early flowering and a late-flowering variety.

MULTI-VARIETY TREES

A multi-variety tree is a single tree onto which two, three, or even four different apple varieties have been grafted (left). If space is severely restricted and you have room for only one specimen, then such a tree solves the pollination problem. Provided the different cultivars have been chosen so that they all flower simultaneously, insects will transfer pollen from one variety to another, effectively fertilizing them all.

It's important that the varieties chosen for a family tree are not only compatible in terms of pollination but also have the same growing requirements and are of more-or-less equal vigor. If they are not, then one will tend to dominate and outgrow the others. Typical combinations include: 'Red Delicious', 'McIntosh' and 'Northern Spy'; 'Anna', 'Dorset Golden' and 'Einsheimer' (low-chill varieties); and 'Yellow Delicious', 'Early Red Summer Red', 'Granny Smith', and 'Fuji'.

APPLE POLLINATION GROUPS

A

'Adams's Pearmain'
'Duchess of Oldenburg'
'Egremont Russet'
'Gravenstein'
'Idared'
'Irish Peach'
'Ribston Pippin'
'Smokehouse'

(top to bottom) **'Egremont Russet'** an early-season eater, **'Idared'** an eater or a cooker, and **'Ribston Pippin'** a dessert apple that stores well. All flower early.

B

'Blenheim Orange'
'Bramley's Seedling'
'Cortland'
'Cox'
'Cox's Orange Pippin'
'Elstar'
'Empire'
'Esopus Spitzenburg'
'Fiesta/Red Pippin'
'Golden Russet'
'Granny Smith'
'Greensleeves'
'Grimes Golden'
'Honeycrisp'
'Hudson's Golden Gem'
'James Grieve'
'Jonagold'
'Kidd's Orange Red'
'Limelight'
'Queen Cox'
'Redfree'
'Rhode Island Greening'
'Stayman Winesap'
'Tompkins King'
'Tydeman's Early Worcester'
'Worcester Pearmain'

Flowering times vary according to location and changing weather conditions from one year to the next. Trees are usually in blossom in mid- to late spring.

C

'Ashmead's Kernel'
'Baldwin'
'Braeburn'
'Criterion'
'Ellison's Orange/Red Ellison'
'Fuji'
'Gala'
'Golden Delicious'
'Golden Noble'
'Goldrush'
'Laxton's Superb'
'Macoun'
'Melrose'
'Rome Beauty'
'Spigold'
'Sundance'
'Tydeman's Late Orange'
'Winston'

(top to bottom) **'Ellison's Orange'** is ready to pick and eat in early fall. **'Golden Delicious'** ripens later and will keep. Both flower in mid- to late spring.

D

'Court Pendu Plat'
'Edward VII'
'Mother/American Mother'
'Roxbury Russet'
'Sheepnose'

(top to bottom) **'Court Pendu Plat'** is a traditional dessert apple, **'Edward VII'** is a cooker, and **'Mother'** is a juicy dessert fruit. All flower late and store well.

Choosing a pollination group

Pollination groups indicate when in spring each apple variety flowers: early, middle, or late in the season. It's best to grow a collection of trees that come from the same pollination group. That way, their blossoms will open at the same time and insects will be able to transfer pollen from one tree to another. Trees belonging to adjacent pollination groups should pollinate one another, too, since their flowering periods are likely to overlap, at least to some extent.

However, there are a few apples with which you must take special care. Called triploids, they are not good at pollinating other varieties. They should therefore be grown with at least two different, compatible cultivars that are not triploids. The best know triploids include 'Blenheim Orange', 'Bramley's Seedling', 'Jonagold', and 'Ribston Pippin'.

RECOMMENDED APPLE COMBINATIONS

The combinations of apples given in this chart are from the same pollination groups, to ensure similar flowering times and, therefore, good fruit set. They will crop from early through to late-season, providing apples for early picking and eating as well as winter storage.

	Eating apple for early picking	Eating apple for winter storage	Cooking apple
Early spring flowering (pollination group A)	'Gravenstein'	'Egremont Russet'	'Idared'
Mid-spring flowering (pollination groups B and C)	'Cortland' 'Ellison's Orange' 'Greensleeves' 'James Grieve' (shown) 'Honeycrisp' 'Worcester Pearmain'	'Ashmead's Kernel' 'Cox's Orange Pippin' (shown) 'Fiesta' 'Fuji' 'Stayman Winesap'	'Bramley's Seedling' 'Golden Noble' (shown) 'Rome Beauty' 'Golden Russet' 'Rhode Island Greening'
Late spring flowering (pollination group D)		'Court Pendu Plat' 'Mother'	'Edward VII' 'Sheepnose'

Growing apples

Most apples are tough, tolerant, and long-lived. Only those grown on very dwarfing rootstocks are overly sensitive about the quality of the soil in which they are grown. That said, all apples are prey to a range of pests and diseases, and all need regular pruning, especially those trained as cordons, fans, and other espalier forms. A well-cared-for tree will repay your attention by producing larger quantities of better-quality fruit.

The year at a glance

	spring			summer			fall			winter		
	E	M	L	E	M	L	E	M	L	E	M	L
plant bare-root	■								■	■		
plant container	■	■	■	■			■	■	■	■	■	■
summer prune					■	■	■					
winter prune									■	■	■	
harvest					■	■	■	■				

Choosing apple trees

Apples are sold as either bare-root or container-grown trees. Specialty nurseries offer a wider choice than garden centers but most of their trees will probably be bare-root and available only in fall (October–November) and spring (March–May).

Newly purchased young trees are usually one, two, or three years old. One-year-olds will be either maiden whips or branched whips (see p.30). They are less expensive than older trees but need to be trained from scratch and will of course take longer to establish and to start fruiting. Two- and three-year-olds will have had some training and pruning already done by the nursery. For a beginner, they are probably the best choice.

When to plant

■ BARE-ROOT Plant in fall or spring, when the trees are dormant. Fall is ideal in Zones 6 and warmer; spring is best for cold-winter areas.
■ CONTAINER-GROWN Plant at any time of year when conditions are appropriate. Avoid late spring and summer months if it is hot and dry.

(left) **Young, newly planted trees** need to be permanently staked if they are on dwarfing rootstocks. It's a good idea to position the stake on the side of the tree that faces into the prevailing wind.

(right) **Traditional orchard trees** are kept short, for ease of picking. Grass, on the other hand, may be allowed to grow fairly long except for an area immediately around the tree, which is kept clear to minimize competition for moisture and nutrients.

PLANTING AN APPLE TREE

Prepare the site in advance. Young apples on dwarfing rootstocks can't be grown successfully in grass, since they will struggle to compete with it for moisture and nutrients. So, if the planting site is already grassed, remove a square of sod, dig out any perennial weeds, work well-rotted compost or manure into the soil, and add some general, all-purpose fertilizer. Use a stake for freestanding trees and a system of wire supports for cordons and fans.

1 Use a sharp spade to slice out an area of sod about 3 ft (1 m) square.

2 Dig a hole deep enough and wide enough to accommodate the plant's roots. If you haven't already done so, work some well-rotted compost or manure into the soil.

3 For a bare-root tree, drive a stake into the ground to a depth of 2 ft (60 cm), about 3 in (8 cm) away from the center of the hole. For a container-grown tree, use a shorter stake, driven in at an angle, to avoid damaging the rootball (see p.35).

4 Make a small mound of soil in the center of the hole and gently spread the roots over it. Check the depth to ensure that the old nursery soil mark on the stem is level with the surface of your soil.

5 Carefully fill the hole with soil, ensuring there are no air pockets among the roots.

6 Gently firm down the soil—don't stamp or you will compact it.

7 Secure the tree to the stake with special tree ties. You may need one at the top and one at the bottom.

8 Water generously now and at regular intervals over the next few weeks.

9 Spread an organic mulch around the plant to help retain moisture and suppress weeds.

10 If the tree has not already been pruned by the nursery, you may need to do it immediately after planting (see p.68).

10

PLANTING DISTANCES

It's hard to be specific about planting distances. Everything depends on the vigor of the rootstock and the variety, on the soil and other growing conditions, and on the form into which the tree is to be trained. Use the distances given below as a general guide to spacings.

Freestanding central leader trees
M27	4–6 ft (1.2–2 m)
M9	6–10 ft (2–3 m)
M26	10–13 ft (3–4.5 m)
MM106	12–17 ft (4–5.5 m)
MM111	17–25 ft (5.5–8 m)

Intensive plantings
M27	5–6 ft (1.5–2 m)
M9	6–8 ft (2–2.5 m)
M26	6–11 ft (2–3.5 m)
MM106	8–13 ft (2.5–4.5 m)

Fans and espaliers
M26	10–11 ft (3–3.5 m)
MM106	11–13 ft (3.5–4.5 m)
MM111	13–17 ft (4.5–5.5 m)

Cordons
30 in (75 cm)

Columnar
24–30 in (60–75 cm)

Where to plant

Choose a warm, sheltered site where trees are protected from strong winds. Avoid frost pockets. Full sunshine is more important for dessert apples. Culinary apples will tolerate some shade.

Soil type

Most apples are easygoing, though they all prefer deep, free-draining soil with a slightly acidic pH of around 6.5. They dislike being water-logged and will grow best if the soil has had plenty of well-rotted compost or manure added to it. Any apple will struggle on shallow, alkaline soil, where it is prone to lime-induced chlorosis (see p.320). The smaller the tree and the more dwarfing the rootstock, the more important it is to give it a rich, fertile soil.

CRAB APPLES

Crab apples are certainly not grown for eating raw. Even when ripe, they are so hard and so sour that it's hard to imagine they could ever be made edible. However, when cooked and sweetened they make a wonderful crab apple jelly.

Crab apples are widely grown as ornamental trees—both for their small, brightly colored fruit and for their blossoms. Many varieties remain in flower for some time and usually for longer than cultivated apples. For this reason, they are valuable in gardens and in orchards as sources of compatible pollen.

(below, left to right) **Most crab apples** are selected for the quality of their fruit or the attractiveness of their white, pink, or red spring blossoms. There are numerous named varieties: 'Evereste', 'Golden Hornet', and 'John Downie' (shown here) are among the best known. **Flowering periods** for crab apples tend to be long, so grow them alongside apples to ensure successful pollination.

Routine care

▦ WATERING Water young trees, cordons, and espaliers regularly throughout the spring and summer, particularly in drought conditions and when the fruit is swelling. Older, established trees are less needy.

▦ FEEDING To ensure that trees produce as much fruit as possible, commercial growers boost the amounts of potassium, nitrogen, phosphorous, magnesium and other elements in the soil with a complex regimen of special fertilizers. However, unless your soil is very poor and your trees are fruiting poorly, an annual application of a general compound fertilizer in early spring, before growth starts, should be sufficient.

▦ MULCHING In spring, after feeding, remove any weeds and spread an organic mulch around the base of young trees, wire-trained forms, and those grown on dwarfing rootstocks or in poor soil. It will help retain moisture and keep down the growth of new weeds.

▦ FROST PROTECTION Although apples usually flower later than pears, plums, cherries, and most other tree fruit, they may still be vulnerable to damage from late spring frost. Protecting large, mature trees is impractical, but it may be possible to use an overnight covering of floating row cover on young trees, cordons, small espaliers, and stepovers. Of course, late-flowering varieties are by definition less prone to frost damage.

(right, top to bottom) **The "June drop"** happens in early summer when most apple trees let a proportion of their young, acorn-sized fruitlets fall to the ground. It looks alarming but is quite normal. It's the tree's way of ensuring that it is not overloaded with fruit. **Further thinning** after the June drop is usually necessary to ensure that the best fruit grow to their optimum size. Thin out crowded clusters by selecting any small, diseased, or misshapen fruitlets and removing them. If they don't come away easily, cut their stalks cleanly using pruners or scissors. Aim to leave 4–6 in (10–15 cm) between dessert apples and 6–9 in (15–23 cm) between larger culinary ones.

GROWING APPLES IN CONTAINERS

Apples can be successfully grown in pots as long as you take care to choose the right variety and the right rootstock. Surprisingly perhaps, the most dwarfing M27 and M9 are not necessarily the best. They are very picky about soil conditions and may or may not be happy in a container. A nonvigorous variety grown on an M26 rootstock might be a better bet. And of course, you'll need to be prepared to prune container apples diligently so they don't overgrow their space.

Start with a young, one- or two-year-old tree and choose a container large enough to accommodate the rootball plus a little extra space all around. Fill it with multipurpose, soil-based medium mixed with some sand or gravel to improve drainage. Feed with a high-potassium fertilizer in spring, and keep the pot well-watered in spring and summer, less so in winter. Every year or two, repot the tree in a slightly larger container, until it reaches the size at which you want to restrict it.

(left) Container-grown apples do best in a sheltered, sunny location. If late frosts are a threat after the blossoms have opened, they can be protected with row cover or moved under cover. They can be netted, too, if birds pose a problem.

Harvesting and storing apples

How do you tell when an apple is ready to pick? The simplest test is to cup it lightly in your palm and twist gently. If it comes away easily with the stalk attached, it is ready. If it doesn't, leave it. Don't tug or tear it off or you may damage the spur. Early dessert varieties should be ready for picking in late summer, or even midsummer. They are best eaten immediately, before their seeds turn brown. Mid-season apples will keep for a little longer—for perhaps a month or two. And certain late-season apples can be stored for up to six months. Apples intended for storage should be picked and handled very carefully. If they are bruised, they won't store well; nor will they if they are left on the tree for too long before picking. Only very few varieties can be left beyond mid-fall.

Apples store best if they are kept somewhere dark, reasonably well-ventilated, and cool but frost-free. Most garages or sheds are fine. Cellars, basements, and attics may be too warm, dry, or stuffy. Spread out apples on slatted wooden or plastic trays, or in special molded grocers' fruit liners, ensuring that they don't touch. Alternatively, wrap each apple in tissue paper or store them in plastic bags perforated with air holes. Inspect stored fruit regularly and immediately remove any that show signs of rot. Varieties that store well through winter include 'Bramley's Seedling', 'Idared', 'Laxton's Superb', 'Jonagold', and 'Golden Delicious'.

Yield

Yields are hard to quantify as they vary widely according to variety, tree form, rootstock, growing conditions, and a host of other variables. However, average quantities you can expect are:

■ FREESTANDING STANDARD or SEMI-DWARF 175–350 lb (80–160 kg).
■ FREESTANDING DWARF 33–55 lb (15–25 kg)
■ FAN 12–33 lb (5.5–15 kg).
■ ESPALIER 22–33 lb (10–15 kg).
■ CORDON 5.5–11 lb (2.5–5 kg).

Season by season

Midwinter
■ If necessary, spray trees with dormant oil to deter aphids, winter moths, and other pests.

Late winter
■ Prune young and established trees before the dormant period ends.

Early spring
■ Begin planting bare-root trees as conditions allow.

Mid-spring
■ Most apple varieties flower now or in late spring. Protect blossoms from frost if necessary.
■ Codling moths will begin mating, so hang pheromone traps to attract and catch males.
■ Inspect dwarf trees and hand-pick pest caterpillars.

Late spring
■ If pollination is successful, fruitlets form now and begin to swell.
■ Water newly planted and wire-trained trees regularly if the weather is dry.
■ Check for powdery mildew and scab on fruitlets.
■ Hang apple maggot traps in trees now or in early summer, depending on when the adult flies emerge in your area.

Early summer
■ Following the "June drop", thin out young fruitlets.
■ Summer prune young espaliers from now to early fall.
■ Check for aphids and spray if necessary.

Midsummer
■ Summer prune established espaliers and cordons now and in late summer, cutting back new laterals and sideshoots.
■ As fruit begins to drop, pick it up regularly and destroy it to help reduce future pest problems.

Late summer
■ Continue summer pruning of cordons, cutting back new laterals.
■ Harvest early season apples and eat soon after picking.
■ Remove and destroy any fruit infected with scab or brown rot.

Early fall
■ Harvest mid-season apples. Eat or store according to the variety.
■ If you have mulched around your trees, rake the mulch out from under the canopy. After leaf fall, replace the mulch and add a new top layer.

Mid-fall
■ Harvest late-season apples and store for the winter.
■ In Zone 6 and warmer, buy and plant new bare-root trees.

(far left to right) **Buds swell** on bare branches in early spring as the days lengthen. **Leaves burst** and begin to unfurl in spring sunshine. **Blossoms** appear on most apple varieties by mid-spring. In cold regions, they may need protection from frost. **Fruitlets** start to swell and will soon need thinning. **Ripe apples** are ready for harvesting, depending on the variety, between late summer and mid-fall. **Once harvested** eat early and mid-season varieties; late-season varieties are best for storing.

Late fall
■ Remove any rotten fruit still hanging on the tree. Rake up any diseased leaves.
■ Check stored fruit for signs of rot.

Pruning and training apples

Every apple tree needs pruning at least once a year. Without this, it will lose its shape, become congested and perhaps diseased, and gradually produce less and less fruit. The basic principles are simple. At the start of their lives, all young trees need training into shape. Thereafter, freestanding trees should be pruned in winter, when they are dormant, and wire-trained trees such as cordons and espaliers should be pruned twice a year, once in summer and once in winter. Beyond that, the only other key thing to know is whether your tree is a spur-bearer or a tip-bearer, because each is pruned slightly differently.

SPUR-BEARERS AND TIP-BEARERS

Most apples produce fruit on branches that are two years old, or older. Each year, fruit buds appear on short little stubs called "spurs." As the years go by, more and more spurs appear until knobby clusters called spur systems are formed. Obviously, the more spurs you have, the more you fruit you'll get—until you reach the point where they become so overcrowded that they require thinning.

A few apple varieties, however, are different. They produce fruit primarily on fresh, new wood that grew only last year. So most of their crop is borne on the ends of the branches instead of along their length. They are known as tip-bearers. When pruning them, the aim is to replace branches and sideshoots that have already borne fruit with new ones that will fruit in the next year or two. This technique is sometimes called renewal pruning.

To complicate things further, some apples produce fruit both on spurs and on the tips of branches and sideshoots. They are known as tip-and-spur-bearers or partial tip-bearers.

(left, top to bottom) **Spur-bearing apple** trees have short, stubby sideshoots that carry flower buds, and later fruitlets. **Tip-bearing apple** trees bear flower clusters, and therefore fruit, mostly at the ends of branches. **Spur thinning** is carried out to reduce overcrowding and involves removing old spurs to improve air circulation, leaving a cluster of younger spurs, each with a flower bud.

General pruning tips

Pruning apple trees regularly with the help of sharp pruners and a good-quality pruning saw will keep them healthy and productive. Get into the habit of removing any dead, damaged and diseased wood, as well as thinning overcrowded growth.

(top to bottom) **Cut back** dead branches completely. **Remove** water sprouts. **Prune out** any diseased shoots or stems.

(opposite) **Orchard pruning** is a big job, one that can last right from early winter right through early spring. These trees are at least thirty years old and are pruned every year to maintain their form.

Pruning a multi-leader apple tree

The objective is to create a tree with multiple well-spaced leaders. This allows removal of a leader if it becomes infected with fire blight, and the rest of the tree can remain productive. A dwarf tree should have a clear trunk of at least 30 in (75 cm) in height; on a semidwarf it should be 4 ft (1.2 m).

1st spring pruning
EARLY SPRING

- Your new tree may already have been pruned by the nursery. If not, prune immediately after planting.
- If you have planted a one-year-old maiden whip, cut it off at a height of 24–30 in (60–75 cm), pruning just above a bud. Buds below the cut will shoot and form laterals next year.
- If you have planted a one- or two-year-old branched whip (as shown above), cut off the central leader or main stem to about the same height, leaving 3 or 4 healthy laterals below the cut.
- Prune back each of the laterals by two-thirds of its length. Cut to buds that face outward or upward.

2nd spring pruning
EARLY SPRING

- Select the laterals and sublaterals that you want to become main branches and cut them back by about half.
- Cut back everything else to 4 or 5 buds.
- Remove any weak, crowded, or crossing stems and any new shoots growing from the main trunk.

3rd spring pruning
EARLY SPRING

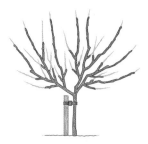

- Tip-prune the main branches by removing about one-quarter of last year's new growth.
- Prune strong sublaterals or sideshoots to 4–6 buds and weaker ones to 2–3 buds. This should encourage growth next year.
- Remove any stems that are crossing or growing into the center of the tree.

(right) **Light and air** are the two watchwords when pruning. Removing branches that grow into the center of the tree opens it up and lets air circulate, which will help to reduce the risk of disease. It also allows sunlight to reach the ripening fruits.

Winter pruning an established spur-bearing tree
LATE WINTER

- By the 3rd or 4th summer after planting, the tree should be fruiting, so winter pruning can be lighter.
- Concentrate on maintaining the overall shape, keeping the center open, encouraging the growth of new spurs, and thinning old, overcrowded ones.
- Cut out any dead, damaged, or diseased wood.
- Thin any badly congested or tangled areas to let light and air into the center of the tree.
- Tip-prune the leaders of strong sublaterals or sideshoots and cut back any weaker ones by about a half of last year's new growth.
- Prune new sideshoots to 4–6 buds.
- Remove completely any new shoots growing from the main trunk.

(left to right) **Prune new sideshoots** to encourage the growth of new spurs. **Prune out any branches** or shoots that show signs of disease such as canker or powdery mildew. **Cut back** to buds facing the direction in which laterals should grow.

Winter pruning an established tip-bearing tree
LATE WINTER

(above) **Remove any new shoots** growing straight into the center of the tree.

- Tip-bearers fruit on last year's new growth, so beware of removing too much.
- Concentrate on maintaining the overall shape, keeping the center open, cutting back a few older sublaterals and sideshoots that have been fruiting for a while, and encouraging the growth of new ones to replace them.
- Cut out any dead, damaged, or diseased wood, and thin the center of the tree if it is congested.

- Lightly tip-prune the leaders of the main branches.
- Remove or cut back to a new shoot or strong bud some of the sublaterals longer than 12 in (30 cm).
- Don't touch any sublaterals shorter than 12 in (30 cm).

Central leader training

On a central leader tree, the main stem rises up as the central leader with several evenly spaced scaffold branches around it. This training system works well for most freestanding apple trees. The tree forms a roughly conical shape. Dwarf central leader trees may need permanent staking. Semidwarf trees should not need staking once established.

(below) **Central leader trees** have an upright main stem and several productive lateral branches.

1st spring pruning
EARLY to MID-SPRING

- Start with a one- or two-year-old branched whip, and prune immediately after planting.
- Select 4 well-angled laterals at a height of 2–3 ft (60–90 cm) above ground level. These will become your main branches.
- Remove any laterals below your chosen 4.
- Cut off the central leader or main stem to about 3 buds above the highest lateral.

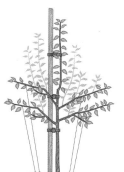

1st summer pruning
EARLY SUMMER

- Prune out all new shoots growing vertically upward.
- If the 4 main branches are developing narrow branch angles, you can use branch spreaders or tie them down so they grow more horizontally. Horizontal growth encourages the production of more fruit.

2nd spring pruning (not shown)
EARLY SPRING

- Cut off the central leader or main stem to about 2 feet above the highest lateral.

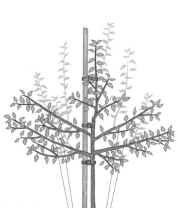

2nd summer pruning
EARLY SUMMER

- Check and adjust or remove the branch spreaders or ties on the 4 main branches.
- Select another set of lateral branches, at least 18 inches above the first set. Use spreaders or ties as needed.
- Prune out all new shoots growing vertically upward.

Winter pruning an established central leader tree
LATE WINTER

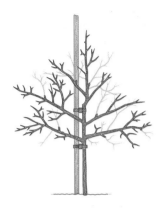

- Focus on the overall shape, cutting back a few older branches, and encouraging growth of new shoots to replace them.
- For a few more years, continue shortening the central leader by one-third or one-quarter of last year's growth until the main form of the tree is complete.
- Thin overcrowded growth from lower branches, especially if it is growing vertically upward.
- Over time, remove older limbs that are shading out more productive sideshoots, and also remove any dead, diseased, or rubbing branches.
- You may also want to summer-prune your established apple trees to thin out crowded growth and improve air circulation among the branches.

(top to bottom) **Older branches** should be cut back to the central leader. **Beneath the stub** will be a dormant bud that will start to grow.

(left) **Spreading branches** by tying them to a lower branch (as shown here) or by putting weights on the branch tips helps to make them grow horizontally, which slows down growth and increases fruit production.

Modified central leader training

You may decide you don't want to add scaffold branches over several years of training. There's a simple alternative. Once your tree has 4 or 5 strong scaffold branches, cut back the central leader to the topmost scaffold branch. The tree will continue to produce sublaterals off the scaffold branches. Prune to maintain form and let light and air reach the center of the tree. Cut back any strongly vertical sublaterals, especially from the topmost scaffold.

(below) **A well-trained dwarf apple tree** is one of the best choices for a small yard. Prune the tree lightly in late winter and again in summer to control its size.

Pruning an apple cordon

Cordons are single-stem trees. Any lateral branches are regularly pruned back to form short sideshoots or spurs on which the fruit is borne. For this reason, tip-bearers don't make good cordons; choose a spur-bearer instead. Prune them twice a year, in winter and in summer, and grow them against a wall or fence or supported by posts and wires. Cordons may be upright or oblique, and can also be trained into double ("U") or multiple (double-"U") forms. Low, horizontal cordons are called stepovers. Compact, upright cordons are called columns or ballerina trees.

(top to bottom) **Oblique cordons** are grown at a diagonal angle, usually in a closely planted row or line. The main trunks can then grow longer than those of upright cordons before they become so tall that the fruit is difficult to pick. **Stepovers** are small horizontal cordons, usually no more than knee-high. They are grown by bending over the central leader of a very young, flexible whip and tying it to a horizontal wire.

1st winter pruning
LATE FALL–LATE WINTER

- Construct a support by tying a bamboo cane to three horizontal wires at angle of 45 degrees.
- Start with a one- or two-year-old branched whip. Plant it at an angle, tie it in to the cane, and prune immediately after planting.
- Cut back to 3 or 4 buds any laterals longer than 4 in (10 cm).
- Don't touch the central leader or any laterals shorter than 4 in (10 cm).

1st summer pruning
MIDSUMMER

- New laterals and sideshoots will have started to emerge by summer.
- Cut back new laterals growing directly from the main trunk to 3 leaves, not counting the basal cluster.
- Cut back sublaterals or sideshoots growing off existing laterals to just 1 leaf beyond the basal cluster.
- This should encourage the development of spurs on which fruit will be borne in coming years.

Winter pruning an established cordon
LATE FALL–LATE WINTER

- Established cordons should not need much winter pruning.
- As trees age, the spur systems may become overcrowded. If so, thin them out by removing weak, overlapping, or congested spurs.
- Cut out completely any very old spur systems that are no longer productive. New growth should replace them.

Summer pruning an established cordon
MIDSUMMER

- Continue cutting back new laterals growing directly from the main trunk to 3 leaves, not counting the basal cluster.
- Cut back sublaterals, or sideshoots growing off existing laterals or spurs, to just 1 leaf beyond the basal cluster.
- When the tree reaches its full height, cut the central leader back to 1 leaf of new growth each spring.

(top to bottom) **By midsummer** new laterals may be growing alarmingly quickly. **Summer pruning** allows light and air to reach the ripening fruit.

Pruning an apple espalier

Espaliers are among the most dramatic of the trained forms. They're large, too—up to 20 ft (6 m) wide unless grown on dwarfing rootstocks—so they need a strong support system and plenty of space. Training them takes time. It will be several years before an espalier with multiple horizontal tiers becomes established.

1st winter pruning
LATE FALL–LATE WINTER

- Construct a support system by securing horizontal wires 14–20 in (35–50 cm) apart to a wall, fence, or upright posts.
- Start with a one-year-old maiden whip, or a one- or two-year-old branched whip if it already has 1 or more pairs of appropriate laterals. Plant it, tie it in to a cane, and prune immediately after planting.
- Cut back the central leader to a strong bud just above the lowest wire, about 18 in (45 cm) from the ground. Make sure there are at least 3 healthy buds below your cut. The lower two should form the first laterals, and the top the new leader.

This mature espalier is in need of a winter pruning to remove those long vertical shoots from the spurs on the upper arms. The fact that they have grown so long may be because they were pruned too early the previous summer, before growth had slowed down.

1st summer pruning
EARLY SUMMER–EARLY FALL

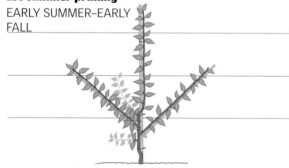

- Secure 2 canes to the horizontal wires at angles of 45 degrees.
- Tie in the new main laterals to the diagonal canes.
- Tie in the new central leader to the vertical cane.
- Cut back any other laterals or young shoots to 2 or 3 leaves.
- During the summer, gradually and carefully begin lowering the 2 diagonal canes.

2nd winter pruning
LATE FALL

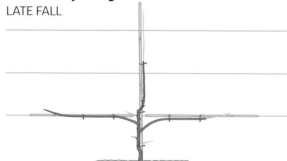

- Lower the 2 arms into a horizontal position and tie them to the bottom wire.
- Tip-prune the laterals by about one-quarter if they do not seem to be growing strongly. Cut to buds pointing downward.
- Cut back the new central leader to just above the 2nd wire and to a bud facing in the opposite direction from last year's. Make sure you leave 3 strong buds—1 for another new leader, and 2 for new left and right laterals.
- Remove completely any laterals below the first 2 arms in order to leave the main trunk clean.

2nd summer pruning
EARLY SUMMER–EARLY FALL

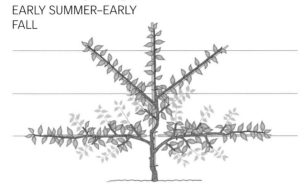

- Secure an additional 2 canes to the horizontal wires at angles of 45 degrees.
- Tie in the 2 main laterals that will form the new left and right arms to the diagonal canes, as you did last year.
- Tie in the new central leader to the vertical cane.
- Prune sublaterals or sideshoots growing from the lower 2 arms to 3 leaves beyond the basal cluster.
- Cut back any other laterals or young shoots growing directly from the main trunk to 2 or 3 leaves.
- During the summer, slowly lower the 2 diagonal canes.

3rd winter and summer pruning
LATE FALL and SUMMER

- Repeat the process of forming horizontal arms until you have as many tiers as you want.
- Then remove the vertical leading shoot.

Summer pruning an established espalier
MID–LATE SUMMER

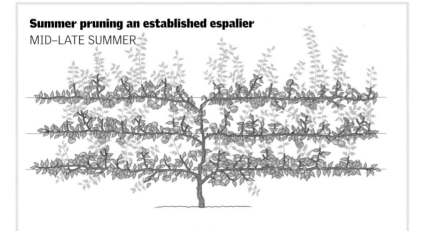

- Prune each arm of the espalier as if it were a cordon.
- Continue cutting back new laterals growing directly from the main left and right arms to 3 leaves, not counting the basal cluster—especially the vigorous growth that will probably shoot up from the top tier.
- Cut back all new sideshoots to just 1 leaf beyond the basal cluster.
- Keep the main trunk clean of all unwanted laterals and sideshoots.

Winter pruning an established espalier
LATE FALL–EARLY SPRING

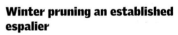

Before pruning

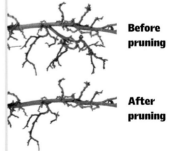

After pruning

- Established espaliers should need only light winter pruning.
- Thin out overcrowded spur systems by removing weak, overlapping, or congested spurs.
- Cut out completely any very old unproductive spur systems so that new growth can replace them.

PRUNING AN OLD, NEGLECTED TREE

The kind of pruning required to rescue a neglected apple tree and bring it back to healthy, productive shape is called renovation. You can't, however, renovate a tree all at once. It will take at least two years, perhaps more. If you attempt it in a single season by pruning the tree too hard, all you'll do is put it into shock and force it into producing a lot of new foliage and little or no new fruit.

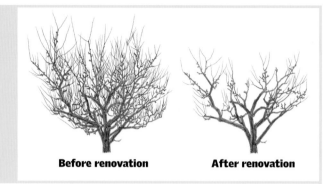

Before renovation   **After renovation**

1st winter pruning
LATE FALL–LATE WINTER

- Start by cutting out all dead, damaged, and diseased branches and stems.
- Look for branches that are crossing and may be rubbing against one another. Remove them.
- Thin out some of the most densely crowded areas so that light and air can circulate.
- Don't remove more than about 25 percent of the tree in any one year.

2nd winter pruning
LATE FALL–LATE WINTER

- Continue pruning overly long branches and any that are hanging too low to the ground.
- Keep an eye on the overall shape, and try to open up the center of the tree by cutting back to laterals facing in the appropriate direction.
- Cut off any water sprouts that have appeared around last year's pruning cuts.
- Start thinning out old, overcrowded spur systems.

Crossing branches are in danger of rubbing against each other. If they split or if the bark is rubbed away, infections can enter and may cause disease.

Diseased wood should be removed promptly, before the infection spreads. Cut back as far as clean, healthy wood that shows no sign of disease.

Tangled, congested areas should be thoroughly thinned out. If they're not, they keep out light and air, increasing the risk of disease.

What can go wrong

Buds and blossoms

1 Blossoms turn brown and wilt
First the flowers and then young leaves turn brown and wither.
■ See **Blossom blight** (p.325) and **Brown rot** (p.326).

Blossoms discolor and die
Frost can damage young leaves and destroy blossoms, especially in the case of apple varieties that flower early in the year. Fire blight can also cause blossoms to turn brown and die.
■ See **Frost** (p.316) and **Fire blight** (p.327).

Leaves, stems, and branches

2 White, powdery coating on leaves
When young leaves and shoots are covered in a dry, powdery, white mold, the cause is the fungus powdery mildew. New growth withers and dies, and affected fruit buds do not produce fruit.
■ See **Powdery mildew** (p.329).

3 Leaves curled and spun with silk
A number of different species of leafrolling caterpillars spin a silk web, wrapping leaves around themselves as a protective cover. On apples, the tortrix moth caterpillar can be one cause of this problem.
■ See **Tortrix moth** (p.341).

4 Leaves eaten and tattered, with holes
Caterpillars feeding on leaves are the most likely cause of the damage. A severe infestation can strip leaves completely. Winter moths are the probable culprits—their caterpillars can often be found inside tightly curled new leaves.
■ See **Winter moth** (p.341).

5 Leaves curled and sticky
The undersides of tightly curled, distorted leaves will probably reveal aphids. The sticky upper surface is due to the honeydew that they excrete, and it may also develop a gray sooty mold. Several different species of aphids—varying in color from green or blue to pink or brown—attack apples.
■ See **Aphids** (p.334), **Rosy apple aphid** (p.339).

6 Small, brown-edged holes in leaves
Red-brown spots on young leaves are caused by tarnished plant bugs. The spots develop into large, torn holes.
■ See **Plant Bugs** (p.338).

7 Looping, meandering lines on leaves
These yellow-brown, scribble-like markings are caused by tiny caterpillars tunneling "mines" as they eat.
■ See **Apple leafminer** (p.334).

8 Brown patches on leaves
Irregular blotches or spots that may be dark green or brown, perhaps turning gray or black in the center, can indicate scab. Infected leaves may yellow and fall. The fruits themselves may be affected, too. Pear leaf blister mites can cause similar blotches.
■ See **Scab** (p.330), **Pear leaf blister mite**, (p.338).

9 White woolly fluff on stems and branches
Cottony tufts on branches and shoots are signs of woolly apple aphids, especially around old cuts and splits in the bark.
■ See **Aphids** (p.334).

10 Cracked, flaky areas of bark
Discolored, sunken, split, or flaky areas of bark can indicate apple canker. As it spreads, cracked rings form, the area around the site may become swollen, and growth ceases above and below it. Whole branches may die.
■ See **Apple and pear canker** (p.324).

Leaves mottled and bronzed
If upper surfaces of leaves are mottled and discolored then become brittle, look underneath with a magnifying glass for tiny spider mites. In severe cases, you may also see fine silk webbing.
■ See **Spider mites** (p.340).

Small yellow spots on leaves
Cedar-apple rust is a fungus that spends part of its life cycle in apple trees and part in juniper species. It also affects the fruit.
■ See **Cedar apple rust** (p.326).

Sawdust on trunks; gummy sap on bark
Boring beetles that feed on foliage and fruits, but the serious damage is done by larvae eating the inner bark and heartwood.
■ See **Appletree borers** (p.334).

Shoot tips wilt and turn brown
Oriental fruit moths lay eggs in twigs or on the undersides of leaves. The larvae hatch and burrow into the tips of shoots.
■ See **Oriental fruit moths** (p.338).

Fruit

11 Pale brown, corky patches
Tarnished plant bugs feeding on young fruitlets can cause them to become disfigured and develop scars or corklike patches.
■ See **Plant bugs** (p.338).

12 Brown scabs and split skin
Scablike patches appear on the fruits. As they spread, the skin dries out and is likely to split or crack, possibly allowing other infections to enter.
■ See **Scab** (p.330).

13 Fruits develop patches of brown rot
Ripening fruits turn brown and may develop concentric rings of white fungal spores, sometimes around a central hole. They either fall to the ground or remain on the tree, gradually shriveling to a mummified state
■ See **Brown rot** (p.326).

14 Ragged holes in fruits
Birds, wasps, and flies feed on ripe fruits, often where the skin has already been pierced or damaged.
■ See **Birds** (p.334) and **Wasps** (p.341).

15 Ribbonlike scars on skin
A meandering, slightly raised scar indicates where a young apple sawfly maggot has hatched and fed just below the skin. If the grub survives, it may continue tunneling inside, causing the fruitlet to fall prematurely. If the grub doesn't survive, the apple may ripen normally—though it will still bear the scar
■ See **European apple sawfly** (p.336).

16 Dark, sunken spots in skin
Small, round, concave spots appear on the skins, particularly in large cooking apples. They may spread down into the flesh and cause the fruit to taste bitter.
■ See **Bitter pit** (p.325).

17 Holes ringed with black-brown "frass"
The hole reveals where the larva of the codling moth ate its way out of the fruit after hatching and feeding. Inside, much of the apple may have been eaten and filled with frass (excrement). European apple sawfly grubs make similar holes.
■ See **Codling moth** (p.335) and **European apple sawfly** (p.336).

Leaf stuck to skin
A leaf attached to the skin of the fruit by a silk web may well be camouflage concealing a tortrix moth caterpillar.
■ See **Tortrix moth** (p.341).

Unsightly brown tunnels in flesh
Apple maggot flies pierce the skin of young fruits and lay their eggs. The maggots tunnel through the fruit, which often drops.
■ See **Apple maggot** (p.334).

Cuts in skin of fruit; deformed fruit
Plum curculios cut a small flap in the skin of fruits to lay eggs. Larvae feed on fruit flesh.
■ See **Plum Curculio** (p.339).

Dry rot of the fruit
This rot starts at the blossom end, and it is caused by a fungus called black rot. It also causes lesions on leaves.
■ See **Black rot** (p.325).

Pears

For some reason, home growers plant fewer pears than apples. Pears are certainly just as delicious—if not more so. And yet, while an apple tree is a common sight in even the most modest, small yard, a pear tree is more unusual. It's hard to know why. The reason may have to do with perception: pears are thought to be more troublesome and trickier to grow than apples. It's true that they're choosy about exactly where they will grow—they dislike being buffeted by wind and they need slightly more warmth and sunshine than apples. And in the eastern part of the country, humidity makes fire blight a potentially serious problem. But if you choose blight-resistant varieties and can give the trees the conditions they like, they should thrive and produce a good crop every year. Moreover, pruning is easier than with apples, and, once established, the trees live longer. So, get the basics right, and you may even find that they're actually easier to grow.

Harvest pears while they are still slightly hard but come away easily in your hand. They will continue to ripen after you bring them indoors.

Which forms to grow

■ **Dwarf and semidwarf trees** These small trees are easier to care for than standard trees and produce fruit within a few years.
■ **Standard trees** These will reach up to 20 ft (6 m) tall, but may be better adapted to cold-winter areas.
■ **Central leader training** Pear trees do well with this method.
■ **Multi-leader training** If one leader contracts fire blight, you can prune it out and still have other leaders to work with.
■ **Cordon** Wire-trained single or multiple stems that produce fruits on short sideshoots.
■ **Espalier and fan** Wire-trained forms with arms growing on either side of a central stem or radiating from a short trunk.

Must-grow pears

1 'Buerré d'Anjou'
Pollination group B
Excellent aromatic flavor. Good for baking, flavor improves with cold storage. Moderately resistant to fire blight.
- **Harvest** late September
- **Eat** September–October

2 'Comice'
Pollination group C
Regarded by many as the best-tasting pear of all. Fruit are a russet yellow-green when ripe, and the flesh is rich, sweet, and juicy. It grows best in the West. Known as the "gift box pear."
- **Harvest** October
- **Eat** October–December

3 'Conference'
Pollination group B
One of the most widely grown of all pears—both commercially and in home gardens. Hardy, dependable, and heavy-cropping. Fruits are long and narrow, and the flesh is sweet and juicy.
- **Harvest** September
- **Eat** October–November

4
'Warren' and 'Clapp's Favorite' are popular with home gardeners in most parts of the country. 'Warren' is very resistant to fire blight and it keeps well. 'Clapp's Favorite' is sweet and productive, and its fruit is best eaten soon after picking. Both of these pears ripen in August.

5 'Gorham'
Pollination group C
An old American variety with a sweet, musky flavor and a green-yellow skin. It is reliable and easy to grow, but doesn't always crop heavily.
■ **Harvest** September
■ **Eat** September–October

6 'Bartlett'
Pollination group B
An early cropping dessert pear, often claimed to be the world's most widely grown variety. Known in the UK as 'Williams'. Very popular for eating fresh and canning, but it is susceptible to fire blight. Does not keep.
■ **Harvest** September
■ **Eat** September

7 'Packham's Triumph'
Pollination group A
Originally bred in Australia at the end of the 19th century, with 'Bartlett' one of its parents. The fine flavor makes it popular both as a grow-your-own fruit and commercially. However, it flowers early and may fall prey to frost.
■ **Harvest** October
■ **Eat** November–December

8 Blight-resistant pears like 'Magness' and 'Moonglow' are a great choice for gardeners in areas where the disease is a problem. 'Magness' is slow to reach bearing age, but has sweet and juicy fruit. 'Moonglow' reaches bearing age quickly; fruit develops best flavor after several weeks in storage. 'Moonglow' ripens in late August; 'Magness' ripens in September.

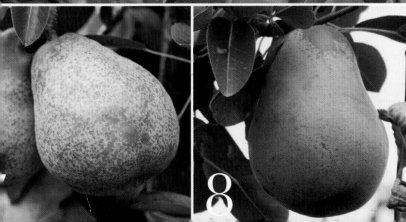

9 'Louise Bonne of Jersey'
Pollination group A

An old-fashioned French dessert pear with a lovely sweet, aromatic flavor. Flowers early in spring but seems able to survive all but the most severe frosts.
- ■ **Harvest** September
- ■ **Eat** October

10 'Beth'
Pollination group C

An excellent early dessert pear. Slightly small but with an outstanding, rich, sweet flavor. Trees fruit when young and generally produce high yields.
- ■ **Harvest** August–September
- ■ **Eat** September

11 'Glou Morceau'
Pollination group C

A winter pear first bred in Belgium in the 18th century. Large fruit with a fine flavor and texture. Needs warmth and sun to develop fully. Stored carefully, they should keep until early January.
- ■ **Harvest** October
- ■ **Eat** December–January

12 'Onward'
Pollination group C

A cross between 'Doyenné du Comice' and 'Laxton's Superb', it shares the same excellent flavor. Easy to grow, reliable, and heavy-fruiting. Good for the average-sized yard. Keeps poorly, so should be eaten soon after picking.
- ■ **Harvest** September
- ■ **Eat** September

13 'Buerré Hardy'
Pollination group B

Dates back to the early 19th century. Large, russeted fruit with smooth, white flesh and a fine flavor. Pick while slightly underripe and store until ready to eat.
- ■ **Harvest** September
- ■ **Eat** September–October

14 'Concorde'
Pollination group C

A cross between the English 'Conference' and French 'Doyenné du Comice'. It is as easy to grow and as heavy fruiting as the former, and has the excellent flavor of the latter. A good choice for a small garden.
- ■ **Harvest** September–October
- ■ **Eat** October–December

'Max-Red Bartlett' (not illustrated)
Pollination group C
A distinctive and unusual red-skinned variety of 'Bartlett'. Texture and flavor are excellent and it should be ready to pick and eat early in the season.
- **Harvest** August–September
- **Eat** September

'Seckel' (not illustrated)
'Seckel' pears are quite small and have golden brown skin. The trees are very hardy and resistant to fire blight. The fruit is very sweet.
- **Harvest** early September
- **Eat** September

'Beurre Bosc' (not illustrated)
This variety is related to the classic 'Bosc' pear, and are very tough and hardy trees. They bear long fruit with russet skin and aromatic flavor. Trees are susceptible to fire blight.
- **Harvest** October
- **Eat** October–December

'Harrow Delight' (not illustrated)
A hardy variety that resists fire blight and scab. Medium-size, smoothed skin fruit with good flavor.
- **Harvest** September
- **Eat** September

ASIAN PEARS

'Chojuro' (not illustrated)
A very long-keeping pear. Distinctive flavor and brown russeted skin that is a bit astringent. Individual fruit may weigh nearly a pound.
- **Harvest** September
- **Eat** September–February

'Hosui' (not illustrated)
Round pears with excellent flavor and golden brown skin. Tree is somewhat willowy in form; resists scab but is susceptible to fire blight.
- **Harvest** August
- **Eat** August–November

'Korean Giant' (not illustrated)
Vigorous and early to come into bearing with very large fruit. Crisp, juicy and sweet; resists fire blight.
- **Harvest** mid-October
- **Eat** October–February

'Tsu Li' (not illustrated)
Looks somewhat like a European pear, very sweet and aromatic flavor. Somewhat fire blight resistant. Early-blooming. Needs to be stored awhile before eating to develop best flavor.
- **Harvest** September
- **Eat** October–November

Choosing and buying pear trees

As with apples, there are a number of things to bear in mind before buying a pear tree. First, the form: do you want it to be freestanding or wire-trained? Second, the rootstock, since that has a major effect on how large the tree will grow. Third, the pollination group to which it belongs, as that determines when it flowers. And, finally, the variety or cultivar.

Choosing a tree form

As a general rule, pears need a more sheltered and sunnier site than apples. If you can provide this and you have room, you might choose a semidwarf or dwarf tree or, in the North, a standard tree. If space is tight, then a row of cordons, an espalier, or a fan on a warm, sunny wall might be a better option.

Choosing a variety

The choice of varieties or cultivars is not as wide for pears as it is for apples. Nevertheless, there are still plenty to choose from—either one of the reliable, disease-resistant, heavy-fruiting modern varieties or, if you search them out, traditional varieties whose ancestry may go back hundreds of years.

Like apples, pears are classified as either dessert or culinary. Culinary pears, which are less common, never ripen sufficiently to eat raw.

Very few pears are self-fertile. They need pollen from another tree for successful fertilization and fruit production. So, all pears should be planted with neighboring trees from the same flowering or pollination group. However, if space is restricted, growing a multi-variety tree may be the solution: it is a single tree with more than one pear cultivar grafted onto the same rootstock (see p.53). The different varieties should cross-pollinate each other.

(opposite, clockwise from top left) **An arch** formed of cordons trained vertically, then bent into curves overhead.
Container trees are best grown on less vigorous rootstocks.
A pear pyramid results from training trees on metal frames.
Orchard pears should all be from the same pollination group.

CHOOSING A ROOTSTOCK

Traditionally, pears were grown on quince rootstocks. many of which are susceptible to fire blight; better pear rootstocks have now been developed. The OHxF series is good for semidwarf and standard European pears, and seedling rootstock of various *Pyrus* species is often used for Asian pears.

| 15' (5 m) |
| 12' (4 m) |
| 9' (3 m) |
| 6' (2 m) |
| 3' (1 m) |

OHxF 333   Quince A

OHxF 333
- VIGOR Semidwarfing.
- CHARACTERISTICS Resistant to fire blight and other diseases. Strong rooting, results in excellent yields. Fruit may be slightly smaller than other rootstocks.
- SUPPORT Stake for the first 2 years.
- HEIGHT 12–20 ft (3.5–6 m).

Quince A
- VIGOR Semivigorous.
- CHARACTERISTICS Stronger growing and a little less fussy about soil conditions. A better choice for poor soil and for slightly larger trees.
- SUPPORT Stake for first 2 years.
- HEIGHT 15–20 ft (5–6 m).

Winged insects transfer pollen between blooms of different pear trees and usually ensure cross-pollination. Always check that the trees you buy will be in blossom at the same time, as well as compatible with each other.

PEAR POLLINATION GROUPS

A
'Chojuro'
'Korean Giant'
'Packham's Triumph'
'Seckel'
'Tsu Li'

B
'Bartlett'
'Beurré d'Anjou'
'Conference'
'Harrow Delight'
'Hosui'
'Magness'
'Warren'
'Winter Nelis'
'Hessle'

C
'Beurré Bosc'
'Clapp's Favorite'
'Concorde'
'Comice'
'Gorham'
'Moonglow'
'Max-Red Bartlett'
'Winter Nelis'

'Packham's Triumph' blossoms in early spring so may need protection from frost.

'Conference' is a popular, firm-fleshed pear that fruits reliably in early fall.

'Doyenné du Comice' flowers late in spring. Its large fruit have a superb flavor.

Choosing a pollination group

Pear blossoms open earlier than those of apples—starting in early spring. The pollination group the pear belongs to will give you an indication. It's important to grow at least two or three different trees from the same pollination group—or at least from an adjacent group—so that their flowers bloom simultaneously and insects can transfer pollen from one tree to another.

However, some pears are not good at pollinating other varieties. Called triploids, they should be grown with at least two different, compatible cultivars that are not triploids.

Some specific varieties of pears cannot be relied upon to pollinate others. For example, 'Comice' and 'Bosc' will not pollinate 'Conference' or vice versa, and 'Bartlett' pears will not pollinate 'Seckel' pears. Asian pears begin to come into bloom earlier than European pears, but later-blooming Asian varieties will pollinate European varieties.

Growing pears

Growing apples and pears is very similar. In some ways pears are easier as they grow vigorously, tend to be more resistant to pests and diseases, and are less complicated to prune. But, in one respect, they are slightly more demanding: they need more warmth and sunshine than apples, and better protection from strong winds and frost, so deciding where to plant them and which form to choose needs careful consideration.

The year at a glance

	spring			summer			fall			winter		
	E	M	L	E	M	L	E	M	L	E	M	L
plant bare-root	▬	▬	▬				▬	▬	▬			
plant container	▬	▬	▬				▬	▬	▬	▬	▬	▬
summer prune				▬	▬	▬						
winter prune	▬											
harvest				▬	▬	▬						

Planting pear trees

Pears are sold as either bare-root or container-grown trees. Specialty nurseries offer a wider choice than garden centers, but most of their trees will probably be bare-root and available only in fall (October–November) and spring (March–May).

Newly purchased young trees are usually one, two, or three years old. Two- and three-year-olds are slightly more expensive to buy but, because the nursery will have already carried out a certain amount of training and pruning, they are probably the best choice for a beginner.

When to plant

■ BARE-ROOT Plant in fall or spring, when the trees are dormant. Fall is ideal in Zones 6 and warmer; spring is best for cold-winter areas.
■ CONTAINER-GROWN Plant at any time of year when conditions are appropriate. Avoid late spring and summer months if it is hot and dry.

ASIAN PEARS

The Asian pear is a different species from the European pear. It has crisp, sweet flesh, and unlike European pears, it can be left to ripen fully on the tree. It's a good choice for growing in the South and West, but it doesn't grow as well in very cold-winter areas.

Asian pears are an increasingly popular alternative to European pears because of their sweet flavor and crisp texture. 'Chojuro' and 'Hosui' are popular varieties.

Where to plant

Pears need a warm, sheltered site protected from strong winds. Avoid frost pockets. Grow cordons, espaliers, and fans against a sunny fence or wall.

Soil type

Pears grow best in deep, free-draining soil with a slightly acidic pH of around 6.5. Although they dislike being waterlogged, they seem to tolerate heavy clay soils better than apples. They struggle on sandy soils, and also on alkaline soils, where they are prone to lime-induced chlorosis (see p.320).

Routine care

■ WATERING Take particular care to water young, recently planted trees and wire-trained forms such as fans and espaliers. Don't let them dry out.
■ FEEDING Fertilize in spring after new growth starts, but take care not to overfeed with nitrogen because it will promote tender growth that is easily infected by fire blight. Do not fertilize trees that have shown fire blight symptoms in the past.
■ MULCHING Remove weeds and spread organic mulch around young trees. Or let grass grow around the trees to use excess nitrogen in the soil and prevent lush tree growth that is susceptible to fire blight.
■ FROST PROTECTION Pear blossoms are vulnerable to frost damage. Protecting large, mature trees is

PLANTING DISTANCES

Recommended spacings vary according to the vigor of the rootstock and the variety, the soil and other growing conditions, and the form into which the tree is to be trained.

Standard trees
20–25 ft (6–7.5 m)

Fans and espaliers
11–13 ft (3.5–4.5 m)

Semidwarf trees
15 ft (4.5 m)

Cordons
30 in (75 cm)

Dwarf trees
8–12 ft (1.2–1.5 m)

Double cordons
3 ft (1 m)

PLANTING A ROW OF PEAR CORDONS

A south-facing wall provides a sunny, sheltered site that is ideal for cordons, espaliers, and fans. Prepare the site in advance by working some well-rotted compost or manure into the soil, and add some general, all-purpose fertilizer. Attach horizontal wires to the wall at intervals of 12–18 in (30–45 cm). For single cordons, start with a branched whip and, immediately after planting, prune as for an apple (see p.72). For double cordons, start with a maiden whip and cut back harder (as shown here).

1 Plant the trees about 12 in (30 cm) away from the wall. Any closer and their roots will be at risk of drying out. Lean them in toward the wall slightly. Plant out the rest of the cordons in the row, allowing a space of about 3 ft (1 m) between each tree.

2 Tie the main stems securely to the lowest of the horizontal wires.

3 Cut off the central leader at a height of about 10 in (24 cm), just above the lowest wire, ensuring that there is one strong bud on each side of your cut.

TRAINING THE ARMS OF THE CORDON

The following summer, train the new laterals by tying them to bamboo canes, set first at an angle and then vertically. Cut back all new sideshoots to one leaf.

1st winter pruning
LATE FALL–EARLY SPRING

1st summer pruning
MIDSUMMER

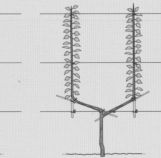

(left) **Double cordons** are perfect for a yard where space is limited. Not only do they look very decorative, they will also provide a reasonable crop, providing they are given support and a sunny, sheltered spot.

The "June drop" takes place in early summer when a proportion of young fruitlets fall to the ground. This is quite natural and is simply the tree's way of discarding diseased or damaged fruit and ensuring that its branches aren't crowded and overloaded.

(below) **Thinning pears** by removing more of the young fruitlets, shortly after the "June drop," will help those that remain to grow to full size. If the crop is heavy, leave just one pear per cluster, about 4–6 in (10–15 cm) apart; if the crop is light, leave two pears per cluster.

impractical, but it may be possible to use an overnight covering of floating row cover on young trees, dwarf trees, and espaliers or fans.

Harvesting and storing pears

There's an art to picking pears at just the right moment. Unlike most fruit, they are best picked while they are still slightly unripe. The sure way to test whether or not early season pears are ready to pick is simply to taste one. It will still be hard, of course, but if it tastes sweet, it's ready; if it doesn't, it's not. Once picked, bring pears indoors and eat them when their flavor has developed and they have softened slightly. If you leave pears on the tree too long or let them overripen indoors, they turn unpleasantly soft, grainy, and perhaps even brown in the middle.

Late-season pears are for keeping. You can't tell by tasting them when they are ready to pick. The best test is to lift them in your hand and twist them gently. If they pull away easily, they're ready. To store them, bring them indoors somewhere dark, reasonably well-ventilated, not too dry, and cool but frost-free. Spread them out on slatted trays or molded grocer's fruit liners, ensuring that they don't touch. Don't wrap them in paper. Inspect them regularly and remove any that show signs of rot. Bring a few at a time into a warmer room so they can soften up for eating. Varieties that store well include 'Seckel', 'Red Anjou', 'Comice', and 'Warren'.

Yield

Yields vary widely according to variety, tree form, rootstock, growing conditions, and other variables. However, average quantities are:
- DWARF 33–45 lb (15–20 kg).
- SEMIDWARF and STANDARD 150–200 lb (65–90 kg).
- FAN 11–25 lb (5.5–11 kg).
- ESPALIER 15–25 lb (7–11 kg).
- CORDON 4.5–8 lb (2–3.5 kg).

Season by season

Midwinter
■ If necessary, spray trees with dormant oil to protect against aphids, pear psylla, and other pests.

Late winter
■ Prune young and established trees before the dormant period ends.

Early spring
■ Begin planting bare-root trees as conditions allow.

Mid-spring
■ Most varieties flower now. Protect blossoms from frost if necessary.
■ Hang pheromone traps to attract and catch male codling moths before they mate.
■ Inspect dwarf trees and hand-pick any pest caterpillars you find.

Late spring
■ Water newly planted and wire-trained trees.
■ Check for powdery mildew and signs of scab.

Early summer
■ Further thin out young fruitlets.
■ Summer prune young espaliers and fans between now and early fall.
■ Begin checking for fire blight symptoms. Prune out and destroy any diseased growth as it appears.
■ Check for pear psylla and spray with summer oil or insecticidal soap if needed. Continue monitoring throughout the fruiting period.

Midsummer
■ Summer prune established espaliers and fans and all types of cordons this month and next, cutting back new laterals and sideshoots.
■ As fruit begins to drop, pick it up regularly and destroy it to help reduce future pest problems.

Late summer
■ Continue summer pruning wire-trained trees.
■ Remove and destroy any fruit infected with scab or brown rot.

Early fall
■ Harvest early-season pears.
■ If you mulched around your trees, rake the mulch out from under the canopy. After leaf fall, replace the mulch and add a new top layer.

Mid-fall
■ Harvest late-season pears and store some for the winter.
■ Tie sticky tree bands around trunks to deter winter moths.
■ In Zone 6 and warmer, buy and plant new bare-root trees.

Late fall
■ Remove any rotten fruit still hanging on the tree.
■ Rake up any diseased leaves.
■ Check stored fruit for signs of rot.

(top to bottom) **Buds** swell in late winter. **Blossoms** open in early spring. **Some fruitlets** will fall to the ground in the "June drop." **Dessert pears** ready for picking.

Pruning and training pears

Pears are pruned and trained in almost exactly the same way as apple trees. Both produce fruit on wood that is two years old or older, and need regular pruning to keep them in shape, to thin out or cut back overly vigorous growth, and to encourage healthy fruit production. Almost all pears are spur-bearers; there are very few tip-bearers (see p.67).

Pruning a pear tree

Both newly planted and established trees are pruned in the same way as apples, the aim being to create a framework of well-spaced main branches spreading out from the trunk (see p.68). Prune in winter, between November and February, when the trees are dormant.

Each year, check for any dead, damaged, or diseased wood and cut it out. Remove any crossing or congested branches, as well as any that are growing vertically upward, crowding the center of the tree. Cut to an outward-facing bud to encourage new growth.

On old, established trees, spur systems can get very crowded. Thin them out regularly to remove old, unproductive spurs and to give more room for the fruit.

Multi-leader pruning

Because pears are so susceptible to fire blight, especially in humid conditions, you may want to train your trees to have more than one leader. That way, you'll still be able to reap a harvest even if one section of the tree becomes infected and has to be removed. For detailed instructions on training a multi-leader tree, follow the instructions on page 68.

Pruning a central leader tree

Pear trees need careful pruning and training in the first few years in order to establish their basic shape. Thereafter, they are pruned twice a year: in summer to cut back new growth, and in winter to thin out crowded spur systems.

1st spring pruning
EARLY to MID-SPRING

- Start with a branched whip. Stake and prune immediately after planting.
- Cut off the central leader or main stem to a bud 20–30 in (50–75 cm) above the ground.
- Prune each lateral or sideshoot to a length of about 6 in (15 cm), cutting to an outward-facing bud.
- Remove any laterals that are growing upright, are crossing, or are too close to the base.

1st summer pruning
EARLY SUMMER

- Very little pruning is required in the first summer.
- Cut back to a single leaf any new shoots growing vertically upward, especially near the top of the tree.
- Tie in the central leader to the tree stake.

Dwarf trees not only fit into smaller spaces, but are easier to check for pests and diseases, and the fruit can be picked without ladders.

2nd spring pruning
EARLY SPRING

- ▦ Prune the central leader to leave about 10 in (25 cm) of last summer's new growth. Cut to a bud on the opposite side to the bud you cut back to last winter.
- ▦ Shorten the main laterals to leave 6–8 in (15–20 cm) of last summer's new growth. Cut to buds facing downward and outward.
- ▦ Shorten sublaterals or sideshoots to just 2 or 3 buds. These will go on to form spurs.

Summer pruning an established tree
EARLY SUMMER

- ▦ Cut back the laterals that form the main branches to leave 5 or 6 leaves of this summer's growth.
- ▦ Cut back sublaterals growing off the main laterals to 3 leaves beyond the basal cluster.
- ▦ Cut back new sideshoots to 1 leaf beyond the basal cluster.
- ▦ Leave the central leader untouched.

Winter pruning an established tree
LATE WINTER

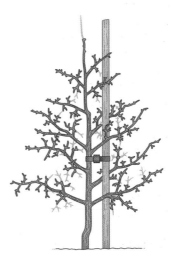

- ▦ When the tree has reached its full height, prune the central leader each winter to leave just 1 bud of last year's new growth.
- ▦ Thin out overcrowded or unproductive spurs.
- ▦ Reduce the number of fruit buds to 2 or 3 per spur.

Pruning a pear cordon

Pears make very good cordons—vertical, oblique, or multiple. They are pruned in the same way as apples (see p.72). Once established, prune them twice a year, in winter and in summer, regularly cutting back lateral branches to form short sideshoots or spurs on which the fruit is borne.

(opposite, clockwise from top) **A row of oblique cordons** with fruitlets in early summer. **Multiple cordon**—the four arms are clearly visible in winter. **A double cordon** is covered in spring blossoms.

(right, from the left) **In summer** new growth on this oblique cordon is very vigorous and must be pruned back to allow light and air to reach the young fruit.

Pruning a pear espalier

Train and prune a pear espalier just as you would an apple (see p.74), although you can perhaps start summer pruning a little earlier. And in winter, be prepared to thin out spurs slightly more ruthlessly; most pears produce them more readily than apples and older spur systems can easily become overcrowded and unproductive.

(below) **In winter** it is easy to see the fruiting spurs on this expertly pruned mature espalier. Congested spurs have been thinned out to keep the tree as productive as possible.

Pruning a pear fan

Like espaliers, pear fans are trained and pruned in the same way as apples. But unlike espaliers, fans do not have a central leader. Instead, the laterals or ribs spread out on either side of a short central trunk. Fans, espaliers, and all wire-trained trees need pruning twice a year, in summer and in winter. It's possible to buy pretrained fans. They are expensive but may give you a year or two's head start on getting the tree established. Otherwise, begin with a maiden whip or a suitable branched whip.

1st winter pruning
LATE FALL–EARLY SPRING

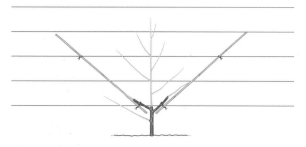

- Construct a support system by securing horizontal wires 12 in (30 cm) apart to a wall, fence, or upright posts. Attach 2 diagonal canes.
- Start with a branched whip. Plant it, and prune immediately after planting.
- Cut off the central leader and any top growth above 2 strong left- and right-facing laterals, at a height of about 18 in (45 cm) above the ground, just below the bottom wire.
- Cut back the 2 laterals to about 18 in (45 cm) and tie them in to the canes. They will become 2 of the main ribs.
- Remove any lower, unwanted laterals.

1st summer pruning
EARLY SUMMER–EARLY FALL

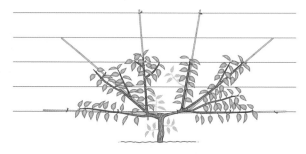

- As sublaterals or sideshoots develop on the 2 main ribs, tie them in to additional canes and to the wires (right), ensuring that they are evenly spread.
- Remove completely any new shoots that are unwanted or growing inward or outward at right angles to the fan.

2nd winter pruning
LATE FALL

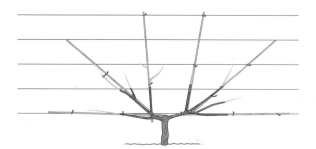

- Tip-prune the laterals by one-quarter or one-third of last summer's new growth.
- Now that leaves have fallen, ensure that the laterals are all tied in securely.
- Remove any unwanted shoots growing directly from the main trunk.

2nd summer pruning
EARLY SUMMER–EARLY FALL

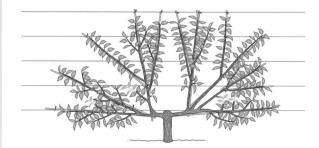

- Attach more canes as required and tie in new sublaterals destined to form additional ribs of the fan.
- Aim for a balanced, even shape, and keep the center uncluttered.
- Where growth becomes crowded, prune sublaterals or sideshoots growing from the main ribs to 3 leaves beyond the basal cluster.

Winter pruning an established fan
LATE FALL–EARLY SPRING

- Established fans should need only light winter pruning.
- Thin out overcrowded spur systems by removing weak, overlapping, or congested spurs.
- Cut out completely any very old spur systems that are no longer productive so that new growth can replace them.
- Remove any dead, diseased, or damaged wood.

(clockwise from top left) **Cut back long shoots** to a healthy spur that is outward-facing. **Prune crowded spurs** to reduce the number of branches they produce. **Remove wood** showing any signs of disease. **A mature pear fan** will remain productive and keep its shape if routine pruning is carried out each winter.

Summer pruning an established fan
MIDSUMMER

- Prune each main rib of the fan as if it were a cordon.
- Continue cutting back new laterals growing directly from the main ribs to 3 leaves, not counting the basal cluster—especially any vigorous vertical growth.
- Cut back all new sideshoots growing from existing laterals and spurs to just 1 leaf beyond the basal cluster.

(clockwise from top left) **Cut back sideshoots** growing from laterals to 1 leaf. **Prune** to 3 leaves any laterals growing from the main branches or ribs. **An established** pear fan in full leaf will need pruning in summer so that new growth doesn't shade the fruit, and to let in light and air.

What can go wrong

Buds and Blossoms

Blossoms discolor and die
Pears flower early in spring and frost often damages young leaves and blossom. Fire blight causes similar symptoms.
■ See **Frost** (p.316) and **Fire blight** (p.327).

Leaves, stems, and branches

1 Leaves curled and tattered with holes
The most likely cause of the damage is moth caterpillars feeding on leaves and curling the edges around themselves.
■ See **Tortrix moth** (p.340) and **Winter moth** (p.341).

2 Orange spots on leaves
Spots may be yellow with an orange or brown center. The cause is rust, a sporadic problem on pears in the Pacific Northwest.
■ See **Rust** (p.330).

3 Yellow-black blisters on leaves
A rash of raised blisters or blotches appears on young leaves, starting off yellow or pink, then turning black as summer passes. Pear leaf blister mites feeding on the leaves are responsible.
■ See **Pear leaf blister mite** (p.337).

4 Brown blotches on leaves
Velvety, dark-brown blotches or spots, usually on leaf undersides, indicate scab; leaves may drop off. The fruit themselves may be affected, too.
■ See **Scab** (p.330).

Brown skeletonlike patches on leaves
Sawfly larvae called pear slugs feed on upper surfaces of leaves, leaving the veins untouched.
■ See **Pear slug** (p.338).

5 Leaves tightly curled and colored red or black
If young leaves curl upward into tight rolls, and turn red, then black, suspect pear leaf-curling midge.
■ See **Pear leaf-curling midge** (p.337).

6 Leaves wither and die back
Leaves and shoots appear scorched and bend over, creating a "shepherd's hook" appearance. Fruits can be affected too.
■ See **Fireblight** (p.327).

7 Leaves curled and sticky
Infestations of aphids cause leaves to curl tightly and become distorted. Upper surfaces may develop gray sooty mold.
■ See **Aphids** (p.334).

Leaves turn yellow

Pear psylla suck on plant juices, causing leaves to turn yellow; sooty mold may grow on leaves. Feeding by San Jose scale also causes leaf yellowing.

■ See **Pear psylla** (p.338); **Scale insects** (p.340).

Cracked areas of bark and dieback

Discolored, sunken, split, or flaky areas of bark can indicate canker. As it spreads, cracked rings form, and whole branches may die.

■ See **Apple and pear canker** (p.324).

Fruit

8 Brown scabs and split skin

Scablike patches appear on the fruit. As they spread, the skin dries out and is likely to split or crack, possibly allowing other infections to enter. Fruitlets are shrunken and misshapen.

■ See **Scab** (p.330).

9 Fruit develop patches of brown rot

Ripening fruit turn brown and may develop concentric rings of white fungal spores, sometimes around a central hole. They either fall to the ground or remain on the tree, gradually drying out and shriveling.

■ See **Brown rot** (p.326).

10 Ragged holes in fruit

Birds, wasps, and flies feed on ripe fruit, particularly if the skin has already been pierced or damaged.

■ See **Birds** (p.335) and **Wasps** (p.341).

Holes ringed with black-brown "frass"

Larvae of the codling moth hatch and feed inside the fruit, then eat their way out, leaving an exit hole. Inside, much of the pear may have been eaten and filled with frass (excrement).

■ See **Codling moth** (p.335).

Misshapen, blackened fruit fall while still young

Small, young fruitlets swell and their skins turn black. They're likely to drop prematurely. Inside, you may still find well-fed midge larvae that are responsible for the damage.

■ See **Pear leaf-curling midge** (p.337).

Pale brown, corky patches

Tarnished plant bugs feeding on young fruitlets can cause them to become disfigured and develop scars or corklike patches.

■ See **Plant bugs** (p.335).

Fruit dimpled and misshapen

Infected pears are lumpy or knobby, and may be hard, woody, or unpleasant-tasting. The cause is a virus which, though it is unlikely to affect all the fruit on a tree, can spread.

■ See **Stony pit virus** (p.328).

Plums

The term "plum" covers a wide variety of related fruit. European plums, along with gages, their green- or yellow-skinned relatives, originated in the Caucasus and southern central Asia, probably as a cross between cherry plums and wild blackthorns or sloes. Japanese plums are extremely sweet and juicy and, because they come into flower very early, are best grown in warm climates. In the US, Japanese plums have long been cross-bred with native species as well as with imported European cultivars to produce modern North American varieties, which grow well in all but the coldest and hottest parts of the country. Damsons and mirabelles are not grown here as much as in Europe, but they are good for cooking, preserving, and making jams.

Plums are not hard to grow, especially now that modern dwarfing rootstocks have helped restrict the size of the trees. They need a lot less pruning than apples and pears. Your biggest challenge is likely to be harvesting the ripe fruit before birds, wasps, and other insects beat you to it.

Plums ripen from July onward, though the best time to pick them depends on the variety—and the weather. Let plums ripen thoroughly on the tree before picking—they will be slightly soft.

Which forms to grow

■ **Semidwarf and dwarf** Good for most backyard settings. Choice of open center or modified central leader training depends on the variety.
■ **Cordon** Plant either single upright trees or perhaps a row of oblique cordons.
■ **Fan** Ideal for a sheltered, sunny fence or wall.

Must-grow plums

1 'Early Laxton'
Pollination group B
One of the very first plums to ripen. Attractive, juicy, medium-sized, yellow-red fruit with an acceptable if unexciting flavor.
- **Fertility** partly self-fertile
- **Harvest** late July–early August

2 'Victoria'
Pollination group B
Still widely regarded as the best all-around plum of them all. Heavy fruiting with fruit of excellent flavor for both eating and cooking.
- **Fertility** self-fertile
- **Harvest** late August–early September

3 'Opal'
Pollination group B
A relatively modern culinary variety from Scandinavia now acknowledged as perhaps the best of the early ripening plums. Heavy-fruiting, its fruit ripen to red and have a good flavor.
- **Fertility** self-fertile
- **Harvest** late July–early August

4 'Warwickshire Drooper'
Pollination group A
An old-fashioned variety with large, yellow plums so heavy that they earn their wonderful name by weighing down the branches of the tree.
- **Fertility** self-fertile
- **Harvest** mid–late September

5 'Jubilee'
Pollination group B
A new variety from Sweden, claimed to be superior to 'Victoria'. The fruit are larger and equally well-flavored. It is also hardy, heavy-fruiting, and disease-resistant.
- **Fertility** self-fertile
- **Harvest** mid–late August

6 'Marjorie's Seedling'
Pollination group C
Large, oval, well-flavored fruit are perfect for cooking but can also be

eaten fresh if left to ripen fully. Purple skin with yellow flesh.
- **Fertility** self-fertile
- **Harvest** late September–early October

7 'Shiro'
Pollination group A
A Japanese plum with medium to large, round, yellow-skinned fruit. The flesh is translucent, sweet, and extremely juicy.
- **Fertility** partly self-fertile
- **Harvest** August

8 'Giant Prune'
Pollination group C
An American plum, also known as 'Burbank's Giant'. It produces heavy crops of large, oval, red–purple fruit that taste and keep well. Frost- and disease-resistant.
- **Fertility** self-fertile
- **Harvest** mid–late September

'Blue Tit' (not illustrated)
Pollination group C
Reliable, dual-purpose plum for eating or cooking. Juicy, medium-sized, and deep blue in color. Blossoms open late, so a good variety for frost-prone areas.
- **Fertility** self-fertile
- **Harvest** early–mid August

'Czar' (not illustrated)
Pollination group B
Traditional cooking plum dating back to the 19th century and still widely grown. Fruit have dark purple skins and yellow-green flesh with a good flavor.
- **Fertility** self-fertile
- **Harvest** early August

'Guinevere' (not illustrated)
Pollination group C
A recently introduced modern variety. The large, sweet, dark-purple fruit will keep well in the refrigerator.
- **Fertility** self-fertile
- **Harvest** September

'Methley' (not illustrated)
Pollination group A
A Japanese plum with red-purple skin and blood-red, very sweet, very juicy flesh. It flowers early and so may need frost protection.
- **Fertility** self-fertile
- **Harvest** July

Gages

1 'Oullins Golden Gage'
Pollination group C
Green-yellow fruit with pale yellow flesh.
Reliable, reasonably sweet, with a good
flavor for both cooking and eating raw.
- **Fertility** self-fertile
- **Harvest** mid-August

2 'Old Green Gage'
Pollination group C
Also referred to as 'Reine Claude-Vraie'
(the "true" greengage) in recognition of
its 16th-century French ancestry. Small
yellow-green fruit with the archetypal,
rich greengage flavor.
- **Fertility** self-infertile
- **Harvest** late August–early September

Damsons & bullaces

1 'Shropshire Damson'
Pollination group C
Sometimes called 'Prune Damson', this old
variety can be harvested as late as October.
Trees are hardy and compact.
- **Fertility** self-fertile
- **Harvest** late September–early October

2 'Langley Bullace'
Pollination group B
The small, almost black fruit are far too tart
to eat raw but make superb jams. Crops are
generous and reliable, but trees can be large.
- **Fertility** self-fertile
- **Harvest** late September–early October

3 'Merryweather Damson'
Pollination group B
An old variety, its classic blue-black fruit
have juicy, yellow flesh. Use them for cooking.
- **Fertility** self-fertile
- **Harvest** late September

3 'Cambridge Gage'
Pollination group C
Bred from the original 'Old Green Gage', this variety is more vigorous and produces more fruit. It retains the same excellent flavor.
■ **Fertility** partly self-fertile
■ **Harvest** late August–early September

'Denniston's Superb' (not illustrated)
Pollination group B
Strictly speaking a plum with green–yellow skin, it is nevertheless usually listed as gage—and indeed sometimes called the 'Imperial Gage'. North American in origin, it is said to date back to the late 18th century.
■ **Fertility** self-fertile
■ **Harvest** late August

Cherry plums (mirabelles)

1 'Golden Sphere'
Pollination group A
Large, apricot-sized, golden-yellow fruit. A recent variety crossbred from plums and cherry plums in the Ukraine, it is very hardy.
■ **Fertility** partly self-fertile
■ **Harvest** August

2 'Gypsy'
Pollination group A
Bright red fruit with a strong cherry-plum flavor are ideal for bottling and for making jam. Also from the Ukraine.
■ **Fertility** partly self-fertile
■ **Harvest** August

Growing plums

Traditionally, plums were grown as standalone bushes or standard trees, but fruit of mature trees were hard to pick and difficult to protect from birds. Thankfully, modern rootstocks restrict growth to about 6–7 ft (2–2.2 m) high on semidwarfing Krymsk 1 and to about 7–9 ft (2.2–2.7 m) high on semivigorous St Julien A. Semidwarf or dwarf plum trees fit well in most yards. If you have a warm, sheltered wall or fence that gets the sun, take advantage of it by opting for a fan shape, or perhaps a row of oblique cordons.

Plums flower in early or mid-spring, depending on the variety you've chosen. For successful pollination to take place, trees that are planted together for compatibility must also be in blossom at the same time.

The year at a glance

	spring			summer			fall			winter		
	E	M	L	E	M	L	E	M	L	E	M	L
plant bare-root	─							─	─	─	─	─
plant container	─	─	─	─	─	─	─	─	─	─	─	─
summer-prune				─	─	─	─	─				
harvest					─	─	─	─	─			

Flowering and pollination

When choosing plums, you need to know the following. First, is the variety self-fertile? And, second, when does it flower? Plums that are self-fertile (or self-compatible) will set fruit from their own pollen. If you intend to plant just a single tree, choose one of these. Others are either partially self-fertile or completely self-infertile, and need cross-pollination by another suitable variety. In practice, this means you'll need to plant two or more compatible trees near one another. Even self-fertile plums, however, are more likely to produce better crops if they are in a position to be cross-pollinated from other trees.

Not all plums flower at the same time. Cross-pollination won't take place between an early-flowering and a late-flowering variety, since insects can only transfer pollen from flower to flower when the blossoms are open. You should, therefore, always make sure you choose varieties from the same flowering or pollination group, or at worst adjacent groups. Plums in, say, group B should pollinate each other because they will all be in flower at the same

PLUM POLLINATION GROUPS

A

Plums
'Avalon'
'Blue Rock'
'Coe's Golden Drop'
'Mallard'
'Valor'
'Warwickshire Drooper'

Gages
'Jefferson'

Cherry plums
'Golden Sphere'
'Gypsy'

B

Plums
'Cox's Emperor'
'Czar'
'Early Laxton'
'Edwards'
'Green Gage'
'Herman'
'Jubilee'
'Opal'
'Pershore'
'Rivers' Early Prolific'
'Sanctus Hubertus'
'Seneca'

Gages
'Denniston's Superb'
'Golden Transparent'

Damsons & Bullaces
'Langley Bullace'
'Merryweather Damson'

C

Plums
'Belle de Louvain'
'Blue Tit'
'Giant Prune'
'Guinevere'
'Kirke's Blue'
'Marjorie's Seedling'

Gages
'Cambridge Gage'
'Early Transparent'
'Old Green Gage'
'Oullins Golden Gage'

Damsons
'Bradley's King'
'Farleigh'
'Shropshire'

(top to bottom)
'Jefferson' and
'Golden Sphere'.

(top to bottom)
'Opal' and
'Merryweather'.

(top to bottom)
'Giant Prune' and
'Shropshire Damson'.

'Early Laxton' belongs to pollination group B. It will cross-pollinate successfully with other plums from the same group.

time. However, provided that the blossoms are open for long enough, there may be some overlap with trees from group A and group B, in which case they may cross-pollinate, too. It's unlikely that trees from groups A and C will.

In general, European plums and damsons are self-pollinating. On the other hand, most Japanese plums require cross-pollination by another Japanese variety or by an American plum. American plums need cross-pollination as well. Hybrid varieties (Japanese plum crossed with American plums) are even more complex. They usually need cross-pollination by an American variety, and some are so choosy that they can be pollinated only by a particular American variety.

If you are unsure about which plums to plant with which, ask at the fruit tree nursery or choose self-compatible varieties such as 'Green Gage'.

Growing in containers

Plums can be grown in large pots or tubs, but only those on semidwarfing rootstock. Compact, bushy Japanese-American hybrids are probably the best choice. Start off young, one- or two-year-old trees in a container with a minimum diameter and depth of 18 in (45 cm) and fill it with multipurpose, soil-based potting mix with added sand or gravel to improve drainage. Feed with a high-potassium fertilizer in spring, and keep the pot well-watered. After two years, repot in a 24-in (60-cm) container.

Choosing trees

Plums are sold as either bare-root or container-grown trees. Specialty nurseries offer a wider choice than garden centers but the trees will probably be bare-root and available only between mid-fall and early spring.

When to plant

■ BARE-ROOT Plant trees in late fall to early spring, when the trees are dormant, unless the

Gages belong to the same family as plums but are green or golden-yellow in color. They are thought to be named after Sir William Gage, who imported them from France in the 18th century.

PLANTING A PLUM TREE

Prepare the site in advance by removing any perennial weeds, working well-rotted compost or manure into the soil, and adding some all-purpose fertilizer. Use a stake for freestanding trees and a system of wire supports for cordons and fans.

1 Dig a hole deep enough and wide enough to accommodate the plant's roots comfortably. If you haven't already done so, add some well-rotted compost or manure and work it into the soil.

2 For a bare-root tree, drive a stake into the ground to a depth of 2 ft (60 cm) about 3 in (8 cm) away from the center of the hole. For a container-grown tree, use a shorter stake, driven in at an angle, to avoid damaging the rootball (see p.35).

3 Make a small mound of soil in the center of the hole and gently spread the roots over it. Check the depth to ensure that the old nursery soil mark on the stem is level with the surface of your soil. Carefully fill the hole with soil, ensuring that there are no air pockets among the roots.

4 Gently firm down the soil—don't stamp and compact it. Water generously now and at regular intervals over the next few weeks.

5 Secure the tree to the stake with a belt tie. You may need one at the top and one at the bottom.

6 Spread organic mulch around the plant to help retain moisture and suppress weeds.

soil is waterlogged or frozen. October is often an optimal month for planting.

■ CONTAINER-GROWN In theory, you may plant at any time of year, providing that trees are available, but fall is best. Avoid late spring and summer months if the weather is hot and dry.

Where to plant

Choose a warm, sunny, sheltered site, away from strong winds and not in a frost pocket. A south- or west-facing wall is ideal for fans or cordons.

Soil type

Plums are tolerant, but prefer deep, free-draining soil with a slightly acidic pH of around 6.5. Like most fruit trees, they dislike being waterlogged and prefer soil with plenty of well-rotted organic matter added.

Planting distances

■ SEMIDWARF 12–15 ft (3.5–4.5 m) apart.
■ DWARF 8–12 ft (2.5–3.5 m) apart.
■ FANS Dwarf 11–13 ft (3.5–4.5 m), semidwarf 13–17 ft (4.5–5.5 m) apart.
■ CORDONS 30 in–3 ft (75 cm–1 m) apart.

(left and right) **From June onward,** begin thinning out young fruitlets. Aim to leave 2–3 in (5–8 cm) between small fruit and 3–4 in (8–10 cm) between larger ones.

Routine care

■ WATERING Water regularly throughout the spring and summer, particularly for wall-trained cordons and fans. Irregular watering during hot, dry weather may cause the skins of the fruit to split.

■ FEEDING In late winter, spread compost around each tree. Apply a blended fertilizer after petals drop in spring.

■ MULCHING In early spring, after fertilizing, remove any weeds and spread an organic mulch around the base of your trees. This will help retain moisture and restrict the growth of new weeds.

■ NETTING Birds can be a problem both in winter, when they eat new fruit buds, and in summer as fruit ripens. Netting large trees may not be practical, but it's easier in the case of cordons and fans.

■ FROST PROTECTION Plums are among the first fruit trees to flower—especially Japanese and cherry plums. They may need to be covered with floating row cover if there is a danger of hard frost.

Harvesting and storing plums

In a year when the fruit set has been good, most plums produce a bigger crop than the trees can physically support. Some fruitlets will fall naturally as part of the "June drop," but you should thin them out further to prevent branches from breaking under the weight. Heavily laden trees may still need supporting with ropes or forked stakes.

Early varieties should be ready for picking in late July. Others, such as damsons and bullaces, may last until October. Even on the same tree, plums do not all ripen at the same time. You'll need to go over each tree more than once, testing the fruit. It will taste at its best when just slightly soft, though plums for cooking, preserving, and freezing can be picked a little earlier. Leave a short length of stalk attached to prevent the skins from tearing and to avoid damaging next year's fruit buds. Eat ripe plums right away; those picked while still slightly underripe should keep for a couple of weeks.

Yield

Yields are hard to quantify as they vary from variety to variety and from year to year. However, average quantities you can expect are:

■ SEMIDWARF 75–100 lb (35–45 kg).
■ DWARF 30–50 lb (14–23 kg).
■ FAN 15–25 lb (7–11 kg).
■ CORDON 8–15 lb (3.5–7 kg).

PLUM/APRICOT HYBRIDS

Plums and apricots have been crossbred to produce hybrid fruit. The first was the California "plumcot," half plum and half apricot. Next came the "pluot," about 75 percent plum and 25 percent apricot, and the "aprium," roughly 75 percent apricot and 25 percent plum.

Season by season

(left to right) **Flower buds** are ready to burst in early spring. **Delicate blossoms** may need protection from frosts. **Fruitlets** start to swell and will soon need thinning.

Midwinter

▨ If necessary, treat trees with dormant spray to protect against aphids.

Late winter

▨ Prune out any branches that show signs of black knot, but wait until spring, after bud break, to prune the tree for training purposes.

Early spring

▨ Begin planting bare-root trees as weather and soil conditions allow.

▨ Weed and mulch around trees.

Mid-spring

▨ Blossoms appear on mid-season and late-flowering varieties. Continue to protect against frost if necessary.

▨ Spring prune young trees this month if you didn't do so in March.

▨ Pinch out unwanted new buds and shoots on wire-trained trees.

▨ If black knot was a problem last year, apply two sprays of lime-sulfur as a preventive, one week apart.

Late spring

▨ Fruitlets form and begin to swell.

▨ Weed and water regularly.

▨ Shake trees to knock loose plum curculios (p.339) onto a dropcloth; destroy the pests. Repeat daily.

Early summer

▨ Start thinning out young fruitlets.

▨ If necessary, lightly summer-prune established trees this month or next. Cut out dead, damaged, or diseased wood, and thin badly congested areas. Tie in new growth and prune back sideshoots.

▨ Hang pheromone traps to help prevent peachtree borer and oriental fruit moth damage.

Midsummer

▨ Harvest the first early-season plums.

▨ Continue light summer-pruning of established trees.

▨ Summer-prune young pyramid and wire-trained trees, cutting back laterals and sideshoots.

▨ As fruit begins to drop, pick it up regularly and destroy it to help reduce future pest problems.

Late summer

▨ Harvest early and mid-season fruit.

Early fall

▨ Harvest mid- and late-season fruit.

▨ Prune wire-trained plums after harvesting.

▨ If you have mulched around your trees, rake the mulch out and under from the canopy. After leaf fall, replace the mulch and add a new top layer.

Mid-fall

▨ Harvest late-season fruit, such as damsons and bullaces.

▨ In Zone 6 and warmer, buy and plant new bare-root trees. October can be an optimal month for planting: the soil is still warm and trees have a chance to get established before growth starts next spring.

Late fall

▨ Remove any rotten fruit still hanging on the tree.

Pruning and training plums

The most important thing to remember is not to prune in winter. Plums, cherries, and other stone fruit are unlike apples and pears; instead of being pruned when the trees are dormant, they are pruned after new growth has begun, making it harder for silver leaf (see p.331) and bacterial canker (see p.324) to enter and infect the tree via pruning wounds. After the first couple of years, freestanding plums need very little pruning—much less than apples and pears. Trained forms, such as cordons and fans, do need regular summer pruning to maintain their shape and productivity.

Pruning a plum tree

Aim for an open-centered tree with a framework of well-spaced main branches. A bush should have a clear trunk of at least 30 in (75 cm) between the lowest branch and the ground; a half-standard or standard will be taller.

Summer pruning an established tree
EARLY TO MIDSUMMER

1st spring pruning
EARLY SPRING

- Whatever time of year you plant, don't prune until the buds begin to open.
- Select 3 or 4 well-spaced main laterals and prune back each by a half or two-thirds of its length—unless the job has already been done by the nursery. Cut to buds that face outward.
- Cut off the central leader to just above the topmost lateral.

2nd spring pruning
EARLY SPRING

- The laterals you left last year will by now have produced new growth in the form of sublaterals. Choose 3 or 4 of each and cut them back by about half.
- Remove all other growth, including any weak, crowded or overlapping stems and any new shoots growing from the main trunk.
- The tree now has a basic framework.

- Prune only if necessary.
- Cut out any dead, damaged, or diseased wood.
- Thin any badly congested or tangled areas to let light and air into the center of the tree.
- Remove any overly vigorous, vertical new shoots.

Pruning upright plum forms

Some European plums are not as naturally spreading in form as Japanese plums. These trees may do well pruned to a modified central leader form.

1st spring pruning
EARLY SPRING

- Start with a branched whip and do not prune before March.
- Cut off the central leader with an angled cut just above a bud at a height of about 5 ft (1.5 m).
- Remove all laterals lower than 18 in (45 cm) from the ground.
- Prune back the remaining laterals by a half. Cut to buds that face outward.

1st summer pruning
MIDSUMMER

- Cut back main laterals to about 8 in (20 cm) from the start of this year's new growth. Cut to buds that face downward.
- Cut back new sideshoots or sublaterals to about 6 in (15 cm).
- Leave the central leader untouched.

2nd spring pruning
EARLY SPRING

- Cut back the central leader to about one-third of last year's growth.
- Thereafter, in early spring each year, continue to prune the central leader by removing two-thirds of last summer's growth until it reaches its maximum height.

Summer pruning an established tree
EARLY TO MIDSUMMER

- Cut out any dead, damaged, or diseased wood.
- Remove old, unproductive growth from congested areas.
- Tip-prune the central leader, cutting it back to about 1 in (2.5 cm) of last summer's growth.
- Remove any vigorous growth from the upper branches in order to preserve the tree's conical shape.

(top to bottom) **Pinch out** the tips of new plum shoots by hand before growth ripens and requires pruning with pruners. **Prune plums** in summer to reduce the risk of infection by canker diseases. **Plums fruit** along the length of laterals that are two or more years old, rather than on spur systems, like apples and pears.

Pruning a plum fan

Grow a plum fan against a sheltered, sunny wall, fence, or a series of wooden posts strung with horizontal wires 12 in (30 cm) apart. Allow a space 12 ft (4 m) wide and 8 ft (2.5 m) high for a fan on St Julien A rootstock and 10 ft (3 m) wide and 6 ft (2 m) high for one on Krymsk 1 rootstock. Established fans put on a lot of new growth each year and need regular pruning to keep them under control and to avoid overcrowded areas.

(left to right) **Cut back laterals** that are growing out at right angles, away from the wall, and tie in those that will form the main arms.

1st spring pruning
EARLY SPRING

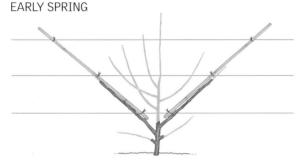

- Start with a branched whip planted 10 in (25 cm) from a wall or fence. Do not prune before early spring.
- Remove all laterals except 2 strong, equal-sized ones on either side of the central leader, about 10 in (25 cm) above ground.
- Prune back them back to about 16 in (40 cm), cutting to a downward-facing bud, and tie them in to canes.
- Prune lower laterals to 1 bud as reserves for the main laterals.
- Cut off the central leader with an angled cut just above the higher of the 2 laterals.

1st summer pruning
MIDSUMMER

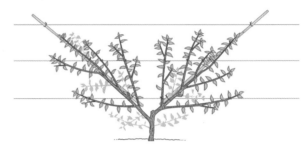

- The 2 main laterals will have lengthened. Tie in their new growth to the bamboo canes.
- New sideshoots or sublaterals will have been produced, too. Select the ones you want to keep, fan them out, and tie them in to the horizontal wires.
- Cut back unwanted sideshoots to just 1 leaf.
- Remove any new shoots growing from the trunk beneath the 2 main arms of the fan.
- For 2nd and 3rd year pruning, see Peaches (p.153).

Spring pruning an established tree
EARLY TO MID-SPRING

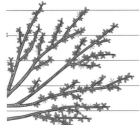

Spring prune only when trees have started into new growth, not when they are still dormant.

- Remove any new buds or shoots growing into or directly out from the wall or fence.
- Pinch out new shoots growing in the "V" between laterals and sideshoots (as you would with tomatoes).
- To avoid congestion, thin remaining sideshoots to at least 4 in (10 cm) apart.

Summer pruning an established tree
EARLY TO MIDSUMMER then again in EARLY FALL

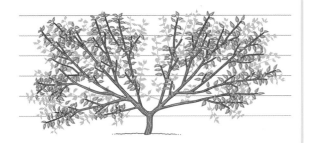

- In early summer, select new laterals to fill out any gaps in the framework of the fan and tie them in.
- Prune new growth on sideshoots back to 5–6 leaves.
- Remove old, crowded, unproductive growth, and any dead or diseased wood.
- After harvesting, cut back to just 3 leaves all the sideshoots you pruned in midsummer.

(below, far left to right) **Newly planted fans** need careful training to stimulate growth and ensure an even spread of equally spaced laterals. **After a few years** the main structure should be in place. **Established fans** can quickly get out of control if not pruned regularly. The naturally vigorous vertical growth seen here urgently needs taming.

What can go wrong

Buds and Blossoms

New buds eaten by birds
Birds may attack the buds during winter and early in spring, damaging them or eating them entirely. They may also peck ripe fruit in summer.
■ See **Birds** (p.335).

Blossoms discolor and die
Because plums flower early in the year, there is always a danger that frost will damage young leaves and flowers.
■ See **Frost** (p.316).

Blossoms turn brown and wilt
First the flowers and then young leaves turn brown and wither. The cause is the same fungus responsible for brown rot.
■ See **Blossom blight** (p.325) and **Brown rot** (p.326).

Leaves, stems and branches

1 Sticky leaves and stems covered with aphids
A covering of sticky honeydew and the gray sooty mold that grows on it are signs of aphids. In early summer, they are likely to be mealy plum aphids. They are green and may or may not be covered in a white, powdery, waxlike coating.
■ See **Mealy plum aphid** (p.337).

2 New leaves curled and distorted
On the undersides of the tightly curled leaves you will see tiny yellow-green aphids. They feed on sap in the leaf tissue.
■ See **Leaf curl plum aphid** (p.337).

3 Leaves with holes eaten out of them
Winter moth caterpillars have pale green bodies with stripes along their sides, and have black heads. When not feeding, they are often found inside tightly curled new leaves.
■ See **Winter moth** (p.341).

4 Leaves appear silvery
A silvery sheen develops on leaves, and shoots and branches may start to die back.
■ See **Silver leaf** (p.331).

5 Leaves have spots or holes; bark oozes gum
The symptoms of bacterial canker show in both leaves and bark. Leaves develop small brown spots with pale edges that turn into round holes. They may turn yellow and wither. Infected bark dies, and orange gum oozes from flat, sunken patches. Bacterial leaf spot causes similar leaf symptoms, without bark symptoms.
■ See **Bacterial canker** (p.324) and **Bacterial leaf spot** (p.324).

Leaves mottled and bronzed
If upper surfaces of leaves become mottled and discolored, then begin to dry up and die, look underneath with a magnifying glass for tiny spider mites. In severe cases, you may also see fine silk webbing.
■ See **Spider mites** (p.339).

Tarry black galls on stems
This fungus stimulates abnormal cell development, resulting in black galls and swellings on stems and roots.
■ See **Black knot** (p.325).

Fruit

6 **Ragged holes or splits in fruit**
Birds, wasps, and flies find plums irresistible. The holes they create when feeding not only make the fruit unappetizing but also accelerate decay.
■ See **Birds** (p.335) and **Wasps** (p.341).

7 **Small holes ringed with black frass**
A small hole surrounded by sticky black excrement called frass is a sign that the plum contains a codling moth larva.
■ See **Codling moth** (p.335).

8 **Fruit develop patches of brown rot**
Brown rot is a fungus that commonly infects plums, usually via holes in the skins. The fruit turn brown and may develop concentric rings of white fungal spores. Plums either fall to the ground or remain on the tree in a shriveled, mummified state.
■ See **Brown rot** (p.326).

Scars on young fruit
Plum curculios cut a small flap in the skin of fruit to lay eggs. Larvae feed on fruit flesh.
■ See **Plum curculio** (p.339).

Shriveled, hollow fruit
Deformed, hollow green fruit without any stones may be the product of a fungal disease known as plum pocket. As the plums shrivel and dry out, they may be covered with white spots.
■ See **Plum pocket** (p.329).

Small olive-green spots on fruit
Green or brown spots on the fruit, and sometimes on the leaves too, are a form of scab. Fruit may be deformed, and the skin may split open.
■ See **Scab** (p.330).

Cherries

It's only relatively recently that cherries have become easy to grow. Just a generation or so ago, they were a real challenge for home growers. The trees grew so large that picking the fruit required ladders. Pollination was hit-and-miss: even if spring frost spared the fragile blossoms, most varieties were not self-fertile. Nowadays, most modern varieties are self-fertile, so a single tree can be grown on its own. And new dwarfing rootstocks mean that trees are much smaller—making them more practical for an average yard, easier to net against birds, and less difficult to harvest.

Despite these improvements, though, cherries still grow best in climates with not-too-cold and not-too-mild winters. Gardeners in the humid Southeast, in the Southwest, and in Zones 4 and colder will find growing cherries a challenge.

Cherries fall into two main categories: sweet varieties, which can be eaten raw; and sour, or tart, varieties, which are too acidic to eat without cooking. 'Montmorency' is the best known of the latter. Duke cherries are a sour-sweet cross between the two. Tart cherries are a bit more tolerant of unfavorable growing conditions than are sweet cherries.

The color of cherries can vary. They're certainly not all red. Some are bright pink, others almost black. In addition, there are so-called white cherries, which are actually a pale yellow, sometimes flecked with orange.

Which forms to grow

■ **Standard trees** Can be grown as a landscape tree, but beware: mature height can be as tall as 50 feet.

■ **Dwarf sweet cherries** Good for most garden settings. Prune to a central leader or modified central leader form.

■ **Dwarf sour cherries** Good for most garden settings. Prune to an open center form.

■ **Fan** A wire-trained form usually grown against a wall or fence.

Must-grow cherries

1 'Sweetheart'
Pollination group D
This is the one to choose for late-season cherries. Unlike most varieties, the dark red fruit ripen gradually, usually lasting until the end of August.
- **Fertility** self-fertile
- **Harvest** mid–late August

2 Sour cherries such as the classic
'Montmorency' and the new 'Surefire' are great for pies. The cherries are bright red and crack-resistant. 'Surefire' is sweet enough to eat fresh, too. Both are self-fertile and ready for harvest in July.

3 'Morello'
Pollination group D
This sour cherry is cold-hardy but not highly productive. The fruit is crack-resistant and ideal for cooking and preserving.
- **Fertility** self-fertile
- **Harvest** August–September

4 Yellow cherries such as 'Rainier'
and 'WhiteGold' often have a beautiful red blush. The flesh is firm and yellow and flavor is excellent. 'WhiteGold' is very hardy; 'Rainier' does well in dry climates. They ripen from June through August, depending on location.

5 'Napoléon'
Pollination group C
Large, pale yellow fruit flushed or mottled with red. Other Bigarreau-type varieties are similarly sweet-tasting.
- **Fertility** not self-fertile
- **Harvest** late July–early August

6 'Stella'
Pollination group C
A breakthrough variety when introduced in Canada in the 1960s—one of the first modern, self-fertile, sweet cherries that could be successfully grown on it own, without another pollinator. It produces large, dark-red, delicious fruit.
- **Fertility** self-fertile
- **Harvest** mid–late July

7 **Duke cherries** combine the qualities of both sweet and sour cherries, so they can be eaten fresh, but have more of a tang than sweet cherries. These may be hard to find at garden centers; try asking for them at a nursery that specializes in tree fruit.

8 'Lapins'
Pollination group C
Also known as 'Cherokee', this late-season sweet cherry has large fruit that are almost black when ripe.
- **Fertility** self-fertile
- **Harvest** late July–early August

'Regina' (not illustrated)
Pollination group C
A hardy cherry with tasty fruit. It fruits long after most other varieties are done.
- **Fertility** not self-fertile
- **Harvest** mid-August

'Sunburst' (not illustrated)
Pollination group C
The first black, self-fertile, sweet cherry, perfect for an average-sized yard.
- **Fertility** self-fertile
- **Harvest** early–mid July

'North Star' (not illustrated)
Pollination group D
Light red, crack-resistant fruit from a very cold-hardy tree. A naturally dwarf variety with good disease resistance.
- **Fertility** self-fertile
- **Harvest** mid- to late July

'Hudson' (not illustrated)
Pollination group D
A sweet dark red cherry that ripens very late. Very productive with widely spreading branches.
- **Fertility** not self-fertile
- **Harvest** August

Choosing and buying cherry trees

These days, most of the widely available cherries are self-pollinating. They are by far the easiest varieties to grow. By all means try one of the older, traditional varieties, but bear in mind that they are unlikely to be self-fertile and must be planted with a compatible neighbor to ensure pollination. Cherries are naturally vigorous, so unless you have a sheltered site with plenty of space, you'll need a tree that has been grafted onto a modern dwarfing rootstock.

CHOOSING A ROOTSTOCK

Two popular cherry rootstocks are Mazzard and Gisela, although several others are also widely used. These modern rootstocks allow the cultivation of small, manageable trees for home landscapes.

15' (5 m)
12' (4 m)
10' (3 m)
6' (2 m)
3' (1 m)

Mazzard   Gisela 5

Mazzard
- VIGOR Semidwarfing.
- CHARACTERISTICS Performs well in heavy and wet soils. Produces trees about twice as tall as those on Gisela 5 rootstocks. Resistant to root-knot nematodes.
- SUPPORT Stake or support permanently.
- HEIGHT 12–15 ft (4–5 m).

Gisela 5
- VIGOR Dwarfing.
- CHARACTERISTICS First developed in Germany, and now used widely around the world. Trees grown on Gisela 5 are small, heavy-fruiting, and easier to protect against frost, rain, and birds. They do, however, still require good growing conditions.
- SUPPORT Stake or support permanently.
- HEIGHT 6–10 ft (2–3 m).

Choosing a tree form

All sweet cherries need a sheltered, sunny site. If you can provide this, you can grow a freestanding standard or dwarf sweet cherry tree. If not, then you're likely to have more success with a fan trained against a sheltered wall or fence, or with dwarf varieties grown in containers. Sour cherries are less particular: they can even be grown as fans against north-facing walls or fences.

Choosing a variety

There is a wider choice of sweet cherry varieties than of sour. However, bear in mind that many sweet cherries are demanding: not only do they

Bees and other insects transfer pollen from tree to tree to ensure that fertilization takes place and fruits can form. They can only pollinate flowers, however, when those on neighboring trees are also open. Cross-pollination won't take place between trees that flower early in the season and those that flower late.

CHERRY POLLINATION GROUPS

A	B	C	D
'Early Rivers'	'May Duke'	'Bing'	'Hudson'
'Mermat'	'Merchant'	'Hertford'	'Morello'
'Noir de Guben'	'Merton Favourite'	'Hedelfingen'	'North Star'
	'Napoléon'	'Lapins/Cherokee'	'Surefire'
	'Rainier'	'Montmorency'	'Sweetheart'
	'Starkrimson'	'Regina'	
	'Van'	'Stella'	
	'Vega'	'Sunburst'	
	'WhiteGold'		

Flowering time is the factor that determines which pollination group a particular cherry variety belongs to. Cherries in group A flower first in spring, and group D cherries flower last. Unless they are actually incompatible, all the cherries in one group should fertilize each other, since they are in flower at the same time, allowing insects to carry pollen from one to another. Because flowering times can overlap, they may even pollinate varieties in an adjacent pollination group.

'Van' is not self-fertile and needs another early-flowering partner from group B, but it is a good pollenizer for other varieties.

'Lapins' is self-fertile and doesn't itself need a partner but it is often used as a pollenizer for other cherries.

'Morello', like all sour cherries, is both self-fertile and a good late-flowering pollenizer for cherries that need a partner.

need a warmer site and better growing conditions, many are not self-fertile and need a compatible partner for successful pollination, particularly if they are heirloom varieties. Almost all sour cherries are self-fertile and most can therefore be grown on their own if necessary. Sweet cherries will not pollinate sour cherries, and although sour cherries should in theory be able to pollinate sweet cherries, their blossoms are unlikely to be open at the same time.

Choosing a pollination group
Although all cherries flower early in the spring, not all come into blossom at the same time. If you are growing trees that are not self–fertile and that need pollinating by one or more compatible neighbors, it's important to choose varieties from the same pollination group. If you do so, their flowers should open simultaneously and insects will be able transfer pollen from one tree to another.

A few cherries, however, are incompatible and will not cross-fertilize. 'Emperor Francis' and 'Bing', for example, will simply not pollinate one another. Fortunately, incompatibility is less of an issue with modern, self-fertile cultivars, but if you plan to grow traditional varieties it is worth getting advice from a specialty nursery.

Growing cherries

Modern hardy, self-fertile varieties have made growing cherries easier than it has ever been. However, to fruit successfully, trees still require a sunny, sheltered site, and they still need protection from frost, from birds, and even from rain when the cherries are ripening. There's a lot to be said, therefore, for growing a fan against a sheltered wall or fence, where it can be covered if necessary. Buying a pretrained fan is worth the extra expense.

The year at a glance

	spring			summer			fall			winter		
	E	M	L	E	M	L	E	M	L	E	M	L
plant bare-root	▬											
plant container	▬	▬	▬									
spring prune	▬	▬										
summer prune					▬	▬	▬					
harvest						▬	▬					

Choosing trees

Cherries are sold as either bare-root or container-grown trees. Buying a bare-root tree from a specialty nursery will give you a wider choice than buying a container-grown tree from a garden center, but bare-root trees are available only in the spring.

Fan-trained cherries grow particularly well against warm, sunny walls, and the form of the tree is very decorative. You will get the best crops from trees in such protected spots.

PLANTING A CHERRY TREE

Prepare the site in advance—the preceding fall, if possible. Remove all perennial weeds, and work plenty of well-rotted compost or manure into the soil, adding some general, all-purpose fertilizer. Use stakes for freestanding trees and a system of wire supports for fans.

1 Dig a hole deep and wide enough to accommodate the plant's roots. Ensure that the old nursery soil mark on the stem is level with the surface of your soil.

2 For a bare-root tree, drive a stake into the ground to a depth of 2 ft (60 cm) about 3 in (8 cm) away from the center of the hole. For a container-grown tree, use a shorter stake, driven in at an angle, to avoid damaging the rootball (see p.35).

3 Set the tree in the hole, carefully spreading out the roots, and replace the soil around them.

4 Gently firm down the soil, ensuring there are no air pockets among the roots. Step down firmly, but don't stamp. Water generously.

5 Spread organic mulch around the tree to help retain moisture and suppress weeds.

6 Secure the tree to its stake with special tree ties. You may need one at the top and one at the bottom.

7 Your tree now has everything it needs to develop a strong root system and healthy top growth.

Cherry blossoms open early in the year and are vulnerable to frost. If cold nights are forecast, make sure you protect the flowers with a covering of fine netting or floating row cover so you get a reasonable crop.

PLANTING DISTANCES

Recommended spacings vary according to the vigor of the rootstock and the variety, the soil and other growing conditions, and the form into which the tree is to be trained.

SWEET CHERRIES

Standard
35–40 ft (11–12 m)

Dwarf
5–12 ft (1.5–3.5 m)

Fan
15–17 ft (4.5–5 m)

SOUR CHERRIES

Standard
20–25 ft (6–7.5 m)

Dwarf
8–12 ft (2.5–3.5 m)

Fan
12–15 ft (3.5–4.5 m)

When to plant

■ BARE-ROOT Plant in early spring, while the trees are dormant, as soon as the ground can be worked (not when too wet or still frozen).
■ CONTAINER-GROWN Plant at any time in spring, but avoid late spring if it is hot and dry.

Where to plant

Choose a warm, sunny, sheltered site where trees are protected from strong winds. Avoid frost pockets. A south- or west-facing wall is ideal for a sweet cherry fan. Sour varieties are less demanding; a sour fan should fruit successfully even if grown against a north-facing wall.

Soil type

All cherries grow best in deep, free-draining but moisture-retentive soil with a slightly acidic pH of around 6.5. They dislike being waterlogged, and will struggle on shallow or sandy soils.

Growing in containers

Cherries can be grown in large pots or tubs, but bear in mind that they are naturally vigorous trees. Choose a self-fertile, compact variety on a dwarfing rootstock. Start with a container that has a minimum diameter and depth of 18 in (45 cm) and fill it with all-purpose, soil-based potting mix blended with some sand or gravel to improve drainage. Cherries are hungrier than most container-grown trees, so feed with a high-potash fertilizer in spring, and keep the pot well-watered. After two years, repot the tree in a 24-in (60-cm) container.

Routine care

■ WATERING Water young, recently planted trees and wall-trained fans regularly, particularly in drought conditions. If you let them dry out and then soak them, the cherry skins are likely to split.

■ FEEDING In early spring, spread compost around each tree. Apply a blended fertilizer in the spring until trees begin to bear fruit. Following that, fertilize after harvest only.

■ MULCHING In spring, after feeding, remove any weeds and spread an organic mulch around the base of young trees and fans.

■ THINNING Cherries do not need thinning.

■ NETTING Birds are a major problem, both in winter when they eat the new fruit buds and in summer as fruit ripens. Netting dwarf trees and fans is an absolute must.

■ FROST PROTECTION When in bloom, cover young trees and small fans with floating row cover.

Harvesting and storing

Leave cherries on the tree to ripen fully—unless the skins start to split, in which case they should be harvested and eaten immediately. Cut them off with scissors or pruners, leaving the stems on the fruit.

Eat or cook cherries as soon as possible after picking, though they will keep for a day or two if washed, dried, and stored in the refrigerator. Red and black cherries can be frozen successfully, but white and yellow varieties may not keep their color.

Yield

Yields are hard to quantify as they vary widely according to a host of variables, including how successful you are at preventing birds from taking the fruit. However, average quantities you can expect from mature, manageable-sized trees are:

■ STANDARD SWEET CHERRY up to 300 lb (135 kg).

■ STANDARD SOUR CHERRY up to 100 lb (45 kg).

■ DWARF SWEET CHERRY 50–100 lb (22–45 kg).

■ DWARF SOUR CHERRY 25–30 lb (11–14 kg).

■ FAN 11–33 lb (5–15 kg).

(below left to right) **Netting** is the only way to stop hungry birds from decimating your crop. **Pick ripe cherries** by cutting them from the tree with their stems intact. Leaving the stems behind can cause disease.

Season by season

(left to right) **Flower buds form** at the same time as the new leaves. **Blossoms** are susceptible to frost damage. **Fruitlets** form in late spring. **Clusters** of ripe fruits are ready for picking.

Midwinter
■ If necessary, treat trees with dormant oil spray to protect against aphids, winter moths, and other pests.

Late winter
■ Prune out any branches that show signs of black knot, but wait until spring, after bud break, to prune the tree for training purposes.

Early spring
■ Begin planting bare-root trees as conditions allow.
■ Weed and mulch around trees.

Mid-spring
■ Most cherries flower now. Protect blossoms against frost if possible.
■ If black knot was a problem last year, apply two sprays of lime-sulfur as a preventive, one week apart.

Late spring
■ Keep newly planted and wire-trained trees regularly watered.
■ Shake trees to knock loose plum curculios onto a dropcloth; destroy the pests. Repeat daily.

Early summer
■ Summer prune cherry fans now or in midsummer, tying in new replacement shoots and cutting back unwanted growth.

■ Net trees against birds.
■ Harvest early season cherries.
■ Hang pheromone traps to help prevent peachtree borer and oriental fruit moth damage

Midsummer
■ Prime time for harvesting sweet cherries.
■ As fruit begins to drop, pick it up regularly and destroy it to help reduce future pest problems

Late summer
■ Most sour cherries will be ready for picking this now or in early fall.
■ After harvesting, summer prune a second time to reduce congestion, remove some of the wood that has just fruited, and cut back shoots that have regrown over the summer.
■ Remove and destroy any remaining fruit infected with brown rot.
■ Fertilize bearing trees after the harvest ends.

Early to mid-fall
■ Last chance for pruning before trees enter their dormant period and the risk of disease returns.
■ If you have mulched around your trees, rake the mulch out and under from the canopy. After leaf fall, replace the mulch and add a new top layer.

Pruning and training cherries

Sweet and sour cherries produce fruit quite differently, so they need different pruning regimens. Sweet cherries fruit at the base of last year's new growth and mostly on stems and branches that are two or more years old, while sour cherries fruit only on shoots and stems that grew the previous year. Don't prune either sweet or sour cherries in winter or you'll risk the trees suffering cold injury or infection from bacterial canker (see p.324). Wait until spring or summer, when the trees are in growth and their sap is flowing.

(left to right) **Sour cherries** bear fruit along much of the length of one-year-old stems. **Sweet cherries** fruit in clusters at the base of one-year-old stems as well as on older wood.

Pruning a sweet cherry tree

Training and pruning is the same as for upright varieties of plum (see p.115). Aim for a central leader or modified central leader tree with a well-formed, somewhat pyramidal shape. Once the tree is established, very little pruning should be necessary. In mid- to late spring, cut out any dead, damaged, or diseased wood, and thin out congested areas.

Pruning a sour cherry tree

Initial training and pruning of a young trees is the same as for an open variety of plum (see p.114). However, after three or four years, when the shape has been established, it can be treated more like a peach (see p.156). Both sour cherries and peaches fruit solely on new growth from the previous year, so remove old wood that will no longer fruit. This will encourage new shoots on which cherries will be borne the year after. Prune twice a year: once in early spring, to reduce congestion and to cut longer, older branches back to young sideshoots or growth buds, and again in summer, after picking your crop.

Summer pruning an established sour cherry tree
LATE SUMMER

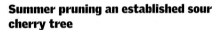

- After harvesting, prune up to one-quarter of the shoots that have just fruited this year. Cut each one back to a new, lower sideshoot so that next year's fruit is borne closer to the center of the tree.
- Cut out any dead, damaged, or diseased wood.
- Thin out a few old laterals and sublaterals that no longer bear fruit, especially if the tree is overcrowded.

Pruning a sweet cherry fan

Grow against a south- or southwest-facing wall or fence. Allow a space 12 ft (4 m) wide and 6 ft (2 m) high for a small fan, more for a vigorous variety grown on Mazzard rootstock. Start with a suitable branched whip or a two- or three-year-old pretrained fan, and train and prune the tree very much as you would a plum fan (see pp.116–17).

Once the fan is about four years old and its basic framework is established, carry out regular pruning, perhaps as often as three times a year: once in early to mid-spring to remove unwanted new growth, again in early summer to shorten new shoots, and finally in early fall to prune back additional growth put on during the summer.

- Remove any new growth that is projecting directly out from or back into the wall.
- Cut out any dead, damaged, or diseased wood.
- Prune back to new sideshoots any older branches that are growing too tall or that are getting overcrowded.

Spring pruning an established sweet cherry fan
EARLY–MID-SPRING

(right, top to bottom) **In spring,** as soon as new growth starts, it is inevitable that a number of vigorous new shoots will start to grow directly out from the wall or fence, seeking the light. Prune them back immediately. If you don't, they will give the fan a shaggy, unkempt look and cast shade over the fruit developing beneath them.

(far left to right) **Dead or damaged stems** are not only unsightly but also pose a potential risk. They are prone to disease, which may then spread and infect otherwise healthy wood. Cut them out completely.

Summer pruning an established sweet cherry fan
EARLY SUMMER then again in EARLY FALL

- Select new laterals to fill out any gaps in the framework of the fan and tie them in.
- Prune other sideshoots back to 5–6 leaves beyond the basal cluster.
- Cut back to sideshoots any vigorous vertical growth, or bend and tie them down horizontally.
- In early fall, after harvesting, cut back to 3 leaves all the sideshoots you pruned to 5–6 leaves in midsummer. This should help produce fruit buds next year.

(right, top to bottom) **Tie in** the new shoots on the fan that you want to keep, and prune back those you don't.

Pruning a sour cherry fan

Plant, train, and prune a sour cherry fan in almost exactly the same way as a peach fan (see p.153). Once it has become established, prune it twice a year. In early to mid-spring, remove old wood to stimulate new growth, and cut back any awkward, outward- or inward-pointing shoots. The second pruning is carried out in late summer or early fall, after the fruit has been picked, to tidy things up and to prune back this year's stems—they have now fruited and will not do so again.

In the early years, concentrate on developing strong laterals that will form the main ribs of the fan. Don't worry if there is an empty space in the middle: the tree will naturally fill that in later on.

Summer pruning an established sour cherry fan
LATE SUMMER–EARLY FALL

1 Cut back stems that have fruited this year to a lower replacement sideshoot. It will form the stem that fruits next year.

2 Spread out replacement shoots so that they fill any gaps in the framework of the fan and tie them in to the canes or wires.

3 Remove any new growth that is congested, crossing, or growing directly outward. This will help keep the fan flat against the wall.

What can go wrong

Buds and blossoms

Blossoms discolor and die
Cherries flower early in spring and frost often damages young leaves and blossoms.
■ See **Frost** (p.316).

Blossoms turn brown and wilt
First the flowers and then young leaves turn brown, wither, and die.
■ See **Blossom blight** (p.325) and **Brown rot** (p.326).

New buds eaten by birds
Birds damage or strip new buds in winter and early spring, returning in summer to take the fruit.
■ See **Birds** (p.335).

Leaves, stems, and branches

1 Young leaves curled, distorted, and sticky
Feeding by black cherry aphids causes new leaves to curl tightly and become distorted. Upper surfaces are sticky and may develop gray sooty mold. Heavy infestations damage new shoots.
■ See **Aphids** (p.334).

2 Small brown or purple spots or holes appear on leaves
Leaves develop small spots with pale edges that can turn into round "shot-holes." Foliage may turn yellow and wither. Various fungal infections may be responsible, or possibly bacterial canker if bark also dies and orange gum oozes from flat, sunken patches.
■ See **Bacterial canker** (p.324), **Fungal leaf spot** (p.328), **Shot-hole disease** (p.330).

3 Irregular holes eaten in leaves
The most likely cause of the damage is moth caterpillars feeding on the foliage. Some species spin silk webs and curl the leaves around themselves.
■ See **Winter moth** (p.341).

4 Yellow leaves with green veins
Yellowing of leaves between the veins may indicate lack of the nutrients iron or manganese (lime-induced chlorosis), or magnesium.
■ See **Iron deficiency** (p.320), **Manganese deficiency** (p.321), **Magnesium deficiency** (p.321).

5 Looping, meandering lines on leaves
These yellow-brown, scribble-like markings are caused by tiny caterpillars feeding inside the leaves, tunneling "mines" through the plant tissue as they eat.
■ See **Apple leafminer** (p.334).

6 Bark or stems ooze gum

Orange resin or gum oozing from branches is not unusual in cherries. It can be a symptom of injury or poor growing conditions, or, more seriously, bacterial canker.
■ See **Bacterial canker** (p.324).

White coating on leaves

Various fungi cause a white powdery coating of mildew to appear on leaves—usually on the upper surface but sometimes on the underside as well. Leaves turn yellow and fall off.
■ See **Powdery mildew** (p.329).

Leaves with skeletonlike brown patches

Pear (or cherry) slugs are yellow larvae covered in slimy black mucus. They feed on upper leaf surfaces, leaving veins untouched.
■ See **Pear slug** (p.338).

Shoots wilt and die

The larvae of oriental fruit moths burrow into the tips of shoots. Later in the growing season, larvae burrow into fruit, too.
■ See **Oriental fruit moth** (p.338).

Black galls on stems

This fungus stimulates abnormal cell development, resulting in black galls and swellings on stems and roots.
■ See **Black knot** (p.325).

Trees grow poorly; limbs may die back

Peachtree borers in the inner bark can weaken and kill trees.
■ See **Peachtree borers** (p.338).

Fruit

7 Ragged holes eaten in fruit

Wasps and flies feed on ripe fruit, particularly if the skin has already been pierced or damaged. Birds are even more voracious and can strip a tree of the whole crop.
■ See **Birds** (p.335) and **Wasps** (p.341).

Webbing on fruit

Fruit may look normal, but inside the fruit are cherry fruitworms, larvae of moths that lay their eggs in spring.
■ See **Cherry fruitworm** (p.335).

8 Fruit develop patches of brown rot

Ripening fruit turn brown and may develop concentric rings of white or cream fungal spots, sometimes around a central hole. They either fall to the ground or remain on the tree, gradually withering and becoming mummified.
■ See **Brown rot** (p.326).

Splits in skins of fruit

A common problem caused by sudden heavy rainfall or irregular watering, which causes the flesh of ripening cherries to swell after their skins have stopped growing.
■ See **Routine care** (p.129).

Apricots

Apricots have much in common with peaches and nectarines: they are equally succulent, juicy, and wonderful to eat, but also equally difficult to grow successfully unless you can provide precisely the right growing conditions: warmth (but not too much heat) and low humidity in summer, and moderate spring weather without late freezes. Apricots are very hardy and happily survive cold winters, but they flower very early in spring. If you don't have the ideal climate, you can try growing apricots as wall-trained fans, in containers, or in a greenhouse or hoophouse. In recent years, a number of new cool-climate varieties have come onto the market, increasing the chances of success. Bred in North America and in France, they flower later and more abundantly than traditional varieties, thus reducing the risk of frost damage and increasing the likelihood that fruit will form. If you plant one, you'll still need to choose your site carefully and you'll still be dependent on a long, hot summer for the fruit to ripen fully, but it's certainly worth a try.

Apricots are tough plants but will only produce a decent crop in cool regions if you grow them against a warm wall. They don't keep particularly well, so eat them fresh or preserve them soon after picking.

Which forms to grow

■ **Freestanding trees** Prune to an open center form, or to a modified central leader in colder climates.
■ **Fan** Grow against a sheltered, sunny wall—a good alternative for less-than-ideal climates.

Must-grow apricots

1 'Alfred'
A reliable, well-established variety with lovely orange flesh. Fruit are sweet, juicy, and medium-sized. Thin them out or the tree may bear fruit only every other year.
■ **Harvest** midsummer

2 'Tomcot'
This is a French-bred variety that grows well in cooler climates. It, too, flowers later and produces more blossoms than most other apricots. Fruit have an excellent flavor, a lovely color, and can grow very large.
■ **Harvest** midsummer

3 'Petit Muscat'
As its name suggests, a variety that produces clusters or bunches of small but intensely flavored fruit with very small stones.
■ **Harvest** late summer

4 'Moorpark'
This old, long-established variety is still popular and widely grown. Its large, juicy, orange-red fruit ripen later than many. The closely related 'Early Moorpark' is similar but crops earlier.
■ **Harvest** late summer

5 'Flavourcot'
Like 'Tomcot', this is another modern variety bred for cooler climates. It flowers quite late and produces a lot of blossoms, increasing the likelihood of a good crop. The large fruit have an excellent flavor.
■ **Harvest** late summer

'Gold Cot' (not illustrated)
A North American variety, this golden yellow apricot is also suited to cool temperate regions. The fruit store very well in the refrigerator.
■ **Harvest** late summer

'New Large Early' (not illustrated)
This 19th-century variety is an early apricot with a good flavor. The large, oval fruit have thin, pale-yellow skin.
■ **Harvest** midsummer

Growing apricots

Apricots are not hard to grow. In many ways they are easier than peaches and nectarines, as they seem less prone to pests and diseases—peach leaf curl, for example, rarely affects them. Probably the key requirements are a sunny, sheltered site; low humidity during the growing season; and protection from frost in spring. If you can't provide these conditions for freestanding trees, grow apricots as small, wall-trained fans, or try genetic dwarf varieties in containers.

The year at a glance

	spring			summer			fall			winter		
	E	M	L	E	M	L	E	M	L	E	M	L
plant bare-root	▬						▬	▬	▬			
plant container	▬	▬	▬	▬								
spring prune		▬										
summer prune				▬	▬	▬	▬					
harvest					▬	▬						

When to plant

■ BARE-ROOT Plant in early spring, while trees are still dormant, as soon as the soil can be worked. In mild-winter areas, you can also plant dormant bare-root trees in the fall.

■ CONTAINER-GROWN Plant at any time in spring, but avoid late spring if it is hot and dry.

Flowering and pollination

Apricots flower very early in the year—usually even earlier than peaches and nectarines—so protection against frost is essential, and hand pollination is advisable (see p.148). However, the trees are self-fertile, so a single tree can be planted on its own and will bear fruit.

Protecting early-spring blossom

Vulnerable flowers must be protected from frost by covering them overnight with row cover, burlap, or plastic. Remove it during the day, or leave it open at the sides to give access to any pollinating insects that may be active early in the season.

Choosing trees

Young trees are sold either bare-root or container-grown. Bare-root trees are generally available in early spring, and in mild-winter areas, also in the fall. Container-grown trees can be bought at most times during the growing season, but are best planted in the spring.

Protect delicate apricot blossoms from frost and rain with some kind of covering. This specially built frame around wall-trained apricots is draped with plastic and the sides have been left open to allow pollinating insects to fly in.

Leave apricots to ripen on the tree for as long as possible. Pick them when they are slightly soft and at their sweetest, and if possible eat them immediately.

Where to plant
Unless you live in the ideal apricot growing areas of California, freestanding trees will do best with a sunny, sheltered site. In areas with late spring frost, plant trees on the north side of a building so they will remain dormant longer in spring. Other options are to train a fan against a south- or southwest-facing fence or wall, plant in containers, or grow apricots in a greenhouse.

Soil type
Apricots like deep, fertile, free-draining soil with a neutral or slightly alkaline pH of 6.7–7.5. Sandy soil will need to be enriched with organic matter.

How to plant
A month or two before planting, dig in plenty of well-rotted compost or manure. Before planting a fan, attach horizontal wires to your wall or fence about 12 in (30 cm) apart. Plant new trees so the nursery soil mark is level with the soil surface.

Planting distances
■ STANDARD 20–25 ft (6–7.5 m) apart.
■ GENETIC DWARF 8–12 ft (2.5–4 m) apart.
■ FAN 12–16 ft (4–5 m) apart.

Growing in containers
A number of different dwarf varieties are available for growing in containers. Use a loam-based potting mix blended with sand or gravel to improve drainage. Apply a general liquid fertilizer in spring and summer, and keep the pot well-watered. Once a year, topdress with fresh medium, and every two years pot on into a larger container. In late winter and spring, bring the trees under cover to protect them against frost, and in summer move them to a warm, sunny spot so that the fruit will ripen fully.

Routine care
■ FROST PROTECTION Outdoor trees should be covered to protect blossoms from frost damage.
■ WATERING Water regularly during spring and summer, particularly newly planted young trees and wall-trained fans.
■ FEEDING In the spring, feed lightly with a general blended fertilizer.
■ MULCHING In early spring, after feeding, weed thoroughly and mulch around the base of the tree.
■ THINNING FRUIT In a good year, when the crop is heavy, thin fruit to leave about 3–4 in (8–10 cm) between each one. Remove any diseased or damaged fruit first.
■ NETTING Birds can be a problem in summer as fruit ripens. If necessary, net fans and trees grown in containers. In the case of large trees, where all-over netting may not be practical, it may be possible to net individual clusters of fruit.

Harvesting and storing
In most places, apricots are harvested in mid- or late summer. When they start to soften, test to see if they are ready. Cup one in your hand and give it a gentle twist. If it pulls away easily, leaving the stalk behind, it is ripe. Apricots will keep for a day or two if kept somewhere cool, but they are best eaten soon after picking. To store them for longer, you must remove the stones and can or freeze them.

Yield
Yields vary from tree to tree and from year to year. However, average quantities you can expect are:
■ STANDARD 150–200 lb (70–90 kg).
■ DWARF 50–100 lb (23–45 kg).
■ FAN 15–33 lb (7–15 kg).

Season by season

Early spring
- In a warm spring, buds may start to burst.
- Protect blossoms from frost and hand-pollinate if necessary.
- Weed and mulch around trees.
- Prune newly planted and young fan-trained trees.

Mid-spring
- Spring prune established fans now and in late spring.
- As fruitlets form, begin thinning them out.
- Fertilize established trees.
- If black knot was a problem last year, apply two sprays of lime-sulfur as a preventive, one week apart.

Late spring
- Weed and water regularly.
- Shake trees to knock loose plum curculios onto a dropcloth; destroy the pests. Repeat daily.

Early summer
- Finish thinning out young fruitlets.
- On young, fan-trained trees, start tying in new sideshoots and cutting back unwanted growth.
- On established trees, cut out old, unproductive branches and remove some of the shoots that fruited last year.
- Hang pheromone traps to help prevent peachtree borer and oriental fruit moth damage.

Midsummer
- Early-season varieties are ready to harvest.
- As fruit begins to drop, pick it up regularly and destroy it to help reduce future pest problems.

Late summer
- Harvest mid- and late-season varieties.
- After harvesting, summer prune established fan-trained trees.
- Fertilize bearing trees after the harvest ends.

Early to mid-fall
- Complete all pruning before the dormant period begins.
- In warm-winter areas, plant bare-root trees while the soil is still warm and trees have a chance to establish roots.

(top to bottom) **Flower buds** may break in late winter. **Foliage** begins to unfurl as the blossoms fade. **Fruit** need plenty of warmth and sunshine in order to ripen fully.

Pruning and training apricots

Apricots are like peaches, plums, cherries, and all other stone fruit: they should be pruned in spring or summer, not in winter when they are dormant. In winter they are most at risk of infection from bacterial canker (see p.324), which enters through pruning cuts. When their sap is flowing, they are more resistant. Rather like plums, apricots bear fruit both on shoots and stems that grew last year and on clusters of older fruiting spurs.

Pruning an apricot tree

Prune and train apricots in the same way as plums (see p.114). Aim for an open center with a balanced framework of well-spaced uncrowded branches. But in cold-winter areas, prune to a modified central leader instead, with a tapering shape that allows light to reach all the branches of the tree. Once trees are established, prune them once a year in early summer.

Pruning an apricot fan

A newly planted fan is trained and pruned in the same way as a peach fan (see pp.152–53). Slightly shorten the leaders of the main ribs in late winter or early spring, and then either thin out, cut back, or tie in new growth between early summer and early fall. Once the fan is established, prune as you would a plum (see p.117).

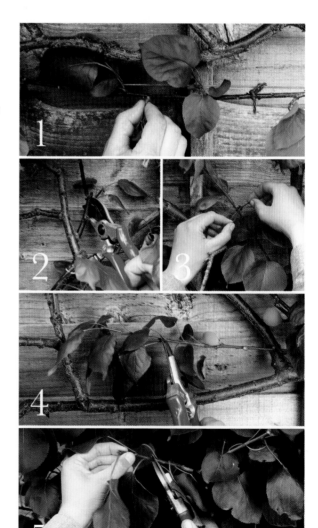

1 In spring, pinch out overcrowded new shoots. There should be a minimum of 4 in (10 cm) between them.

2 Prune out completely any new shoots growing downward, directly into the wall, or straight out toward you from the fan.

3 Select new shoots that you want to keep for future growth, and tie them in so that they fill in any gaps.

4 In early summer, shorten shoots that you don't want to grow. Cut them back so that just 5 or 6 leaves remain beyond the basal cluster.

5 After harvesting, cut back to 3 leaves the shoots you pruned to 5 or 6 leaves earlier in the summer. Cut back to just 1 leaf any new sideshoots that have grown from them.

What can go wrong

Buds and blossoms

Blossoms discolor and die
Apricots flower earlier in the year than almost any other fruit tree and are extremely prone to frost damage.
■ See **Frost** (p.316).

Blossoms turn brown and wilt
First the flowers and then young leaves turn brown and wither.
■ See **Blossom blight** (p.325) and **Brown rot** (p.326).

Leaves, stems, and branches

1 Leaves and stems wither, then turn brown
Young shoots, leaves, and stems wilt, turn brown, and die. The cause is usually a fungus.
■ See **Dieback** (p.326).

2 Small spots and holes appear in leaves
Leaves develop small brown spots with pale edges that turn into round "shot-holes." Foliage may turn yellow and wither. Fungal infections may be responsible, or possibly bacterial canker if bark also dies and orange gum oozes from flat, sunken patches. Bacterial leaf spot also causes shot-holes.
■ See **Bacterial canker** (p.324), **Bacterial leaf spot** (p.324), and **Shot-hole disease** (p.330).

Leaves are curled and yellow-green
Aphids feeding on sap on the undersides of leaves cause them to curl up and become misshapen. Foliage may be sticky with honeydew.
■ See **Aphids** (p.334).

Leaves mottled and bronzed
When spider mites feed, the upper surfaces of leaves become speckled or mottled with pale yellow-bronze spots. In severe cases, you may also see fine silk webbing.
■ See **Spider mites** (p.339).

Small, brown, shell-like insects on stems
Scale insects feed on stems and branches, weakening plants overall. They are elliptical in shape and covered with a domed shell.
■ See **Scale insects** (p.339).

Shoots wilted or dying
Oriental fruit moth larvae burrow into the tips of shoots, causing them to wilt. You may find the pinkish worms inside fruit, too.
■ See **Oriental fruit moth** (p.338).

Trees lack vigor; limbs may die back
Peachtree borer larvae tunnel through inner bark, disrupting nutrient and water flow.
■ See **Peachtree borer** (p.338).

Fruit

3 Red-brown spots on fruit
A measles-like rash of spots, especially when coupled with leaves that are tattered with holes, may indicate shot-hole disease.
■ See **Shot-hole disease** (p.330).

4 Ragged holes in fruit
Birds, wasps, flies, and other insects feed on ripening fruit. They either make holes in the skin or aggravate existing ones. The damage they cause will accelerate rot and decay.
■ See **Birds** (p.335) and **Wasps** (p.341).

Fruits develop patches of brown rot
Brown rot is a fungus that may infect fruit via a hole in the skin. The fruit turn brown and may develop concentric rings of white fungal spores.
■ See **Brown rot** (p.326).

Scars on young fruit
Curculios are hard-shelled beetles that cut a small flap in the skin of fruit to lay eggs. Larvae feed on fruit flesh.
■ See **Plum curculio** (p.339).

Peaches and nectarines

Peaches are thought to originate from ancient China. Confucius wrote about them in the first century BCE, and they appear in drawings hundreds of years before that. The Greeks and Romans grew and ate them. However, it wasn't until the sixteenth century that they spread to northwestern Europe, and cultivation was even later in North America, during the 17th century. Smooth-skinned nectarines, which have a similar flavor, are thought to be an accidental mutation or "sport" of the peach.

Growing peaches and nectarines can be a challenge because of pest problems and the trees' climatic requirements. Peach trees are fairly hardy, and do, in fact, need a cold spell during the months when they are dormant in order to spur them into fruiting successfully. Spring frost is the principal cause of much trouble, damaging the fragile, early blossoms. Also, lack of sufficient heat and sunshine in summer can often prevent the fruit from ripening. The best locations are warm, stable climates in the western United States that have reliably hot summers. East of the Rockies, plum curculios and various diseases make peach-growing more difficult. If you don't have ideal conditions, be prepared to grow peaches against a sheltered, south-facing wall, in containers, or even in a greenhouse.

Growing perfectly ripe peaches outdoors relies on good summers and a very sheltered site. Nectarines require similar conditions. If you can't provide them, try growing compact varieties of both in pots, moving them into the warmest, sunniest location when they are most in need of heat and sunshine.

Which forms to grow

- **Standard trees** Prune to an open center form.
- **Genetic dwarf trees** Prune to an open center form.
- **Fan** Grow against a sheltered, sunny wall—a good alternative for less-than-ideal climates.

Must-grow peaches and nectarines

1 'Fantasia'
Nectarine
Easy to grow, resistant to frost and canker. The large, yellow-fleshed fruit have a good flavor.
■ **Harvest** August

2 'Garden Lady'
Peach
A specially bred dwarf variety that produces a compact tree ideal for growing in containers.
■ **Harvest** July–August

3 'Bonanza'
Peach
A dwarf variety originally bred in California specifically for growing in containers. Good choice for a sunny patio, deck, or balcony.
■ **Harvest** August

4 'Duke of York'
Peach
An early-fruiting variety that is reliable and widely grown. Large, delicious, yellow-fleshed fruit.
■ **Harvest** July

5 'Red Haven'
Peach
A vigorous, heavy-fruiting variety that is well-suited to fan-training. Fruit have firm yellow flesh with a fine flavor. Some resistance to peach leaf curl.
■ **Harvest** August

6 'Lord Napier'
Nectarine
Perhaps the best-known and most widely grown nectarine in temperate regions. Given the right conditions, it bears large, juicy, white-fleshed fruit.
■ **Harvest** August

7 'Peregrine'
Peach
One of the best peaches for temperate climates. Reliable, heavy-fruiting, white-fleshed fruit with excellent flavor.
■ **Harvest** August

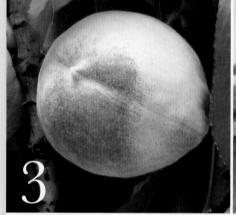

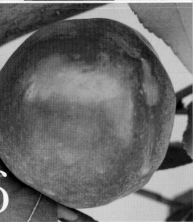

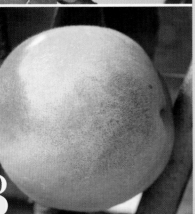

8 'Hale's Early'
Peach

An early variety that may be ready for picking as soon as mid-July. Fruit are a very pale yellow with red markings when ripe. In a good year, crops can be so heavy that thinning the fruit is vital.
■ **Harvest** July

'Avalon Pride' (not illustrated)
Peach

A modern variety with resistance to peach leaf curl. Discovered by chance as a seedling in Washington State. Sweet, juicy, yellow flesh.
■ **Harvest** August

'Rochester' (not illustrated)
Peach

One of the best and least troublesome peaches for growing outdoors in temperate climates. What it lacks in flavor it makes up for in dependability.
■ **Harvest** August

'Saturn' (not illustrated)
Peach

An unusual flat peach that originates from China. Excellent, sweet, honeyed flavor. Resistant to frost but needs a warm, sunny site to ripen fully.
■ **Harvest** August

'Elberta' (not illustrated)
Peach

A classic freestone yellow peach for Southern gardens, dating from 1875.
■ **Harvest** July

'Contender' (not illustrated)
Peach

Firm, large freestone peaches borne on hardy and productive trees. Beautiful coloring.
■ **Harvest** August

'White Lady' (not illustrated)
Peach

Well-colored, high-quality fruit with sweet white flesh. An excellent dessert peach. Grows well in the East.
■ **Harvest** August

'Redgold' (not illustrated)
Nectarine

Freestone fruit with appealing color and flavor. Firm yellow flesh allows for good storage life. Good winter hardiness.
■ **Harvest** late August

'Arctic Jay' (not illustrated)
Nectarine

Highly rated for its mix of sweet and tart flavor. Susceptible to bacterial leaf spot. Good for California and Pacific Northwest.
■ **Harvest** August

'Early Rivers' (not illustrated)
Nectarine

Worth tracking down from specialty suppliers as this is one of the first nectarines to ripen: fruit may be ready to harvest by mid- or late July. Generally produces good crops with pale yellow-red skin and juicy, yellow flesh.
■ **Harvest** July

'Nectarella' (not illustrated)
Nectarine

A dwarf variety that is easy to grow and unlikely to grow taller than about 5 ft (1.5 m). For planting outdoors or in a container. Produces heavy crops of large, tasty fruit.
■ **Harvest** August

'Pineapple' (not illustrated)
Nectarine

Outstanding flavor, but because it doesn't ripen until late in the season, it needs a very good summer. Alternatively, grow in a greenhouse.
■ **Harvest** early September

'Redwing' (not illustrated)
Peach

Large fruit turn a deep red as they ripen and develop a sweet, juicy flavor. 'Redwing' comes into blossom late and is therefore less prone to frost damage. A good choice for northern regions.
■ **Harvest** August

Growing peaches and nectarines

Peach and nectarine trees both need warmth and sunshine, and in less-than-ideal climates, they need protection from wind also. If you can't provide this, try growing these crops in containers or as a wall-trained fan, or perhaps in a greenhouse or hoophouse.

The year at a glance

	spring			summer			fall			winter		
	E	M	L	E	M	L	E	M	L	E	M	L
plant bare-root	▬											
plant container	▬	▬	▬									
spring prune	▬	▬									▬	
summer prune				▬	▬	▬						
harvest				▬	▬	▬						

Flowering and pollination

Peaches and nectarines are self-fertile, which means that a single tree planted on its own should pollinate itself without pollen from neighbors. However, the blossoms open early in the year when it may still be too cold for many insects to be active, so hand-pollination may be necessary.

Choosing trees

Young trees are sold either bare-root or container-grown. Bare-root trees are generally available in early spring. Container-grown trees can be bought at most times of the growing season, but are best planted in the spring. Peaches are grafted onto a variety of rootstocks. 'Citation' is dwarfing; 'Nemaguard' is resistant to nematodes. Seedling rootstocks may be best in areas where spring frosts are common.

When to plant

- BARE-ROOT Plant in early spring, while trees are still dormant, as soon as the soil can be worked.
- CONTAINER-GROWN Plant at any time in spring, but avoid late spring if it is hot and dry.

Where to plant

Choose a warm, sunny, sheltered site where trees are protected from strong winds. If spring frosts may be a problem, plant on the upper part of a north-facing slope so that trees will stay dormant longer. Avoid frost pockets. Try growing a fan against a south- or southwest-facing fence or wall.

Soil type

Peaches and nectarines need deep, fertile, free-draining soil with a slightly acidic pH of 6.5–7.0. Like most fruit trees, they dislike being waterlogged.

Hand-pollinate peaches if there are no insects around in the yard. Use a small, soft brush to transfer pollen carefully from one flower to another.

(left to right) **Spring blossoms open** very early. Grown outdoors, both peaches and nectarines are likely to need protection against frost damage at flowering time.
A plastic rain cover over a peach fan may be unattractive, but without it there is a high chance of infection from rainborne peach leaf curl (see p.328).

How to plant

Prepare the site a month or two in advance by digging in plenty of well-rotted compost or manure. Before planting a fan, attach horizontal wires to your wall or fence about 12 in (30 cm) apart. Plant new trees so that the old nursery soil mark on the stem is level with the surface of your soil.

Planting distances

- STANDARD TREES 15–20 ft (5–6 m) apart.
- GENETIC DWARFS 4–10 ft (1–3 m) apart.
- FANS 12–16 ft (4–5 m) apart.

Growing in containers

Compact dwarf varieties are available that are ideal for container growing, and there are distinct advantages to growing peaches and nectarines in pots. Most importantly, containers are mobile, so you can bring them indoors under cover to protect against frost and peach leaf curl. You can also move them to the warmest, sunniest part of your yard or deck when the fruit is ripening.

Start off young trees in small containers with a diameter of 15–18 in (38–45 cm), filled with loam-based potting mix blended with a little sand or gravel to improve drainage. Feed with a high-potash fertilizer in spring and summer and keep the pot well-watered. Once a year, topdress with fresh soil, and every two years pot on to a larger container.

Growing under glass

In New England and some other areas, summers may not be warm enough for peaches and nectarines to ripen outdoors. In these areas, growing peaches in containers may be your best choice—you can put the container in the sunniest, warmest spot possible. And if you have a green house or hoophouse, that's an option too. If you plan to grow peaches or nectarines in a greenhouse, it should be unheated—the trees require a cold spell during their dormant period. They need rich, fertile soil, plentiful watering, and high humidity, both before and after the period when they are in flower. Blossoms may need hand-pollination.

Routine care

- WATERING Water regularly throughout the spring and summer, particularly wall-trained fans.
- FEEDING In early spring, just before growth starts, apply a general blended fertilizer. In cold regions, feed in spring only. In other areas, in early summer, while fruit are developing, water with a diluted, high-potassium tomato fertilizer.
- MULCHING In early spring, after feeding, remove any weeds and mulch around the base of your trees.
- NETTING Birds can be a problem in summer as fruit ripens. Netting fans is an option.
- FROST PROTECTION Outdoor trees need floating row cover in spring to protect blossoms from frost damage.

Give peaches plenty of room by thinning them out when they are still small, as early as mid-spring if fruitlets have already formed. The fewer there are, the larger they will grow.

(left to right) **Thinning peaches** and nectarines to give them space to grow is done in two stages: in mid-spring and early summer. At the first stage, thin each cluster to a single peach. At the second, remove fruit that are still too close together.

- RAIN PROTECTION A plastic cover to keep rain off buds and flowers between early winter and late spring reduces the risk of peach leaf curl (see p.328).

Thinning peaches

Both peaches and nectarines must be thinned, or the tree will be overburdened and fruit won't grow to its full size. Thin once, to one fruit per cluster, when they are very small, and space them out again when they are larger. Peaches should be 8–10 in (20–25 cm) apart, nectarines 6 in (15 cm) apart.

Harvesting and storing

Fruit are ready for picking when they become slightly soft at the top, around the stalk. Cup them in your hand and give them a gentle twist. If they don't come away easily, leave them a little longer. Kept somewhere cool, peaches and nectarines will last for a few days, but if you want to store them for longer, remove the pits and can or freeze.

Yield

Yields vary from tree to tree and from year to year. However, average quantities you can expect are:
- STANDARD 100–150 lb (45–65 kg)
- DWARF 30–60 lb (14–27 kg).
- FAN 10–25 lb (4.5–11 kg).

Season by season

Early spring
- Blossoms open. Protect from frost and hand-pollinate if necessary.
- Weed and mulch around trees.
- Bring container-grown trees indoors under cover.
- Prune newly planted and young fan-trained trees now or in mid-spring.
- Apply a general blended fertilizer around existing trees.
- Plant bare-root trees.

Mid-spring
- Spring prune established fans now and in late spring.
- As fruitlets form and begin to swell, begin thinning them out.
- If black knot was a problem last year, apply two sprays of lime-sulfur as a preventive, one week apart.

Late spring
- Weed and water regularly.
- In hot climates, feed trees with liquid fertilizer while fruits are developing.
- Shake trees to knock loose plum curculios onto a dropcloth; destroy the pests. Repeat daily.

Early summer
- Finish thinning out young fruitlets.
- On young, fan-trained trees, start tying in new sideshoots and cutting back unwanted growth.
- On established trees, cut out old, unproductive branches and remove some of the shoots that fruited last year.
- Hang pheromone traps to help prevent peachtree borer and oriental fruit moth damage.

Midsummer
- Early-season varieties are ready to harvest.
- As fruit begins to drop, pick it up regularly and destroy it to help reduce future pest problems.

Late summer
- Harvest mid- and late-season varieties.
- After harvesting, summer-prune established fan-trained trees.

Early fall
- Complete all pruning before the dormant period begins.

Early winter
- In mild-winter areas, put up plastic rain covers to protect against peach leaf curl.

(top to bottom) **In warm springs** buds are ready to burst in early spring. **Blossoms** may need hand-pollination. **Fruitlets** on a nectarine fan have been thinned to one per cluster. **Nectarines** should be ripe enough for picking by mid- or late summer.

Pruning and training peaches and nectarines

The most common training method for peach and nectarine trees is as open center trees, similar to plums (p.114). In areas where bacterial canker is a problem, don't prune in winter. Wait until spring when new growth has begun. Peaches and nectarines both fruit only on shoots and stems that grew last year, so pruning removes some of the old growth that has already fruited and encourages the tree to produce new growth that will fruit the following year.

For successful fruiting, give peaches plenty of room by thinning them out when they are still small—as early as mid-spring if fruitlets have already formed. The fewer there are on the stem, the larger they will grow.

Pruning a fan

Grow against a south- or southwest-facing wall or fence. Allow a space 12 ft (4 m) wide and 6 ft (2 m) high. Either start with a suitable branched whip or pay a little more and buy a two- or three-year-old pretrained fan. The latter will give you a head start in getting the tree established.

1st spring pruning
LATE WINTER–EARLY SPRING

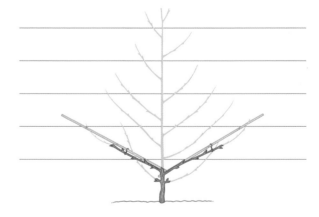

- Construct a support system by securing horizontal wires 12 in (30 cm) apart to a wall or fence. Attach 2 diagonal canes.
- If you are starting with a branched whip, cut off the central leader and any top growth above 2 strong left- and right-facing laterals, at a height of 10–12 in (25–30 cm) above the ground, just below the bottom wire.
- Cut back the 2 laterals to about 14 in (35 cm) and tie them in to the canes. They will become the 2 main arms.
- Remove any lower, unwanted laterals.

1st summer pruning
EARLY SUMMER–EARLY FALL

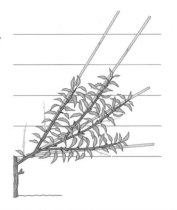

- As sideshoots grow from the main laterals, select 2 above and 1 below to form the ribs of the fan. Tie them in to additional canes.
- Cut back all other shoots to 1 leaf.

2nd spring pruning
LATE WINTER–EARLY SPRING

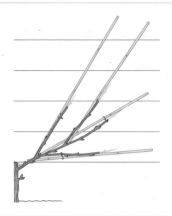

- Cut back the leader of each lateral and sublateral by one-quarter of last year's growth.
- Cut to buds facing in the direction you want the branch to grow.

2nd summer pruning
EARLY SUMMER–EARLY FALL

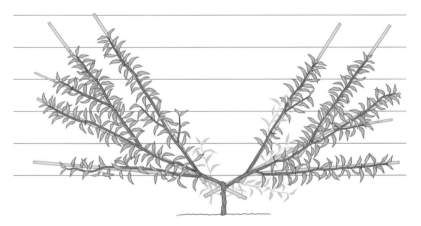

- Continue adding canes and tying in new sideshoots.
- Remove completely any new buds or shoots growing into or out from the wall or fence.
- Prune out new shoots growing vertically into the center or below the main arms.

3rd spring pruning
LATE WINTER–EARLY SPRING

- Again, cut back the leaders of the main branches by one-quarter of last year's growth.

3rd summer pruning
EARLY SUMMER–EARLY FALL

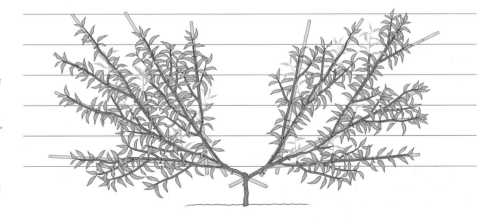

- In early summer, thin out new sideshoots growing off the main ribs of the fan to 1 every 4–6 in (10–15 cm).
- Later, prune back crowded, crossing, or outward-growing sideshoots to 2–4 leaves, not counting the basal cluster.
- Continue adding canes and tying in new sideshoots.

Spring pruning an established fan
MID–LATE SPRING

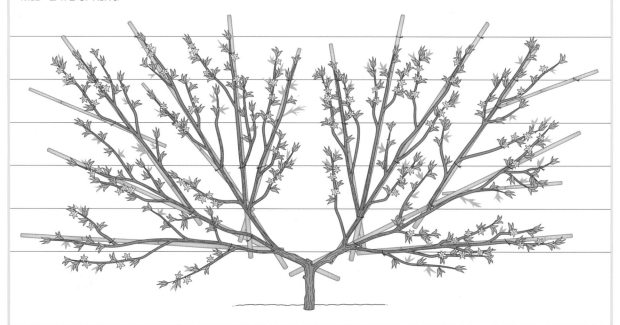

- On each of the main laterals and sublaterals, select 2 new sideshoots to grow on and bear fruit next year, choosing the first just below the lowest flower and the second to keep in reserve. Cut back all others to 1 leaf.
- Remove completely any new buds or shoots growing directly into or out from the wall or fence, as well as any that are closer than 4–6 in (10–15 cm) apart.
- Cut out any dead, damaged, or diseased wood.

(opposite) **A fan-trained nectarine** can put on an impressive amount of growth, as can be seen from this half-pruned mature fan growing in a large greenhouse. Spring pruning keeps new growth in check as well as reducing shading and ensuring good air circulation around the fruitlets.

(below, left and center) **Cut back new shoots** that are growing outward. They produce unnecessary growth that will spoil the shape of the fan and create too much shade. (right) **Start thinning** fruits and tie in any vigorous new sideshoots.

Summer pruning an established fan
LATE SUMMER–EARLY FALL

- After harvesting, cut back the stems that bore fruit this year to one or both of the two new replacement sideshoots you selected to grow on.
- Tie in the new shoots to the canes so that they fill in the gaps.

Pruning a freestanding tree

Initial training and pruning of a young, newly planted tree is the same as for a plum (see pp.114–15). Aim for an open-centered bush with a balanced framework of main branches. Thereafter, prune established trees once a year in early summer.

Summer pruning an established tree
EARLY–MIDSUMMER

- Remove up to one-quarter of the shoots that fruited last year.
- Cut back to a pointed growth bud rather than a fat fruit bud (see p.43) in order to stimulate new shoots.
- Cut out any dead, damaged, or diseased wood.
- Thin out a few old laterals and sublaterals that no longer bear fruit.

What can go wrong

Buds and Blossoms

Blossoms discolor and die
Peaches and nectarines flower early and are highly prone to frost damage.
■ See **Frost** (p.316).

Blossoms turn brown and wilt
Fungal infection causes flowers and then young leaves to turn brown and wither.
■ See **Blossom blight** (p.325) and **Brown rot** (p.326).

Leaves, stems, and branches

1 New leaves are distorted, blister, and turn red
Almost as soon as they appear, new young leaves pucker, turning bright red or purple. The cause is peach leaf curl.
■ See **Peach leaf curl** (p.328).

2 Leaves are curled and yellow-green
Leaves curl up and discolor due to aphids feeding on sap on the undersides. Foliage may be sticky with honeydew.
■ See **Aphids** (p.334).

3 Leaves mottled and bronzed
Spider mite feeding causes upper surfaces of leaves to become speckled or mottled with pale yellow-bronze spots. You may see fine silk webbing.
■ See **Spider mites** (p.339).

4 Yellow leaves with green veins
Yellowing of new leaves between the veins may indicate lack of iron or manganese, common in alkaline soils.
■ See **Iron deficiency** (p.320), **Manganese deficiency** (p.321).

Holes appear in leaves
Leaves with bacterial canker develop small brown spots with pale edges that turn into round holes. Infected bark dies, and orange gum oozes from flat, sunken patches. Holes in leaves are also symptoms of bacterial leaf spot.
■ See **Bacterial canker** (p.324) and **Bacterial leaf spot** (p.324).

Small shell-like insects on stems
Scale insects feed on stems and branches, resulting in leaf yellowing and limb dieback.
■ See **Scale insects** (p.339).

Shoots wilted or dying
Oriental fruit moth larvae burrow into the tips of shoots, causing them to wilt. You may find pinkish worms inside fruits.
■ See **Oriental fruit moth** (p.338).

Trees lack vigor; limbs may die back
Peachtree borer larvae tunnel through inner bark, disrupting nutrient and water flow.
■ See **Peachtree borer** (p.338).

Abnormal shoots and discolored leaves
Plants with peach rosette mosaic virus produce rosettes of leaves. Leaves may be discolored.
■ See **Peach rosette mosaic virus** (p.329).

Fruit

Ragged holes in fruit
Birds, wasps, and other insects feed on ripening fruit, making or enlarging holes.
■ See **Birds** (p.335) and **Wasps** (p.341).

5 Fruit develop patches of brown rot
Brown rot is a fungus that causes fruit to turn brown. Concentric rings of white fungal spores may develop.
■ See **Brown rot** (p.326).

Scars on young fruit
Beetles with long snouts—plum curculios—cut a small flap fruit skin to lay eggs. Larvae feed on fruit flesh.
■ See **Plum curculio** (p.339).

Olive-green spots on fruit
Fungal scab causes these spots. Fruit become cracked and misshapen.
■ See **Scab** (p.330).

Sunken lesions on fruit
Tarnished plant bugs suck juice and inject saliva that causes fruit distortion.
■ See **Plant bugs** (p.338).

Quinces

Quinces are small- to medium-sized trees best grown as bushes with one to three main trunks. It's possible but not easy to grow them as wall-trained fans. They are originally from the central and southwest regions of Asia, where hot summers mean they ripen fully and become soft and sweet enough to eat raw. In northern, temperate regions, they remain rock-hard and sour, and require cooking. However, they make excellent jellies, jams, and pastes, and when stewed with apples, or baked in the oven with roast meats, their flesh turns pink and releases a wonderful, aromatic flavor.

(above and left) **Quinces** are ready to pick in early to mid-fall, but leave them on the tree for as long as you can. Harvest before they drop and well before the first frost. Ripe fruit will keep until mid- or even late winter. Store them separately in a cool place, or their strong perfume will taint other fruit, such as apples and pears.

Growing quinces

Quinces grow on their own rootstocks—usually Quince A and Quince C, the same as those most commonly used for pears (see p.86). Trees grown on Quince A tend to reach 11–15 ft (3.5–4.5 m) in height, and those on Quince C 10–11 ft (3–3.5 m).

The year at a glance

	spring			summer			fall			winter		
	E	M	L	E	M	L	E	M	L	E	M	L
plant bare-root	▬	▬		▬	▬							
plant container	▬	▬	▬	▬	▬							
winter prune							▬	▬	▬			
harvest							▬	▬				

Quince blossoms are spectacular. It's almost worth planting a tree solely for the flowers. Either pure white or flushed with pink, they resemble wild roses, appearing after the new, bright-green foliage has opened.

Choosing a variety

Unsurprisingly, the choice of varieties or cultivars is much more limited than for apples or pears. The most commonly grown include 'Champion', 'Orange', Pineapple', and 'Smyrna'.

Quinces are self-fertile and will pollinate themselves. A single tree can therefore be grown on its own.

When to plant

■ BARE-ROOT Plant in spring or fall, when the trees are dormant, but not if the soil is waterlogged or frozen.
■ CONTAINER-GROWN Plant at any time during the growing season, but avoid hot, dry weather.

Where to plant

Quinces grow best in a warm, sheltered corner or close to a wall, away from any danger of frost pockets. They need sun if the fruit is to ripen successfully.

Plant quince trees in the same way as apples (see pp.58–59), making sure to stake them for the first few years.

Soil type

Quinces are fairly tolerant, although they grow best in a deep, fertile, moisture-retaining soil with a slightly acidic pH of around 6.5.

Routine care

■ WATERING Take care to water young, recently planted trees.

■ FEEDING and MULCHING In the early years, and especially on light soils, use a general blended fertilizer in early spring before growth starts. Follow it mid-spring with an organic mulch around the base of the trees. Avoid overfeeding in areas where fire blight can be a problem, because lush new growth is especially susceptible to the disease.

■ FROST PROTECTION Quinces flower later in spring than most other tree fruit and, except in northern regions, they are less vulnerable to damage from frost.

Harvesting and storing

It's best to leave quinces on the tree for as long as possible—until mid- or even late fall, provided temperatures stay above freezing. After picking, store them somewhere cool and dark. Don't wrap them, don't let them touch each other, and keep them separate from other fruit. They should last for a month or two.

Pruning

Established trees shouldn't need much pruning. They fruit primarily on the tips of growth from the previous summer, so treat them like tip-bearing apples (see p.69). Prune in winter when the trees are dormant.

(right) **Young fruit** are often covered in a soft, fuzzy, white or gray-brown down, although as they ripen this disappears and the skins deepen to a lovely, almost luminous golden yellow.

WHAT CAN GO WRONG

Many of the pests and diseases that afflict apples (see pp.78–79) and pears (see pp.100–101) may also affect quinces. The most common include brown rot (p.326), powdery mildew (p.329), fire blight (p.327) and quince leaf blight (p.329). Fruit are also prone to splitting if watering is irregular.

(below, left to right) **Quince leaf blight** is a form of fungal leaf spot. Red-brown spots appear on leaves, which turn yellow, wither, and die. **Brown rot** seems to afflict quinces particularly badly, both while the fruit is ripening and also when it is in storage. **Fruit may split** if a period of drought is suddenly followed by a spell of wet weather. Rot is then likely to develop.

Mulberries

Mulberries seem strangely out of place here among the tree fruit. Instead, they look as if they should be found growing on canes or bushes, like blackberries or loganberries, rather than on trees. But tree fruit they are—and large, handsome trees, too. Mulberries are not commonly grown these days. They should be. First, the fruit is wonderful: a ripe, black mulberry bursts in your mouth with an intense, sweet-tart flavor that is quite unique. Second, you're unlikely ever to taste fresh mulberries unless you grow them yourself; the fruits don't travel well and so are extremely unlikely ever to make it into supermarkets.

(above and left) **Black mulberries** and red mulberries are the best known types for pies, but their dark purple juice can make harvesting a nightmare. The white mulberry is related, and there are cultivated varieties that produce flavorful fruit—and no stains.

Growing mulberries

Mulberries are not hard to grow, although they can be hard to establish. Red and white mulberries can become large trees over 50 feet tall. Black mulberries are somewhat smaller, growing to only 30 feet tall. You can train mulberries to remain smaller or as wall-trained espaliers. Black mulberries are hardy only in Zones 7 and warmer. In colder climates, you'll have to grow them in containers.

The year at a glance

	spring			summer			fall			winter		
	E	M	L	E	M	L	E	M	L	E	M	L
plant bare-root	▬	▬	▬				▬	▬	▬			
plant container	▬	▬	▬	▬								
summer prune					▬	▬						
winter prune									▬	▬	▬	▬
harvest						▬	▬	▬				

Choosing a variety

Several cultivars are available. For red mulberry, try 'Wellington', 'Illinois Everbearing', or 'Collier'. 'Black Persian' is a popular black mulberry. 'Oscar' is a white mulberry variety that bears purple fruit; 'Sweet Lavender' has tasty white fruit.

Mulberries are self-fertile and will pollinate themselves, so single tree can be grown on its own.

When to plant

■ BARE-ROOT: Plant in spring, or in fall in mild-winter areas. Do not plant when the soil is waterlogged or frozen.
■ CONTAINER-GROWN: Plant at any time during the growing season; fall or early spring are best.

Where to plant

Choose a site where the tree can grow to full size without dropping fruit on a walkway or driveway. Black mulberries do best in a sunny, sheltered spot.

Soil type

Mulberries will grow happily in most soils but prefer a fertile, free-draining one with a pH of 5.5–7.0. They may struggle in very heavy, wet ground.

Routine care

■ WATERING Take care to water young, recently planted trees.
■ FEEDING and MULCHING If planted in moderately fertile soil, red and white mulberries need no special feeding. Black mulberries can be fed with a general fertilizer for the first few years after planting. Two or three weeks later, spread an organic mulch around the base of the trunk.
■ FROST PROTECTION Mulberries flower late in spring and, except in northern regions, tend not to suffer frost damage.

Harvesting and storing

Mulberries ripen over a long period. Ripe berries tend to fall off the tree. Black mulberries remain on the tree better than red or white will. For eating raw, leave black mulberries on the tree for as long as possible before picking, although when ripe they will begin to drop naturally. For cooking and making jams and jellies, pick all types of mulberries when still slightly underripe.

Pruning

Prune red and white mulberries when young to create a nice shape, and after that to remove dead or damaged wood if needed. If you train a mulberry as an espalier, do so in summer (see pp. 74–75).

What can go wrong

Mulberries are relatively pest- and disease-free. Birds are likely to be the biggest nuisance, and, if you're unlucky, mulberry canker (see p.328).

Medlars

Medlars are one of the oddest-looking fruits in this chapter. When ripe, they are rather like giant, brown rose hips, about the size of crab apples. Even more odd is the manner in which they are eaten. They are deliberately left until almost rotten, then the flesh is squeezed or spooned out once it has turned into a soft, sweet, brown paste. Related to the quince and hawthorn, medlar trees are undoubtedly handsome, with a decorative, drooping form. However, the fruit is an acquired taste.

(above) **After harvesting,** fruits are stored until the flesh "blets" or starts to decompose, when it develops a soft, caramel-tasting quality. If that sounds too unappetizing, medlars can also be used for making jams or jellies, in much the same way as quinces.

(below) **Pretty, pink-tinged spring flowers** and wonderful fall color make medlars attractive, as well as productive, garden trees. For reliable flowering, fruiting and good leaf color, plant trees in a sunny spot.

Growing medlars

Medlars are rarely grown on their own roots. Instead, they are usually sold grafted onto a Quince A rootstock. They are grown as small trees, usually about 10 feet tall, although they can reach up to 20 feet.

The year at a glance

	spring			summer			fall			winter		
	E	M	L	E	M	L	E	M	L	E	M	L
plant bare-root	▨	▨					▨	▨	▨			
plant container	▨	▨	▨				▨	▨	▨			
winter prune									▨	▨	▨	▨
harvest								▨	▨			

Choosing a variety

Only a handful of different varieties or cultivars are available. The most common are 'Nottingham', 'Dutch', and 'Royal'.

Medlars are self-fertile and will pollinate themselves. A single tree can be grown on its own.

When to plant

■ BARE-ROOT: Plant in spring, or in fall in mild-winter areas. Do not plant when the soil is waterlogged or frozen.
■ CONTAINER-GROWN: Plant at any time in the growing season; fall or early spring are best.

Where to plant

Medlars grow best in a warm, sunny, sheltered location. They will tolerate some shade.

Plant medlar trees in the same way as apples (see pp.58–59), making sure to stake them for the first few years.

Soil type

Medlars are not picky, although they prefer a deep, fertile, free-draining soil with a pH of 6.5–7.5.

Routine care

■ WATERING Take care to water young, recently planted trees.

■ FEEDING and MULCHING In the early years, and especially on poor soils, use a general blended fertilizer in late winter or early spring, before growth starts, and follow it with an organic mulch around the base of the trees.
■ FROST PROTECTION Medlars flower later in spring than most other tree fruit and, except in northern regions, are less vulnerable to damage from frost.

Harvesting and storing

As they ripen, medlars turn from green to brown, fatten up, and develop a russetlike covering. Leave them on the tree for as long as possible before picking—until mid- or late fall if there is no danger of frost. When they are ready, they will pull away easily with their stalks attached. Don't eat them right away. Instead, dip the stalks in a concentrated salt solution, then store them somewhere cool and dark, upside-down, stalks in the air. After a few weeks they will have "bletted": that is, the flesh inside should be soft and sweet, and on the point of decomposing without actually having begun to rot.

Pruning

Prune medlars as you would an apple (see pp.68–69), in winter when they are dormant. Established trees shouldn't need much pruning at all.

What can go wrong

Medlars are generally trouble-free. They sometimes become infected with a form of fungal leaf spot (see p.328), and you may find that moth caterpillars feed on the leaves at certain times of year. The effects can be unsightly but are rarely serious.

Figs

Many claims are made about the ancestry of figs. They are routinely declared to be one of the oldest of all cultivated plants, dating back to the Neolithic period, more than 11,000 years ago. Certainly, they predate the farming of wheat and other cereals, and there are records of their popularity among the ancient Egyptians, Greeks, and Romans, both for their flavor and as a reputed aphrodisiac. The foliage also played a key part in preserving the modesty of classical sculptures. Figs are by nature best suited to warm climates. Growing them in gardens is easy in Zones 8 and warmer, but in colder zones, getting them to fruit reliably can be a challenge. Summers are simply not long and hot enough for fruit to form and ripen in the same year. Instead, embryonic fruit formed one year must be protected over winter in the hope that they develop and ripen the following year. In a greenhouse, fruiting becomes more reliable, and if the greenhouse is heated, figs may fruit twice or even three times a year.

Figs with pale green, yellowish-green, or even green-and-yellow-striped skins tend to have pale-colored flesh, while that of the classic, dark purple-skinned varieties tends to be a rich, deep red.

Which forms to grow

■ **Freestanding tree** Attempt only in warm, sheltered sites unless growing in a container. They do well in the Southeast and mild parts of the West, but require protection in cold-winter areas.
■ **Fan** A fan-trained tree against a sheltered, sunny wall may bear fruit even in Zones 6 and 7.

Must-grow figs

1 'Brunswick'
A hardy variety that can be grown outdoors in mild-winter regions. Large, pear-shaped fruit with pale green skins flushed with brown or purple. Inside, the flesh is sweet and yellow-red in color.
- ■ **Color** green
- ■ **Harvest** late summer

2 'Rouge de Bordeaux'
This one is for only the sunniest, most sheltered of sites or for growing under glass. Often claimed to be the best-tasting fig of them all, the small to medium-sized fruit have purple skins, red flesh, and a wonderfully rich, aromatic flavor.
- ■ **Color** purple
- ■ **Harvest** late summer–early fall

3 'Panachee'
Dating back to the 17th century, 'Panachee' is almost worth growing for its looks alone. The fruit are striped yellow and green, and the flesh is bright red and sweet-tasting. Best grown as a fan against a warm, sheltered wall, or in a container.
- ■ **Color** yellow and green stripes
- ■ **Harvest** late summer

4 'Brown Turkey'
The tried-and-tested favorite for growing outdoors in mild-winter areas. It produces good crops of sweet, purple-brown figs with red flesh. You may also come across it referred to as 'Brown Naples' or 'Fleur de Rouge'.
- ■ **Color** purple-brown
- ■ **Harvest** late summer–early fall

5 'White Marseille'
Sometimes sold as 'White Genoa', 'White Naples', or even 'Figue Blanche', this variety produces large, pale green fruit with sweet-tasting white flesh that is almost transparent. It needs a warm, sheltered location if it is to be grown outdoors. Otherwise, grow it in a container or under glass.
- ■ **Color** pale green
- ■ **Harvest** late summer–early fall

'Violetta' (not illustrated)
Originally from Bavaria, and sometimes referred to as the 'Bavarian Fig' or in full as 'Bayernfeige Violetta', this is an extremely hardy variety that will tolerate low temperatures and is easy to grow. In favorable conditions it may produce two crops a year. The large, red-fleshed fruit have a good flavor.
- ■ **Color** green-purple
- ■ **Harvest** late summer–early fall

Growing figs

Growing figs is fairly easy, but unless you live in an area with long, hot summers, it can be hard to get them to produce a worthwhile crop of ripe fruit. It's important to understand how their annual fruiting cycle works. In hot, subtropical climates, or when grown in a heated greenhouse, figs can produce fruit two or three times a year, but outdoors in areas with moderate or cool summers, you can expect only one crop—from fruit that form in late summer, overwinter as pea-sized embryonic figs, then ripen the following summer.

The year at a glance

	spring			summer			fall			winter		
	E	M	L	E	M	L	E	M	L	E	M	L
plant	▓	▓	▓									
spring prune		▓	▓									
summer prune				▓	▓							
harvest indoors		▓	▓	▓								
harvest outdoors				▓	▓	▓						

Flowering and pollination

Figs grown in temperate regions are parthenocarpic. This means that they don't need pollinating or fertilizing in order to produce fruit. In fact, they don't appear to have flowers at all—at least, not visible ones. Actually, the flowers are hidden, contained within the embryo fruit. Figs do not produce seeds either, so propagation is always done from cuttings.

Choosing trees

Young figs are usually supplied container-grown. The trees grow on their own roots and are not grafted onto other rootstocks.

When to plant

The best time to plant a fig is in spring or fall, when the tree is dormant, but not if the soil is waterlogged or frozen. Avoid late spring and summer months if it is hot and dry.

Figs fruit better if potbound, so don't be tempted to pot them on into too-large containers. Keep them well-watered during the spring and summer, and feed with high-potassium tomato fertilizer when the fruits are ripening.

GROWING FIGS UNDER GLASS

In cool climates it may be better to grow figs under glass. Planting them directly into the ground in a greenhouse means they will be under cover year-round, and you'll have the opportunity to grow tender varieties that would struggle outdoors—'Rouge de Bordeaux', for example. You'll also get a much heavier crop, especially if the greenhouse is heated.

Figs are large trees and a wire-trained fan is likely to take up a large area of wall or roof space. In small greenhouses, it's probably much more practical to grow figs in containers. In summer, when the trees are in full leaf, they can be moved to a warm, sunny spot outside.

In fall, figs that won't ripen this year may drop from the tree. This is a natural shedding process and not an indication that the tree is in poor health.

Where to plant

Choose a warm, sunny, sheltered site protected from strong winds. In cool regions, grow a fan against a south- or southwest-facing fence or wall. Avoid frost pockets. Otherwise, grow in containers or under glass.

Soil type

Figs will grow in almost any well-drained ground, even shallow, sandy soils and slightly alkaline soils. In fact, in rich, very fertile, moisture-retentive soils, they tend to grow too vigorously, with too much foliage and too few fruit.

How to plant

Because figs are naturally vigorous, there is a tradition of planting them in sunken containers or specially constructed "fig pits" in order to restrict their roots deliberately. This curbs the growth of the tree, keeping it to a manageable size, and encourages it to produce fruit rather than foliage. Freestanding figs need staking for the first few years after planting.

Planting distances
■ BUSHES and HALF-STANDARDS restricted 12–20 ft (4–6 m), unrestricted 20–25 ft (6–8 m) apart.
■ FANS restricted 8–12 ft (2.5–4 m), unrestricted 12–15 ft (4–5 m) apart.

Growing in containers
Figs are ideal for growing in pots. In fact, they thrive in them. The container restricts root growth so that the tree does not grow too big. And, provided it is not too heavy, the pot can be brought into a cold conservatory or unheated greenhouse during winter, or covered with floating row cover to protect it from frost. The tree can then be moved to the warmest, sunniest part of your yard in summer.

Trees in containers are best grown as dwarf half-standards, with a clear stem or leg of about 16–30 in (40–75 cm) before the lateral branches spread out to form a bushy, open-centered head.

A multi-stemmed dwarf bush is suitable, too. Plant young trees in a container with a diameter of 10–14 in (25–35 cm) filled with loam-based potting mix blended with some sand or gravel to improve drainage and plenty of stones or crocks at the bottom. Keep the pot well-watered, and each spring topdress with fresh soil mixed with some slow-release general fertilizer. Every two or three years repot or transfer to a slightly larger container.

Routine care
■ WATERING Regular watering throughout the spring and summer is very important, particularly for young trees, wall-trained fans, and figs planted in containers or grown in pits to restrict their roots. They will all drop their fruit if allowed to dry out.
■ FEEDING In early spring, at the beginning of the growing season, apply a general blended fertilizer. Between late spring and late summer, while fruit

BUILDING A FIG PIT
A fig pit is basically a concrete-lined box sunk into the ground, with a layer of rubble at the bottom. It is designed to restrict the spread of the tree's roots, and is suitable for both freestanding trees and wall-trained fans.

1 Dig a hole and line it with 24 x 24 in (60 x 60 cm) paving slabs, each set on edge and protruding above the surface of the soil by about 2 in (5 cm). Put an 8-in (20-cm) layer of tightly packed broken bricks or rubble in the bottom to restrict roots but also to provide drainage.

2 Plant the young tree in the center of the pit, filling the hole with good-quality soil or loam-based potting mix blended with well-rotted organic matter and a slow-release general fertilizer.

3 Make sure the old nursery mark on the stem is level with the surface of the soil, firm it down, and water well. If you are planting in late fall, prune the stem to a healthy bud about 18 in (45 cm) above soil level.

are developing, water weekly with a diluted, high-potash tomato fertilizer or similar liquid feed.

■ MULCHING In early spring, after feeding, remove weeds and spread mulch freestanding and wall-trained trees with well-rotted compost or manure.

■ NETTING Birds can be a problem in summer as fruit ripens. Netting large trees may not be practical, but it's easier in the case of fans and trees in pots.

■ THINNING UNRIPE FRUIT In late fall, remove and discard any green fruit that have failed to ripen. It is too late for them to do so now, and outdoors they will not survive the winter. But don't touch the recently formed, tiny embryo figs; they will grow and ripen next year.

■ FROST PROTECTION Figs do not flower, but embryo fruits remain on the tree over winter and, along with young shoots, are at risk of frost damage. Bring container-grown trees under cover, and protect wall-trained fans with row cover. You can also protect fans or freestanding trees with an insulating blanket of dry straw. Pack the dried material in snugly and secure it with netting. Remove it in late spring. Some gardeners dig a trench next to a fig tree, sever the roots on one side, and bend the tree into the trench, insulate it, and then bury it for the winter, resurrecting it in spring.

Harvesting and storing

Fruit are ready for picking when they are fully colored, become slightly soft, and the stalks begin to bend so that the fruits tip downward. A telltale sign is when the skin around the eye splits and a bead of nectar appears. Figs will keep for a while after harvesting, but if they are really ripe they're best eaten straight from the tree. Resist the temptation to pick them before they are ready: they won't ripen any further once they are off the tree.

Yield

Yields vary too widely to quantify.

(below, left to right) **Remove any unripe figs** larger than a pea in late fall. Even the biggest will no longer ripen this year, and in any case they will be killed off during the winter. **Full-grown, ripe figs** as well as smaller, embryo fruitlets are commonly seen on the same tree simultaneously.

Season by season

(above, left to right) **New buds** break and fruitlets start to form almost as soon as the tree emerges from its winter dormancy. **Spring foliage** unfurls dramatically. **Fruits** that have overwintered as tiny embryos swell and ripen. (below) **Ripe figs** don't store well, so eat them as soon as possible after picking.

Early spring
■ Last chance to plant trees before they come out of their winter dormancy.
■ Apply a general blended fertilizer, then weed and mulch around trees.

Mid-spring
■ A first wave of new fruitlets starts to form. In hot climates and under glass, they should ripen by late summer. Outdoors in cool climates, they are unlikely to ripen at all.
■ Spring prune established trees and fans now or in late spring, cutting back unwanted growth and encouraging new fruiting shoots.

Late spring
■ Remove insulation used to protect trees during the winter. Dig up buried trees and provide support to keep them upright while their roots regrow.
■ Begin regular watering.
■ Give trees a liquid fertilizer while fruits are developing, between now and late summer.

Early summer
■ In hot climates and under glass, trees may produce a small, early crop from fruit borne on last year's new growth.
■ Summer prune established trees and fans now and in midsummer. Pinch out growing shoots to encourage the formation of new fruitlets, and tie in new growth on fans.

Midsummer
■ Early-season varieties may be ready to harvest.

Late summer
■ Harvest mid-season varieties.
■ A second wave of new fruitlets appears.

They should overwinter as tiny embryo fruits. In hot climates and under glass, they may produce a small crop in early summer. Outdoors in cool climates, they should ripen and form a main crop in mid- to late summer.

Early fall
■ Harvest late-season varieties.

Mid-fall
■ In cold-winter areas, protect trees with straw or other insulation or bury them in a trench for the winter.
■ Bring container-grown trees under cover before the first frost.

Late fall
■ In mild-winter areas, buy and plant bare-root trees.

Pruning and training figs

Most figs produce new young fruits twice a year. The first wave appears on new shoots in spring, gradually fattening up during the summer. In hot climates and in heated greenhouses, these ripen and can be harvested in early fall. However, outdoors in cooler regions, they never ripen and should be removed. The second wave of fruits starts to appear in late summer and early fall, forming tiny, embryonic figs, each no larger than a pea, at the tips of the year's new growth. Left on the tree, they should overwinter and provide a crop next year—for harvesting in spring in hot climates or under glass, and in late summer in cooler regions.

Whether grown as freestanding trees or wall-trained fans, established figs should be lightly pruned twice a year: once in spring to thin out old or damaged wood and to maintain the overall shape; and again in early summer to stimulate the production of the embryo fruits that will develop and ripen next year.

Fig sap can be an irritant. If you react adversely to it, wear gloves when pruning and take care not to get any on your skin.

Pruning a fig tree

Initial training and pruning is similar to that for a plum (see p.114). Aim for an open-centered tree with a balanced framework of main branches. Thereafter, prune established trees in spring and early summer.

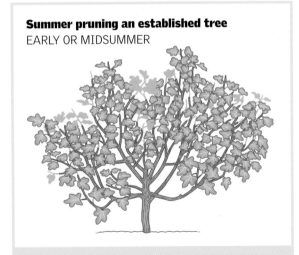

Spring pruning an established tree
MID-SPRING

- Select a few lengthy laterals that are now fruiting only at their tips and prune them back hard to a bud 2–3 in (5–8 cm) from the trunk or main branch. This will promote new growth closer to the heart of the tree.
- Cut back to undamaged wood any shoots that have been damaged by frost during the winter.
- Remove congested growth from the center of the tree.
- Cut out any dead, damaged, or diseased wood.

Summer pruning an established tree
EARLY OR MIDSUMMER

- Pinch out the growing tip of each new shoot as soon as 5–6 leaves have appeared. This will stimulate the formation of the second wave of embryo fruits. It also allows sunlight to reach existing fruits that are now in the process of ripening.

Pruning a fig fan

Grow against a south- or southwest-facing wall or fence. Allow a space
12 ft (4 m) wide and 7 ft (2 m) high. Start with a two- or three-year-old tree.
Initial training and pruning is similar to that for a peach (see pp.152–53),
although the ribs may need wider spacing as fig leaves are larger.

(below, left to right) **In spring**, the structure of the budding fan is clearly visible. **By early summer,** the fig has put on an impressive amount of foliage.

Spring pruning an established fan
MID–LATE SPRING

- Select a couple of the oldest, least productive main laterals and cut them back to a single bud. This should help open up congested areas.
- Prune to 1 bud or leaf about half of the sideshoots growing from the main ribs or arms of the fan. This will encourage new fruiting growth.
- Remove completely any new buds or shoots growing directly into or out from the wall or fence.
- Cut out any dead, damaged, or diseased wood, including any shoots damaged by frost during the winter.
- Tie in new shoots that will help form the framework of the fan as it grows.

(left to right) **Cut out old stems** at the base to encourage new, more vigorous growth. **Prune sideshoots** on either side of the fan in spring, cutting back to one bud.

Summer pruning an established fan
EARLY OR MIDSUMMER

- Pinch out the growing tips of new shoots once they have 5–6 leaves. This encourages the formation of embryo fruits and lets sunlight ripen existing fruits.
- If you can, identify figs that will not ripen this year, and cut off the shoots bearing them. New growth should break from the stumps, producing further embryo fruits. If you can't, don't worry. Pick off unripe fruit later in the year, in fall.
- Continue tying in new shoots.

(right) **Remove shoots** with small, unripe figs by making a clean cut with a pair of sharp pruners.

In a greenhouse, a fig can be trained vertically upward, then fanned out across a series of overhead horizontal wires stretched beneath the roof.

Carefully bend the current year's new lateral shoots into position and tie them in to the wires using string or flexible plant ties. Don't secure them too tightly.

Aim for a framework of well-spaced ribs with plenty of room for air to circulate and for sunlight to reach the ripening fruits.

What can go wrong

Leaves, stems, and branches

1 Leaves mottled and bronzed
If upper surfaces of leaves become speckled or mottled with pale yellow-bronze spots, then begin to dry up and die, look underneath with a magnifying glass for tiny spider mites. In severe cases, you may also see fine silk webbing. Spider mites are much more likely to be a problem in a greenhouse.
■ See **Spider mites** (p.340).

2 Small, white, wax-covered insects on stems
Mealybugs feed on sap that they suck from stems and branches. These pests are recognizable by their coating of fluffy, white wax.
■ See **Mealybugs** (p.337).

3 Bumps on stems and leaves
Several kinds of scale insects may be found on stems and branches, especially on figs in a greenhouse. They are elliptical and covered with a domed shell. If leaves are also covered with sticky honeydew, then the cause is the type known as soft scale.
■ See **Scale insects** (p.340).

Rusty-brown spots on leaf undersides
Fungal rust causes these spots. Infected leaves may die and drop.
■ See **Rust** (p.330).

Plants grow poorly
If your fig trees seem lackluster, check stems carefully for scale insects. If you find none, then suspect root-feeding nematodes.
■ See **Scale insects** (p.340) and **Nematodes** (p.337).

Fruit

4 Unripe figs drop from the tree prematurely
In summer, this is probably due to a shortage of water. In fall or winter, unripe figs fall naturally or are killed by frost.
■ See **Routine care** (p.171).

5 Fruit partially or wholly eaten
The closer figs are to being perfectly ripe, the more irresistible they are to birds, wasps, flies, and other insects. They feed on the ripening fruit, making or enlarging holes in the skin.
■ See **Birds** (p.334) and **Wasps** (p.341).

Soft Fruit

The term "soft fruit" is something of a catchall, meaning—in essence—any fruit that doesn't grow on trees. The main categories are bush fruit (currants, gooseberries, blueberries, and cranberries), cane fruit (raspberries, blackberries, and hybrid bramble fruits), and, in a group of their own, strawberries. Strictly speaking, grapes are a type of soft fruit, too, although in this book they are treated separately. Many of the fruits termed "tender and unusual" (melons, cape gooseberries, kiwifruit, and more) are soft fruits as well, but they have been grouped together because of their particular climatic growing requirements.

Soft fruits have a special appeal as grow-your-own crops. They almost all taste at their absolute best when left to ripen on the plant, then picked and eaten immediately. But at that point they are fragile, and unlikely to survive the long journey to a supermarket shelf. Consequently, commercially grown fruit is usually picked before it is ripe, when it is firmer and more resilient. The result? It will never have the sweetness, juiciness, aroma, and flavor of fruit you have grown and picked yourself.

Blackberries might seem an odd choice of fruit to grow in your backyard or community garden. After all, they're easy to find growing wild. However, cultivated varieties crop more heavily, and some are mercifully thornless.

Growing soft fruit

Planting a selection of soft fruit is a fairly long-term commitment. It's certainly longer-term than growing annual vegetables, which are there one year and gone the next, though it's obviously not such an investment in the future as planting a fruit tree. Apart from strawberries, you can expect most soft fruit bushes or canes to live and to continue producing fruit for several years. Choosing the appropriate site and providing your soft fruit crops with the right growing conditions are, therefore, crucial.

Vertical cordons are a great way of growing red currants. They are economical on space, the fruit is easy to pick, and if trained against a sheltered wall they enjoy a perfect microclimate.

Buying soft fruit

Like fruit trees, new soft-fruit plants can be bought either bare-root or potted in containers. Specialty nurseries usually sell bare-root plants in the fall and again in the spring, when they are dormant. Garden centers in mild-winter areas may offer container-grown plants year-round—though the choice may be more limited.

Always buy plants from a source that can guarantee they are officially certified disease-free.

Planting soft fruit

Most soft fruits are cool-climate plants, and are tolerant about where they are planted. However, they all prefer somewhere sheltered, out of strong winds, and will all ripen better in sunshine. Soil requirements vary, but fertile, free-draining soil is always a good thing, and no plants, except perhaps cranberries, will grow well in heavy, waterlogged ground. Prepare your site by digging in well-rotted manure or garden compost. Add some general fertilizer, and balance the pH of the soil if necessary.

The best time to plant is in early spring, unless you are planting tissue-culture plants. For those, wait until your last spring frost has passed. Strawberries, currants, and gooseberries can also be planted in fall in areas with relatively mild winters. Do not try to plant in winter when the ground is waterlogged or frozen. Also avoid planting in July and August, when the weather is hottest and driest.

Pruning and training soft fruit

Gooseberry, currant, and blueberry bushes usually grow satisfactorily without support, but raspberries, blackberries, and hybrid bramble fruits, as well as any soft fruit grown as cordons or fans, will need training and tying in to fences, walls, or post-and-wire structures. Standard gooseberries and red currants require staking.

Regular pruning helps to keep plants tidy, healthy, and productive. Specific pruning techniques vary from fruit to fruit, but here are a few general guidelines:

■ IMMEDIATELY REMOVE any growth that is **dead**, **damaged**, or **diseased**—sometimes known as **"the three Ds."**

■ THIN OUT CROWDED and congested areas so that light can get in and air can circulate.

■ TIE UP OR CUT BACK any growth that is hanging too low or touching the ground.

■ AFTER HARVESTING raspberries, blackberries, and hybrid bramble fruits, cut out the canes that have fruited, as they won't fruit again.

■ EACH WINTER, remove a few of the older stems from established blueberry, gooseberry, and currant bushes. This will make way for new growth.

■ PRUNE SIDESHOOTS on gooseberries, red currants, and white currants in both winter and summer to encourage them to produce lots of fruiting spurs. But don't do this with black currants: they fruit differently.

■ ROUTINELY REMOVE strawberry runners, using them to propagate new plants if required.

Protecting soft fruit
Apart from the usual range of diseases, disorders, and infestations, birds are by far the most serious threat to soft fruit crops. Scare devices may work for a while, but birds are smart and learn to ignore them very quickly. Nets are the only guaranteed protection, and a specially constructed, walk-in fruit cage is the ultimate defense.

(right, top to bottom) **A system of double protection** ensures a perfect crop of strawberries: below, a thick layer of straw lifts the fruit off the soil and keeps them clean; above, a cover of netting protects them from birds. **Gooseberries** put on a lot of new growth in summer, so cut back sideshoots to let in light and air.

Strawberries

Strawberries are irresistibly seductive—few things rival their luscious aroma and flavor when ripe, sweet, and freshly picked. In the past, however, that pleasure was fleeting. The season for traditional summer-fruiting strawberries came and went over the course of just a few short weeks in June or July. Commercial growers and breeders, therefore, have long been in search of the Holy Grail: the year-round strawberry. They have made some progress. As well as summer-fruiting, we now have fall-fruiting varieties, also known as everbearing, perpetual, or remontant strawberries. Perpetual they're not, but they nevertheless usually produce a small crop in about June, then start producing again from late summer right through to the first frost—or longer if you protect them from freezing temperatures. In addition, there are day-neutral strawberries, a relatively recent innovation. These berries have been bred to grow regardless of the length of the day, which means that it doesn't matter to them what time of year it is. As long as it's neither too cold nor too hot, they should crop within about twelve weeks of planting. So, in theory at least, you can grow your own strawberries for Christmas and Easter.

A new, novelty form of strawberry—the pineberry—has recently become available to home growers. It is white with red seeds and has a slight pineapple flavor.

Traditional, summer-fruiting strawberries still have arguably the best flavor, but their season is short. Modern everbearing varieties keep fruiting right into the fall—or even longer if you cover them to protect them from frost.

Must-grow strawberries

1 EVERBEARING STRAWBERRIES

It's definitely worth including one or two varieties of everbearing strawberries in your garden for a harvest that will last from early summer through fall. Here are some of the best to try:

'Fort Laramie' can withstand punishingly cold winters, and thrives in mild-winter areas too. Excellent sweet flavor; produces June–August. Can be planted in containers or baskets, too.

'Ozark Beauty' is a heavy producer of large, "honeysweet" berries that are good for canning, freezing, and fresh eating. Has resistance to leaf spot. Produces through summer and into fall.

'Albion' is a new variety that's coming on strong. It's resistant to root rot and other diseases as well as mite problems. The berries are long and firm, with good flavor. Produces summer through fall.

2–8 SUMMER-BEARING STRAWBERRIES

Nothing beats the pleasure of the June strawberry harvest. For a satisfying crop in early summer, you'll want to sample some of these varieties:

'Earliglow' ripens early and is disease-resistant. No sugar needed for these berries! Great choice for canning, too.

'Benton' is very easy to grow because it can even tolerate wetter soil than many varieties. Ripens later than many June-bearing varieties.

'Surecrop' is sure to please in any region of the country. Produces reliably large yields of deep red berries with intense flavor. Ideal for processing.

'Chandler' is the berry of choice for gardeners in Florida and California who want to try growing strawberries in the winter, where the plants may fruit as early as March. Firm, juicy berries; food for freezing.

'Shuksan' berries do well in the Northwest and in most other areas too. High yields of large dark red flavorful berries. Great for fresh eating and freezing.

'Honeoye' is one of the best June-bearers. Heavy-cropping, medium-to-large, glossy-red, firm, juicy berries. Fairly good disease resistance.

'Sparkle' is a longtime favorite because of its fabulous sweetness and rich strawberry flavor and heavy yields. Late ripener. Some disease resistance.

'Annapolis' (not illustrated) is an early producer of large fruit. It holds its size well through later harvests. Berries are light red and winter hardy. An excellent early season choice for u-pick farmers and fresh sales.

'Sonata' (not illustrated) is a recent introduction from the breeder of the Dutch 'Elsanta' variety with even larger, sweeter berries, the same excellent flavor, and allegedly improved disease resistance.

'Snow White' (not illustrated) is white with red seeds and a mild, pineapplelike taste. Sometimes called a "pineberry," it was originally a cross between South American and North American forms of strawberry.

9 ALPINE STRAWBERRIES
These small berries are super-flavorful and productive:

'Mignonette' (shown here) is one of the best-tasting alpines and can be as large as 1 inch (2.5 cm) long.

'Alpine Yellow' produces yellow fruits with brown seeds. The flavor is a combination of strawberry and pineapple.

'Rugen' does not produce runners, but will reseed itself to spread and fill in a bed. Produces sweet red berries.

DAY-NEUTRAL STRAWBERRIES
(not illustrated)
As long as it's neither too cold nor too warm these varieties are ready to harvest within about 12 weeks of planting:

'Seascape'
Very popular in the West. Large, disease-resistant, heavy producer. Low chilling requirement. Fruit is firm and appealing.
■ **Harvest** heavy crop in late spring, lighter production for summer to fall

'Tristar'
Medium-size berries that seem to get larger in the fall. Excellent for fresh eating or freezing. Good disease resistance, and a good choice for containers.
■ **Harvest** early summer and again in fall

Growing strawberries

Most people will tell you that strawberries are easy to grow, and in many ways they are. There's certainly no complicated training and pruning to worry about. But they're not quite as easy as you may think: they're prone to a lot of pests and diseases, and they need to be well cared for if they're to produce a satisfactory crop of good-sized, good-looking, tasty fruit. Easy to grow but difficult to grow well—that might be more accurate.

The year at a glance

	spring			summer			fall			winter		
	E	M	L	E	M	L	E	M	L	E	M	L
plant summer-fruiting/everbearing	■	■	■									
plant day-neutral	■											
harvest summer-fruiting			■	■	■							
harvest everbearing					■	■	■					
harvest under cover	■	■	■					■	■			

Strawberries usually flower in mid-spring. The more flowers you get, the better the crop.

PLANTING STRAWBERRIES DIRECTLY INTO THE GROUND

Prepare the soil well in advance by digging in plenty of well-rotted manure or compost and by carefully removing all traces of perennial weeds. Fork in some general, blended fertilizer. Rake over the soil and level it out.

1 Use a line to measure out the positions of your planting holes, about 18 in (45 cm) apart.

2 Trim off any too-long, straggly roots from each runner and carefully spread them out over a small mound created in the bottom of each hole.

3 Check that the crown of the plant is at the same height as the surface of the soil, then backfill and firm down gently with your hands.

4 Water the young plants thoroughly, both now and at regular intervals over the next few weeks, especially if the weather is dry.

Choosing plants

Unless you're propagating your own strawberries (see p.190), you'll need to buy new, certified disease-free plants, since growing them from seed is difficult. They are available as either bare-root or container-grown plants. The strawberries you are most likely to get from a garden center will be container-grown. Bare-root plants are less expensive but tend to come from specialty nurseries via mail-order. They will be open-ground or field-grown runners or greenhouse-grown plants started from tissue culture. Most mail-order nurseries offer strawberry plants for sale in late winter through spring, with shipping to Zone 9 beginning as early as mid-February. All bare-root plants should be planted out as soon as they arrive.

When to plant

The timing varies according to the sort of plants available and the form in which you buy them. Do not attempt to plant in winter, or if the ground is waterlogged.

■ SUMMER-FRUITING and EVERBEARING VARIETIES The best time is in the spring. You should remove flowers for the first three to four months after planting, so you won't be able to start harvesting until fall (for everbearers) or the following spring. Good-sized pot-grown plants (which will be available at local nurseries during the summer), however, may not need flowers removed, so they will crop well in their first year whenever they're planted.

■ DAY-NEUTRAL VARIETIES Plant outdoors in early spring and pinch off flowers for about the first six weeks. After that, allow fruit to form. You can harvest for the rest of the summer. In the South, you can plant again in later summer for a harvest the following year. Plant in pots from June through September for fall and winter crops in greenhouses or hoophouses.

Where to plant

Strawberries grow best in full sun, though they will tolerate a few hours of shade during the day. Choose a sheltered site out of strong winds but avoid potential frost pockets. Don't plant where you've recently grown tomatoes or potatoes.

PLANTING STRAWBERRIES THROUGH PLASTIC MULCH

Planting through slits cut in plastic stretched over a slightly raised bed has a number of advantages. The plastic warms the soil and acts as a mulch to suppress weeds. It also helps to retain moisture, and the berries won't get mud-splashed as they ripen. You can either install a length of soaker hose laid beneath the plastic to keep the plants moist, or water each plant with a watering can or hose.

1 Create a 3-ft- (1-m-) wide bed mounded up slightly in the center. Cover it with a length of plastic 4 ft (1.2 m) wide. Clear plastic warms the soil most effectively as it acts like a greenhouse, but opaque black plastic suppresses weeds.

2 Bury the edges of the plastic firmly into the soil along each side of the bed to anchor them.

3 Using a sharp knife or a pair of scissors, cut X-shaped slits in the plastic at 18-in (45-cm) intervals.

4 Plant the strawberries into the slits and firm down the soil around them. Fold back the edges of the plastic and water. The sloping bed will ensure that excess water drains away.

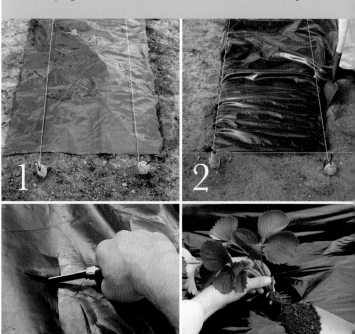

Soil type

Strawberries are not too picky about soil, provided that it is free-draining. Damp, waterlogged conditions lead to root rots and other diseases. A slightly acidic pH of 6–6.5 is ideal.

Planting distances

- PLANTS 18 in (45 cm) apart.
- ROW SPACING 30 in (75 cm) apart.

Routine care

- WATERING Newly planted strawberries need regular watering, as do established plants when the weather is hot and dry. However, the ripening fruits themselves dislike actually getting wet; this can trigger botrytis or gray mold (see p.326). If possible, water the soil rather than the plants, and water in the mornings so that any moisture splashed on the fruits has evaporated by the evening.
- FEEDING In mid- to late spring, particularly if your soil is poor, sprinkle a little blended fertilizer around the plants, taking care that it doesn't touch the leaves. For an additional boost of potassium, give plants a high-potash fertilizer after harvesting.
- NETTING Nets are essential to keep off birds—certainly in summer as the strawberries begin to color and ripen.
- FROST PROTECTION Early-flowering varieties may need protection from floating row cover or cloches overnight if there is a danger of frost. Uncover the plants during the day to allow insects to pollinate the flowers.
- MULCHING Mulch is necessary not just to retain moisture and suppress weeds but to keep

(left) **Protect strawberries** by surrounding them with a layer of straw when they are in flower or as soon as fruits begin to form.

the berries clean. Without mulch, they actually sit on the soil and will soon be splashed with mud. "Strawing down" is the traditional method of protecting them (see opposite), but growing them through plastic or using special strawberry mats achieves the same result. Whichever you choose, weed thoroughly before mulching.

Straw mulch

Spread a generous layer of straw around each plant. Tuck it in carefully so the leaves and berries are lifted off the soil and air can circulate beneath. Barley straw is the best, wheat straw is good, but oat straw may contain nematodes (see p.337).

Strawberry mats

Special fiber mats have a hole in the center and a slit on one edge allowing them to be slipped around the crowns of each plant, like a collar. They're neat and easier to install than laying straw, but in time they become dirty.

Plastic

Keep plastic tightly anchored and stretched taut so that water runs off rather than collecting in puddles: it may cause fruits to rot.

Strawberry mats placed carefully around the crowns well before the fruits ripen will protect the berries.

(below left to right) **Remove surplus runners** that form on fruiting plants when they appear. Cut them off close to the parent plant with sharp pruners. You can pot them and keep growing them (see p.189). **Netting** is vital to keep hungry birds off fruit. In some areas, squirrels may also be a problem.

Harvesting and storing

Strawberries ripen quickly, and you'll need to check plants every day. For eating fresh, try to catch them at the point where they have turned completely red but before they begin to get soft. Pick them in the morning after the sun has dried them, and if possible eat them immediately, while they are at their very best. For storing, pick the berries when they are still slightly white at the end. They will probably continue to ripen and will keep in the refrigerator for a couple of days.

Strawberries do not freeze well—they almost invariably turn mushy when thawed. They are fine for cooking, but otherwise unappetizing.

Yield

Yields vary widely from variety to variety, but a healthy plant should produce something in the range of 8 oz–1 lb (225–450 g) of fruit.

What to do at the end of the season

Tidy up your strawberry patch after the harvest ends if you want the plants to fruit again next year.

Remove any old straw from around the plants and pull out any weeds. After the ground freezes, use fresh straw or evergreen boughs to cover the plants and protect them from frost heaving. Pull the mulch back in early spring.

The lifespan of strawberries

Strawberry plants don't last forever. Viruses and other diseases have a tendency to build up, and crops are likely to diminish as each year goes by. Perpetual and day-neutral strawberries are best replaced after two years or—even better—planted afresh each year and grown as annuals. Summer-fruiting varieties shouldn't be kept going for more than three or four years. It helps to rotate strawberry beds, just as you would with vegetables.

Growing in containers

Strawberries are ideal for container growing. Indeed, there are a number of reasons why you may even prefer to grow them in containers. First, pots, troughs, towers, hanging baskets, and growing bags are all economical in terms of space. Second, they

PROPAGATING STRAWBERRIES

Left to their own devices, most strawberries will virtually propagate themselves. Their natural behavior is to put out stems or "runners" on which plantlets form and take root where they come in contact with the soil. You can choose to cut them off and throw them away if they are unwanted, sever them and let them grow on where they have rooted, or pot them up and replant them elsewhere. A word of warning: strawberries are not immortal. To avoid the buildup of viruses and other diseases, propagate only from young, healthy plants.

1 Once runners have formed and young plantlets are starting to grow, carefully lift them from the soil—no more than four or five per plant. Don't separate them from the parent plant just yet.

2 Sink a small pot into the ground and fill it with potting mix. Plant the rooted runner, peg it down with a U-shaped wire, and keep it watered. In 4–6 weeks, once it has established, sever it from its parent. It is now ready for transplanting.

(left to right) **Hanging baskets** are suitable for growing most strawberries, and they can look attractive. And, of course, it's the one sure way to keep the plants free of slugs. Sadly, growing them in mid-air won't deter birds: you may still need to cover them with nets. **Harvest** strawberries when dry and they'll keep for longer, if you can resist eating them.

are mobile, and can therefore be moved into a sunny, sheltered spot to take advantage of light and warmth or brought inside for protection from cold. Third, they can be raised off the ground to protect them from slugs. And, lastly, they are less prone to soilborne diseases.

Almost any kind of container is suitable, as long as it is deep enough and has sufficient drainage holes. Special terra-cotta or plastic strawberry pots have cup-shaped pockets around their sides in which individual plants are grown. Some have a central watering tube that helps prevent plants at the bottom from drying out. Tower pots are similar but are constructed from a number of stackable, self-contained units. Growing bags are particularly effective. They are best planted in spring and early summer with cold-stored runners or young, container-grown plants, and can be raised off the ground, either on planks or boxes or on a special "table-top" frame.

All containers should be watered regularly. Little and often is the mantra, so that the plants always remain moist, never becoming waterlogged and never drying out. As soon as plants flower, start giving them a weekly liquid feeding with a high-potassium/low-nitrate fertilizer (tomato fertilizer,

for example). After harvesting, when you remove the old foliage, give them one last feeding with blended fertilizer, then nothing more until next spring. Replace the plants every two or three years.

Growing strawberries under cover

The term "under cover" is used here to mean anything from a temporary cloche to a full-sized greenhouse. Whichever method you choose, the objective of growing plants under cover is always the same: to extend the season so that you can harvest fruit earlier or later than you would if you were growing strawberries outdoors.

Forcing outdoor strawberries for an early crop

Early varieties grown outdoors can be encouraged to fruit up to three weeks earlier than usual by covering the plants with glass or plastic cloches or with low hoophouses in late winter or early spring. As soon as the flowers open, begin removing the

Greenhouse-grown strawberries will fruit earlier than those grown outdoors without cover, but may not have as much flavor.

covers on warm days so that insects can pollinate them. Remember that plants under cover will need to be watered by hand.

Forcing greenhouse strawberries for an early crop

Even earlier crops are possible by growing strawberries in containers kept in a greenhouse during the winter. It's best to plant up new runners in summer and leave them outdoors, exposing them to a certain amount of cold weather but protecting them from any severe, late-fall or early-winter frosts and from heavy rain. Then bring them indoors, either into a heated greenhouse in late fall or into an unheated greenhouse in early winter. The plants should flower in February. As soon as they do, and because no insects will be around, hand-pollinate them every day using a small, soft brush. If pollination is successful and the fruit sets, begin watering regularly and feed with a liquid, high-potassium fertilizer. On warm days, open doors or windows to keep the temperature at 68–75°F (20–24°C). You should have strawberries from a heated greenhouse as early as mid-spring, and from an unheated one in late spring.

Growing winter strawberries under cover

Day-neutral strawberries are the ones to choose if you really want to prolong the season. They will continue producing fruit regardless of the length of day as long as the temperature does not drop below 50°F (10°C). Plant them in pots at any time between June and September, bring them into an unheated greenhouse in fall, and they may well fruit right up until the winter holidays. Perhaps not as delicious as an outdoor-grown strawberry in midsummer, they are welcome nonetheless.

ALPINE STRAWBERRIES

Like miniature versions of regular strawberries, Alpine strawberries (right) are closer to the original wild species than cultivated varieties. Also known as *fraises des bois*, meaning "woodland strawberries," they produce tiny fruits—not much larger than peas—throughout the summer months. They have a fragrance and concentrated, intense flavor that makes them highly prized. They're easy to grow and can be bought as small, ready-grown container plants or raised from seed. Sow indoors or under cover in early spring, and plant out in late spring, in a partially shaded area if summers are hot. You may get a few berries in the first year, but you'll get a lot more in the second. Established plants are likely to self-seed and should spread readily.

Season by season

(left to right) **Flowers** begin to open in mid-spring. **Green fruitlets** soon follow. **Ripe berries** are particularly attractive to birds as well as slugs.

Early spring
■ Cover outdoor plants with cloches or tunnels in order to force an early crop.
■ Feed plants with a general, blended fertilizer.
■ Plant bare-root runners or new, pot-grown strawberries outdoors now or in mid-spring—though don't expect a crop this year.
■ Plant day-neutral varieties outdoors now or in mid-spring—they should fruit in late summer.

Mid-spring
■ Most varieties flower now or in late spring. Protect against frost damage if necessary, but uncover to allow pollination.
■ As fruit starts to appear, put strawberry mats in place or spread a layer of straw around and underneath the plants.
■ Harvest greenhouse strawberries.

Late spring
■ Water regularly as berries fatten up and ripen.
■ Protect plants against slugs, and net to keep off birds.
■ Harvest very-early-season summer-fruiting varieties.

Early summer
■ Harvest early- and mid-season summer-fruiting varieties.
■ Plant day-neutral varieties in pots between now and late summer—with frost protection they will fruit through the fall.
■ Propagate by potting up young plantlets from runners between now and late summer.

Midsummer
■ Harvest mid- and late-season summer-fruiting varieties, and the first of the perpetual varieties.
■ New bare-root runners start to become available.
■ Plant new runners outdoors now or in late summer for a crop next year.

Late summer
■ Plant day-neutral varieties outdoors between now and mid-fall—they will fruit next summer.
■ Cut back and tidy up all plants that have finished fruiting.

Early fall
■ Plant bare-root runners or new, pot-grown strawberries between now and late fall—though it is too late to expect much of a crop next year.

Mid-fall
■ Harvest the last of the perpetual varieties until the first frost of winter—unless you cover them with cloches in order to prolong the season.
■ Last chance until next spring for planting new strawberries outdoors.

Late fall
■ Bring pot-grown strawberries into a heated greenhouse for an early crop next March or April.
■ Harvest the last of container-grown, day-neutral varieties protected from frost earlier in the fall.

What can go wrong

Leaves and stems

1 Yellow-red blotches with gray centers

Irregular purple-red spots on leaves may spread and enlarge into gray-centered blotches with red and yellow margins. The blotches may turn into holes and an off-white mold may appear.
■ See **Fungal leaf spot** (p.327).

2 Yellow leaves with green veins

If leaves turn yellow with skeletal green veins, and if the plant is obviously growing poorly, it's usually a sign that the soil is too alkaline and the plant is suffering from lime-induced chlorosis, meaning that it is unable to absorb enough iron and manganese.
■ See **Iron deficiency** (p.320), **Manganese deficiency** (p.321).

Discolored, wilted leaves and fine silk web

Green leaves mottle and turn bronze or pale yellow, wither, and die. A fine silk web spun over infested plants is the telltale sign that this might be spider mites. The problem can occur both in greenhouses and outdoors.
■ See **Spider mites** (p.339).

Curled, sticky leaves

Aphids are the most likely cause. They are at their worst in spring, when they feed on new growth, especially if plants are growing in a greenhouse or hoophouse. Aphids spread viruses.
■ See **Aphids** (p.334).

Distorted, yellow-patterned leaves

Crumpled, crinkled, or stunted leaves with yellow margins, yellow spots and blotches, or yellow mosaic patterning are all signs of different viruses that can attack strawberries.
■ See **Strawberry virus** (p.331).

Dark patches and white powdery coating

Leaves develop dark, red-purple, blotchy patches on their upper surfaces, and a gray-white powder covers the undersides. The leaves curl upward at the edges. Powdery mildew is caused by a fungus, and tends to be worse when the weather is hot and dry. Flowers and fruit may be affected, too.
■ See **Powdery mildew** (p.329).

Leaves discolor and wilt

In summer, older leaves are red or brown, and young leaves are yellow. There may be black streaks on leaf stems, and the whole plant wilts and may die. The cause is likely to be verticillium wilt.
■ See **Verticillium wilt** (p.331).

Leaves wilt and base of stems rots

Leaves turn yellow and wilt, and the plant may die. Symptoms are similar to those of verticillium wilt, but in this case the crown of the plant is also brown and rotten.
■ See **Crown rot** (p.326).

1

2

Stunted growth and discolored leaves

Plants are smaller than normal. Inner leaves are red or orange, and outer leaves are brown and dry. The central cores of roots are red instead of white. The cause is the fungus known as red stele. If plants are stunted and leaves are yellow, the problem may be root-knot nematodes.
■ See **Red stele** (p.330) and **Nematodes** (p.337).

Crinkled leaves with thick stalks

Overall poor or stunted growth, crumpled, distorted leaves, and stalks either shorter and thicker than normal, or longer and colored red, may be caused by an infestation of nematodes.
■ See **Nematodes** (p.337).

Leaves nibbled and roots eaten

Adult strawberry root weevils eat notch-shaped holes out of the edges of the leaves and larvae feed underground on the roots. If severely attacked, plants may wilt and die.
■ See **Strawberry root weevils** (p.340).

Skeletonlike leaves

Japanese beetles feed on leaf tissue but do not eat leaf veins. Their larvae, white grubs, feed on roots, which also weakens the plants.
■ See **Japanese beetles** (p.336).

Fruit

3 Fluffy, gray or brown mold

In wet summers or in damp and humid conditions, fruit may become covered with mold and start to rot. The likely cause is the fungus *Botrytis cinerea*.
■ See **Botrytis** (p.326).

4 Fruit partially or wholly eaten

Both birds and slugs find ripe strawberries absolutely irresistible and will attack them relentlessly.
■ See **Birds** (p.335), **Slugs** (p.340).

Fruit loses its shine

Berries that are dull rather than shiny and that are perhaps also stunted or distorted may be infected with powdery mildew.
■ See **Powdery mildew** (p.329).

Fruit distorted and gnarled

Tarnished plant bugs inject a toxin as they feed that causes this fruit damage. If flowers are damaged by frost, it can also result in fruit with similar damage, known as "catfacing."
■ See **Plant bugs** (p.338) and **Frost** (p.316).

3

4

Raspberries

The aroma and the flavor of a bowl of ripe, fresh raspberries captures the essence of midsummer. Traditionally, however, the raspberry season was woefully short. Most summer-fruiting raspberries lasted no more than three weeks or so, and were then finished until the next year. Admittedly, fall-bearing varieties were available to prolong the season, but their yields were low and the berries didn't taste like much of anything. Nowadays, modern fall-bearing cultivars are much improved, making it possible—at least in theory—to pick and eat fresh fruit from early July right through to the first frost. And there's a wide choice of different colors, too: from orange and yellow, through red, to purple and black.

Once raspberries are established and you've got the hang of their basic pruning requirements, they're fairly easy to grow. They are vigorous plants, and the summer-bearing varieties, especially, will need sturdy supports as well as protection from hungry birds. For a reasonable crop, you'll need a row of canes 6–10 ft (2–3 m) long, and if you're growing both summer- and fall-bearing varieties, make sure you keep them completely separate.

Picking perfectly ripe raspberries on a dry day is one of summer's great pleasures. You can still harvest the berries if the weather is wet, but they won't keep as well. Red berries can be summer- or fall-bearing, but the gold or yellow varieties tend to fruit in the fall.

Which forms to grow

■ **Canes** Summer-bearing raspberries grow tall and need supports. Fall-bearing raspberries are shorter and can be grown without supports, though they will do better with them. Most support systems employ wooden posts and either a single or double row of wires.

Must-grow raspberries

1–5 SUMMER-BEARING RASPBERRIES

Some of the best-known raspberries are summer-bearing types.

'Tulameen' has large, bright red berries with excellent flavor. Crops generously, often for 4–6 weeks. Bred in Canada, it is hardy, with good resistance to disease.

'Meeker' is highly reliable with excellent flavor. Canes are easy to train. Resists botrytis rot.

'Latham' produces sturdy, round, bright red berries that are less likely to crush when picked. Very hardy and adaptable. Good for freezing and canning.

'Taylor' is a favorite for its excellent flavor and high yields. Berries are large, long, and light red. Ripens later than other summer raspberries.

'Cascade Delight' Originally bred in the Pacific Northwest, this raspberry is resistant to root rot and therefore ideal for damp conditions. Heavy crops of large fruit with excellent flavor.

'Glen Fyne' The most recent of the Scottish 'Glen' raspberries, introduced in 2008. Spine-free canes carry early crops of large, bright red berries with an outstanding flavor.

'Glen Prosen' Smooth, spine-free canes and good crops of firm berries that have an excellent flavor. Resistant to viruses.

'Leo' Not the heaviest producer but useful in that it's the latest of the Summer-bearing varieties: you may still be picking until almost the end of August.

'Malling Jewel' An old favorite that fruit slightly earlier than 'Malling Admiral'. Plants are fairly compact and growth is not as rampant as others—a good choice for smaller gardens.

6 YELLOW RASPBERRIES

Glowing yellow raspberries are a treat to look at and to eat. Try one of these great varieties:

'Fallgold' is one of the most popular yellow berries because of their delightful sweet flavor. Plants are very hardy. This is an everbearing type.

'Anne' produces pale yellow fall berries that are large and very sweet. Good for fresh eating and freezing.

7 PURPLE AND BLACK RASPBERRIES

Not everyone likes the flavor of these berries as well as red, but try for yourself and see. If these intensely-hued berries appeal to you, then you'll want to plant a sampling of these varieties:

'Allen' bears intensely sweet, glossy, black fruit. Vigorous canes are very productive and hardy, and grow well in many areas.

'Jewel' produces large black fruit with rich flavor. Vigorous, productive canes are disease-resistant and extremely hardy.

'Royalty Purple' is a high-yielding purple raspberry with a distinctive flavor and aroma. Gourmet-quality fruit ideal for fresh eating, jam, and pie. Resistant to some insect pests.

'Bristol' is a high-yielding summer-ripening black raspberry that is easy to pick because its canes stay upright. Excellent flavor and vigor.

'Black Hawk' black raspberries are sweet and firm. Anthracnose-resistant and very productive. One of the hardiest varieties available.

8-10 FALL-BEARING RASPBERRIES

There's no pleasure to equal fall raspberries, which bring a burst of fresh fruit when most other berry plants are winding down.

'Caroline' grows well in most regions, and ripens earlier when summers are warmer than average. Vigorous, with firm berries that are very high in nutrients and antioxidants. Berries are larger than 'Heritage' and start to ripen earlier, too.

'Autumn Bliss' starts to fruit early and is heat tolerant for the South; large red berries have mild flavor. Canes are relatively short and quite sturdy.

'Heritage' is so vigorous that it doesn't need staking. Large, bright red berries are good for eating, freezing, or jam.

'Autumn Treasure' A modern English variety that produces large, conical berries of a bright red color on sturdy, spine-free canes. Good pest and disease resistance, so it is a sensible choice for organic growers not wishing to use chemicals. Fruits a little later than 'Autumn Bliss'.

'Belle de Malicorne' A French variety that produces large, bright red berries. Given the right growing conditions, it can fruit twice a year, once in midsummer and again in fall—until very late if it is protected from frost.

Growing raspberries

Summer- and fall-bearing raspberries behave differently. Summer varieties fruit on last year's canes, and fall varieties fruit on this year's. They are therefore pruned very differently. To get it right, you must know which you are dealing with, and you must keep them well separated. If they spread and the two types merge, you'll get very confused, not knowing which canes to cut down and which to leave for next year.

(left) **Bare-root raspberry canes** are often sold in bundles by specialty nurseries and garden centers for planting out in early spring. Container-grown canes may be available at other times of year, but in most areas, it's still best to plant them in late spring when the soil is beginning to warm, allowing the plants to establish quickly.

The year at a glance

	spring			summer			fall			winter		
	E	M	L	E	M	L	E	M	L	E	M	L
plant bare-root	■											
plant container	■	■	■				■	■	■			
prune							■				■	■
harvest					■	■	■	■				

Choosing plants

Raspberries can be bought as bare-root, tissue-culture, or container-grown plants. Each plant comes as a single cane not much thicker than a pencil, with its own root system. New long cane raspberries are supplied as single canes about 4 ft (1.2 m) long. They are more expensive but will bear fruit in their first summer.

When to plant

■ BARE-ROOT In most parts of the country, plant in early spring. In California, plant from late fall to early spring.

■ CONTAINER-GROWN Plant in spring; with tissue-culture plants wait until after frost danger is past. Fall planting works well in mild-winter areas.

■ LONG CANE Plant in November and December or in early spring.

Where to plant

Choose a sheltered site, out of strong winds, to protect canes from damage. Raspberries ripen best in full sun, especially fall-bearing varieties, which crop late in the season. In the hot South, though, providing afternoon shade can help promote fruit production.

Soil type

Raspberries need plenty of water, but they must have free-draining soil. If they become waterlogged, even for short periods of time, the roots are likely to die. If you garden on heavy soil, consider planting them in raised beds.

Raspberries like a slightly acidic soil with a pH of around 6.0-6.5. If your soil is alkaline (higher than about 7.5), acidify it to help prevent lime-induced chlorosis (see p.320). If it is dry and sandy, add plenty of organic matter to help retain moisture, and water regularly.

How to plant

Prepare the soil thoroughly in advance and erect your post-and-wire supports. Weed meticulously. Dig a trench, add some well-rotted compost or manure, and mix it in with the soil.

Raspberries don't need to be planted very deep. Spread out the roots at a depth of about 3 in (8 cm), firm down the soil, and cut off the top of each cane to a bud about 10 in (25 cm) above ground level. When new shoots start to emerge from below ground in spring, they'll grow more strongly if you cut the original cane down to the level of the soil. It may feel drastic, but it's worth it.

Planting distances

- CANES 15–18 in (38–45 cm) apart.
- ROW SPACING 6 ft (2 m) apart.

Growing in containers

Raspberries can be grown in pots, although they may not yield a large crop. Shorter, fall-bearing varieties are likely to be more successful. Plant two or three canes together in a single container about 12 in (30 cm) in diameter, and be prepared to support the canes as they grow, perhaps against a fence or trellis. Watering is crucial: they must never get waterlogged or be allowed to dry out.

(below, left to right) **Newly planted canes** will get off to a good start if you dig well-rotted compost into the planting trench to improve soil structure. **New shoots** soon begin to grow in spring and burst into leaf. Mulch the plants thickly to keep moisture locked into the soil, especially after feeding. **Cut down** the original cane to soil level, taking care not to damage the new growth. This will encourage the plant to produce more canes as well as helping it to establish a strong root system.

Routine care

■ WATERING Water regularly, once or twice a week in a dry summer, especially when the berries are beginning to fatten up. Try to avoid splashing the canes or you may spread fungal infections.

■ FEEDING Raspberries are hungry plants and do need feeding. In spring, topdress the soil around the plants with a general, blended fertilizer to boost levels of nitrogen, phosphate, and potash.

■ MULCHING After feeding, water the soil thoroughly. Then spread a 2–3-in- (5–8-cm-) thick mulch of well-rotted manure or compost around the plants, without letting it touch the canes themselves.

■ NETTING Summer-bearing raspberries need nets or a fruit cage to keep off birds. Fall-bearing varieties seem to generate less interest and can be grown without netting.

■ FROST PROTECTION Raspberries flower later in the year than most other soft fruits, and are less susceptible to frost damage.

Harvesting and storing

Most summer-bearing raspberries ripen in July, though a few go on into August. Fall-bearing varieties start in August and may continue producing until October, or when they are halted by the first frost. Unlike blackberries, the "plug" or core remains behind on the bush when you pick the fruit. So if the berries don't come away easily, they're not ready. Ripe raspberries will keep for a few days in the refrigerator, but if you're not going to eat them promptly, freeze them soon after picking. Don't leave ripened fruits on the bush: they will rot and subsequent berries won't grow to their full size.

Yield

Crops tend to be heavier from summer-bearing than from fall-bearing varieties. For each 3-ft (1-m) section of a row of canes, you might get 4.5–6.5 lb (2–3 kg) of summer raspberries and 2.2–3.3 lb (1–1.5 kg) of fall raspberries.

Propagation

Young shoots can be lifted to make new plants very easily. Carefully dig up a healthy-looking sucker with a fork so that it has some roots attached at its base, and cut it off from the main rootball. Replant it in a pot or elsewhere in the ground. Avoid propagating from old or unhealthy canes. It's safer to buy new, disease-free plants.

(top to bottom) **Correct watering** is important when the berries are ripening. Be careful not to splash the foliage or you could inadvertently spread fungal diseases. **Pick raspberries** when it's dry—although, if it's wet, you have the perfect excuse to eat them immediately, as they won't keep. Slightly underripe berries are better for cooking or freezing.

Season by season

(left to right) **Tie in** new canes with soft twine or string.
New leaves sprout from the canes in spring. **Blossoms** appear
relatively late and are unlikely to need protection. **Berries** pull
away easily when fully ripe.

Late winter
■ Tip-prune overwintering summer-bearing canes.
■ Cut down and remove all of last year's fall-
bearing canes if you didn't do so during the fall.

Early to mid-spring
■ New young leaves start to appear on last year's
summer-bearing canes.
■ New canes start to shoot from below ground
on fall-bearing varieties.
■ Feed with a general, blended fertilizer, then
mulch around plants.
■ Plant new bare-root canes now.

Late spring
■ Flower buds form, and blossoms open for
pollination.
■ Begin weeding and watering.
■ Net summer-bearing berries against birds.

Early summer
■ Water generously, at least once a week or more
if the weather is dry.
■ Tie in new growth securely.

Midsummer
■ Harvest summer-bearing berries.
■ Continue watering regularly as fruits ripen.

Late summer
■ Harvest the last of the summer-bearing and
the first of the fall-bearing berries.
■ Cut down and remove summer-bearing canes
that have finished fruiting. Tie in and loop over
new canes for next year.

Early fall
■ Harvest fall-bearing berries.
■ Plant container-grown raspberries starting
now in mild-winter areas.

Mid-fall
■ Continue harvesting until the first frost.

Late fall
■ Cut down and remove all fall-bearing canes
after leaves drop off.

Pruning and training raspberries

Summer- and fall-bearing raspberries are pruned very differently. Each needs pruning only once a year, but you need to know when—or you'll be in for a disappointing crop. Fall-bearing raspberries fruit on this year's canes. So when they're finished, you cut them down to the ground. Next year, the plants grow from scratch all over again. Summer-bearing raspberries, however, fruit on the canes that grew the year before. You can, of course, remove those when all the berries have been picked, but you mustn't cut down the new canes that haven't yet fruited: you need those for next year.

Post-and-wire supports

A specially built system of posts and wires is the best way to support raspberries, especially summer-bearing varieties, which grow tall. Use 3 x 3 in (8 x 8 cm) rot-resistant wooden posts each 8 ft (2.5 m) in length. Sink them into the ground to a depth of 24 in (60 cm) and stretch horizontal lengths of heavy-gauge galvanized wire between them, either in a single row or in double rows attached to cross-pieces.

Summer-bearing raspberries grow tall and definitely need supports. Fall-bearing raspberries are shorter and can be grown without, though they too will do better with supports.

Single-wire supports

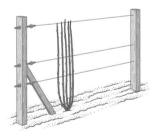

- Use three horizontal lengths of wire, at heights of about 30 in (75 cm), 3 1/2 ft (1.1 m), and 5 ft (1.5 m).
- Tension them with straining bolts.
- As new canes grow, tie them in to the wires with string.

Double-wire supports

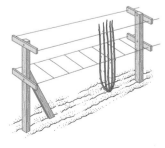

- Attach two cross-pieces 2 ft (60 cm) long to each of the wooden posts, one at a height of about 3 ft (1 m) and the other at 5 ft (1.5 m).
- Stretch parallel wires horizontally between them, and tie further wires or string crosswise at regular intervals.
- Canes will grow up within the grid.

Pruning summer-bearing raspberries

Pruning mostly takes place in late summer, after all the fruit has been harvested. New canes, which will fruit next year, are tied in securely and merely tip-pruned lightly in winter.

1 In late summer, after harvesting, cut down to the base all canes that have fruited this year. This will let in light and air and reduce the risk of disease spreading from old growth

2 At the same time, make sure that this year's new canes are tied in about 4 in (10 cm) apart. If they are too long, arch them over and secure them in tall loops. It keeps them tidy and prevents wind damage.

3 In February, tip-prune the looped-over canes to about 6 in (15 cm) above the highest horizontal wire. These are the canes that will bear fruit this summer.

Pruning fall-bearing raspberries

After the canes lose their leaves in fall, cut or mow them off at ground level. New canes will emerge in spring and fruit in late summer. If you don't remove the canes in the fall, they will resprout the following year and produce a small summer crop, which is why they are sometimes called everbearing raspberries. Concentrating the plant's energy on the fall crop gives better results.

1 Raspberries are hardy plants and can be left to overwinter without the need for protection.

2 In late fall, cut down to the base all the canes that grew last year.

3 New canes may need help reaching the wires. Hold them up by gathering them loosely with string.

4 In early summer, prune out any new canes that are obviously spindly and weak or are growing out at awkward angles.

What can go wrong

Leaves and canes

White powdery coating on leaves
Powdery mildew is caused by a fungus, and tends to be more active when the weather is hot and dry. Leaves may yellow and die, and canes may wilt. Occasionally, fruit will spoil.
■ See **Powdery mildew** (p.329).

1 Yellow leaves with green veins
Yellowing of new leaves may indicate lack of iron, and of older, lower leaves, lack of manganese.
■ See **Iron deficiency** (p.320), **Manganese deficiency** (p.321).

2 Leaves curled, brown, and dying
This may be a sign of drought, lack of potassium, or raspberry crown borer.
■ See **Potassium deficiency** (p.321) and **Raspberry crown borer** (p.339).

3 Purple spots with white or gray centers
These signs of disease appear on both canes and on leaves. Serious infections can cause complete dieback.
■ See **Raspberry leaf spot** (p.329).

Curled, sticky leaves
Aphids cause leaves to become distorted and build up a sticky or sooty coating.
■ See **Aphids** (p.334).

Mottling or mosaic patterns on leaves
Blotchy, yellow-green patches, stunted growth, perhaps with downward curling at the edges, may be signs of a virus.
■ See **Raspberry virus** (p.329).

Small holes eaten in leaves
Tiny, red-brown spots and holes with tattered, brown edges may be signs of attack by plant bugs, which suck sap and are hard to spot.
■ See **Plant bugs** (p.335).

Orange, rustlike patches on leaves
Rust is a fungus that affects many soft fruits. It is unlikely to be fatal.
■ See **Orange rust** (p.329).

Purple patches on canes around new buds
Blotches turn from purple–brown to silvery-gray in fall. New growth on infected canes may die the next spring.
■ See **Raspberry spur blight** (p.330).

Canes split and break
A fungal infection at the base of canes causes them to turn dark brown and brittle, and snap off. Anthracnose (fungal leaf spot) can cause this too.
■ See **Raspberry cane blight** (p.330) and **Fungal leaf spot** (p.328).

Skeletonlike leaves
Japanese beetles feed on leaf tissue but do not eat leaf veins. Their larvae, white grubs, feed on roots, which also weakens the plants. Raspberry fruitworms cause similar leaf damage.
■ See **Japanese beetles** (p.336) and **Raspberry fruitworm** (p.339).

Cane tips wilt
Raspberry cane borer beetles lay eggs near the tips of new canes. The larvae burrow down through the canes.
■ See **Raspberry cane borer** (p.339).

Fruit

4 Fluffy, gray mold
Affected fruit become covered with powdery mold and start to rot.
■ See **Botrytis** (p.326).

5 Fruit eaten
Birds, wasps, and other insects find raspberries irresistible, especially summer-fruiting varieties.
■ See **Birds** (p.334), **Wasps** (p.341).

Maggots in fruit
Ripening berries may shrivel, discolor, and rot. Inside, you may find the pale, creamy-brown grubs feeding.
■ See **Raspberry fruitworm** (p.339).

Fruit small, dry, and flavorless
Plants infected with *Verticillium* wilt may bear fruit that does not ripen properly. The fungus can kill canes.
■ See **Verticillium wilt** (p.331).

Blackberries and hybrid bramble fruits

These berries all started out as wild brambles. In fact, depending on where you live, you may be able to pick as many wild blackberries as you're ever likely to need from fencerows and woodlands or along roadsides. However, in your garden you can grow specially bred, cultivated varieties. The fruit will be bigger and better, the yield will be higher, and new plants should be disease-free.

Some hybrid bramble fruits—which include loganberries, boysenberries, and a handful of less familiar crops—are the result of cross-breeding between blackberries and raspberries, and some of them date back to the 19th century. Plant-breeding programs continue today, of course, though they now tend to concentrate on creating more compact, less rampant varieties, without thorns, and with larger, sweeter berries. All of these are welcome initiatives from the point of view of grow-your-own fruit gardeners.

Most blackberries have a long season. The first fruit may be ready for picking in July and further berries should continue to grow and ripen well into the fall—although they are likely to contain more seeds as time goes on.

Must-grow blackberries

1 'Loch Ness'
A compact, thornless variety that does not require a lot of space or complex training. Good-sized fruit, good yields, and good flavor.
■ **Harvest** from late August

2 'Black Butte'
Originally from the western United States, very large berries as much as double the size and weight of traditional fruit. Good for eating and cooking.
■ **Harvest** from mid-July

3 'Silvan'
Sometimes spelled 'Sylvan', an Australian variety with long, dark blue-black berries that ripen early. Good disease resistance.
■ **Harvest** from early July

4 'Oregon Thornless'
Originally bred from a wild European blackberry, it has distinctive, very attractive foliage. Harvesting can last into October.
■ **Harvest** from late August

5 'Waldo'
An early-producing, modern variety with large, exceptional-tasting berries. It is compact and thornless, so ideal for small gardens.
■ **Harvest** from mid–late July

'Fantasia' (not illustrated)
Heavy crops of large, delicious berries—though the thorny, fast-growing canes need strict taming to stay under control.
■ **Harvest** from late August

'Helen' (not illustrated)
Recent, compact, thornless variety that may be ready to pick very early and is resistant to disease.
■ **Harvest** from early July

'Karaka Black' (not illustrated)
A New Zealand variety with long, cylindrical, strong flavored fruit. It fruits from July through to September.
■ **Harvest** from mid-July

1

2

3

4

5

Must-grow hybrid berries

1 Loganberry
Hybrid raspberry × blackberry. Originally created in California in the 19th century. The berries are tart in taste and better for cooking than eating fresh.
■ **Harvest** from mid-July

2 Boysenberry
Hybrid loganberry × blackberry. Large, juicy, red-purple fruit that taste distinctly of blackberries.
■ **Harvest** from late July

3 Tayberry
Hybrid raspberry × blackberry. First bred in Scotland in the 1960s. The berries are red-purple, have a fine flavor, and are larger and sweeter than loganberries.
■ **Harvest** from mid-July

4 Japanese wineberry
A species in its own right. Clusters of unusual, small red berries are sweet and juicy. Invasive in some areas— check with your local extension office.
■ **Harvest** August

Dewberry (not illustrated)
Also a species rather than a hybrid. Often grown as a trailing bramble.
■ **Harvest** July

Marionberry (not illustrated)
Sometimes classified as a hybrid, sometimes as a true 'Marion' blackberry, this U.S. cultivar certainly has loganberry in its parentage. Very long, trailing canes and berries with a superb flavor.
■ **Harvest** from late July

Tummelberry (not illustrated)
A Scottish-bred variant on the tayberry. Hardier but not so sweet. Closer in flavor to a loganberry.
■ **Harvest** from mid-July

Other hybrid berries you may be able to obtain from specialty nurseries include:
King's Acre Berry
Sunberry
Veitchberry
Youngberry

Growing blackberries

Most blackberries and hybrid bramble fruits grow vigorously and don't demand a lot of attention. If anything, you'll find they need taming rather than encouragement. Pruning them once a year, after you've finished harvesting the fruit, is important, as it will clear out old canes that have no further use and create space for the new growth that will bear fruit the following year.

The year at a glance

	spring			summer			fall			winter		
	E	M	L	E	M	L	E	M	L	E	M	L
plant bare-root	▬	▬	▬									
plant container	▬	▬	▬					▬	▬			
prune							▬	▬	▬			
harvest					▬	▬	▬					

Blackberry bushes will produce heavier crops if you train the new canes along horizontal wires, and keep tying in the long fruiting stems. Some of the best varieties are thornless, which makes for much easier harvesting.

Choosing plants

Blackberries and hybrid bramble fruits are available as bare-root plants or in small pots from mail-order suppliers, or as container-grown plants at some garden centers. They look unimpressive—often just a single cane not much thicker than a pencil. For healthy plants, make sure you buy certified virus-free stock and of a recognized variety or cultivar.

When to plant

■ BARE-ROOT In most areas, plant in early spring;

PLANTING A BLACKBERRY BUSH

This container-grown blackberry is to be trained across a wooden fence. If you plan to use a system of posts and wires, it's best to construct it before you plant. If possible, dig some well-rotted compost or manure into the soil a month or two beforehand. And remember to remove all perennial weeds.

1 Dig a hole deep enough and wide enough to accommodate the plant's rootball comfortably, allowing an additional 4 in (10 cm) all around.

2 Give the plant a good soaking with water, remove it from its container or wrapping, and place it in the hole.

3 Check the depth to ensure that the top of the rootball is level with or slightly below the surface of your soil.

4 Carefully firm down the soil. Water generously and spread organic mulch around the plant, keeping it clear of the stem. If necessary, shorten the cane to a bud at a height of about 8–10 in (22–25 cm), and cut it off completely in midsummer once other new canes emerge.

---

in the Deep South and coastal California, plant in fall and winter.

■ CONTAINER-GROWN Plant in spring or fall, but not during hot, dry summer months.

Where to plant

Choose a sheltered site, out of strong winds. Hybrids need full sun in order ripen successfully in summer. For blackberries this is not so crucial; most varieties are still productive in partial shade.

Soil type

Blackberries are tolerant of most soils as long as they are free-draining. Hybrid bramble fruits are a little pickier: they appreciate deep, rich, fertile soil. Both will grow best if your soil has had plenty of organic matter added to it to help provide nutrients and retain moisture. Add some lime if the pH of your soil is below 5.5.

Planting distances

■ LEAST VIGOROUS 8–10 ft (2.5–3 m) apart.
■ FAIRLY VIGOROUS 10–13 ft (3–4.5 m) apart.
■ VERY VIGOROUS 13–15 ft (4.5–5 m) apart.
■ ROW SPACING 6 ft (2 m) apart.

Routine care

■ WATERING In a dry summer, water generously, at least once a week, particularly when the berries are turning from red to black. Try not to splash the new canes or the fruit so you minimize the risk of spreading fungal infections.

■ FEEDING In early spring, topdress the soil around the plants with a general blended fertilizer.

■ MULCHING About a month after feeding, pull rather than hoe out any weeds and water the ground well. Then spread a 2–3-in (5–8-cm) mulch of shredded bark, wood chips, or leaves around the plants, without letting it touch the canes.

PROPAGATION BY TIP LAYERING

Blackberries and hybrid bramble fruits are easy to propagate. New shoots will quickly develop roots if they come in contact with the soil. Indeed, in the case of dense, overgrown bushes, you may well find it happening naturally, without your help.

1 Between July and September, bend over the tip of a new shoot and bury it in the soil to a depth of about 4 in (10 cm). Firm it down and water it in.

2 By the end of the year, the tip should have rooted. Cut it free from its parent, and either pot it up or leave it until spring, then transplant.

■ NETTING Hybrids are more likely to need nets to keep off birds than are blackberries.
■ FROST PROTECTION Blackberries and hybrids flower relatively late in spring, and are less prone to frost damage than most other soft fruits.

Harvesting and storing

Blackberries are ready to pick when they are plump and shiny-black. They should pull away easily in your hand, with the plug or core still in the fruit. If they resist, they're not ready, and if they squash easily then they are overripe. Ripe blackberries will keep for a few days in the refrigerator but, if you're not going to eat them promptly, they freeze well.

Hybrid berries should be left to ripen as long as you dare, to develop maximum flavor and sweetness. It's tempting to pick them too soon. The best time to harvest them is in the morning, after the dew has dried and before it gets too hot, or in the evening. Wet berries won't store well.

Yield

It's hard to generalize about yields, as the size and vigor of bushes vary so greatly. However, expect something in the range of 10–30 lb (5–15 kg).

(below left to right) **Pick ripe fruits** while they are still firm to the touch. They should come away easily, with the plug, which is edible, still in the fruit. **Freeze ripe berries** if you have a surplus, and use them for cooking during the winter months.

Season by season

Late winter
🔳 Spread out and tie in last year's new canes if you didn't do so the previous fall.

Early to mid-spring
🔳 Leaf buds begin to burst and new young leaves start to appear.
🔳 Feed with a general fertilizer
🔳 Weed and mulch around plants to suppress weeds.
🔳 Plant new bare-root canes now.
🔳 Uproot new plants propagated by tip layering and transplant.

Late spring
🔳 Blossoms should be fully open and pollinating insects will be at work.
🔳 First young fruitlets start to form as the blossom drops.
🔳 Weed and water if necessary.

Early summer
🔳 Water more generously if the weather is dry—once a week or more.
🔳 Net hybrid berries against birds.
🔳 Train new growth away from fruiting canes and tie it in neatly. These new canes will fruit next year.

Midsummer
🔳 Harvest early-season fruits.
🔳 In hot weather, continue watering regularly as fruits ripen.
🔳 From now through mid-fall, propagate new plants by tip layering.

Late summer
🔳 Harvest mid-season fruits.

Early fall
🔳 Harvest late-season fruits.
🔳 Cut down and remove canes that have fruited this summer—either now or at any time before the end of the year.
🔳 Spread out and tie in this year's new canes in place of the fruited canes you have just removed. These new canes will fruit next year.
🔳 In mild-winter areas of the South and California, plant new plants, starting now and continuing through fall and winter.
🔳 New bare-root canes start to become available from specialty nurseries.

Late fall
🔳 Now and in early winter, in cold-winter areas, lay trailing varieties on the ground and cover them with several inches of a fast-draining mulch to prevent chilling injury.

(top to bottom) **New buds** emerge early in spring. **Blossoms** appear a couple of months later, when frosts are usually over. **Pollinated flowers** form fruitlets. **Berries** soon start to ripen.

Pruning and training blackberries

Blackberries and hybrids all fruit on one-year-old canes from the previous summer. Training separates last year's canes (the ones bearing fruit this summer) from this year's canes (the new shoots that will fruit next summer) and pruning after harvesting removes all the old canes that have just fruited.

Wire-training methods

Use strong metal or 3 x 3 in (8 x 8 cm) rot-resistant wooden posts each 8 ft (2.5 m) tall, and sink them to a depth of 24 in (60 cm). Stretch 4 horizontal lengths of heavy-gauge wire between them, 14–18 in (35–45 cm) apart.

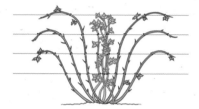

Upright fan This year's fruiting canes are fanned out, and the new ones grow up the center. In fall or winter, the fruited canes are cut out and new canes take their place.

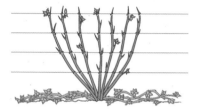

Trailing fan New canes trail on the ground on either side of this year's fan. When old fruited canes are cut down, new canes are raised up and tied in position as a new fan.

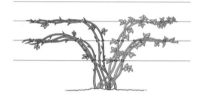

Alternate bay This year's fruiting canes are tied to one side, and all new growth is tied to the other side. So, one side fruits and the other doesn't. Next year everything swaps.

Pruning and training an established blackberry

Pruning takes place in fall, when you simply cut out all the canes that have finished fruiting. Thereafter, it's a matter of tying in new growth to keep new and one-year-old canes separated.

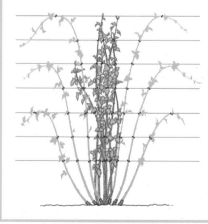

1 In fall, after harvesting, cut down to the base all canes that have fruited this year.

2 During the winter or next spring, move last year's new canes into position for fruiting in the coming season and tie them in place.

3 As the new season's shoots emerge and form new canes, carefully tie them in too, training them out of the way of this year's fruiting canes. They will fruit next year.

What can go wrong

Leaves and canes

1 Purple spots with white or gray centers
These appear on leaves and on canes, and can cause dieback. Blackberries and hybrid bramble fruit may be affected.
■ See **Blackberry leaf spot** (p.325) or **Raspberry leaf spot** (p.330).

2 Brown spots on leaves
Anthracnose and other fungal diseases cause irregular brown spots surrounded by yellow patches on leaves, which may then die.
■ See **Fungal leaf spot** (p.328).

Purple patches on canes around new buds
By fall the patches turn silvery-gray. Hybrid berries such as loganberries are most at risk.
■ See **Raspberry spur blight** (p.330).

Yellow mosaic patterns on leaves
Downward curling at the edges and stunted leaf growth may be signs of a virus.
■ See **Raspberry virus** (p.330).

White powdery coating on leaves
The powdery mildew is caused by a fungus, and tends to be worse when the weather is hot and dry. Leaves may yellow and die, and canes may wilt. Occasionally, fruit will spoil.
■ See **Powdery mildew** (p.329).

Orange-red, rustlike patches
Rust is a fungus that affects many soft fruits. It is unlikely to be fatal, but it is advisable to pick off and destroyed infected leaves.
■ See **Orange rust** (p.330).

Small holes eaten in leaves
Tiny red-brown spots and holes with tattered brown edges may be signs of tarnished plant bug or lygus bug damage.
■ See **Plant bugs** (p.338).

Canes die back
Dying canes may be due to raspberry crown borer damage or *Verticillium* wilt.
■ See **Raspberry crown borer** (p.339) and **Verticillium wilt** (p.331).

Fruit

3 Berries do not ripen fully
Feeding redberry mites cause parts of berries to remain hard and stay red, especially later in the summer.
■ See **Redberry mite** (p.339).

4 Maggots in fruit
Yellow-white beetle grubs called fruitworms feed inside the ripening berries.
■ See **Raspberry fruitworm** (p.339).

5 Fluffy, gray mold
Affected fruit become covered with mold and start to rot.
■ See **Botrytis** (p.326).

Gooseberries

Gooseberries were a popular fruit about a century ago, but they fell out of favor for decades because they are alternate hosts of a serious disease of pine trees called white pine blister rust. Many states banned planting of gooseberries (and currants) because of this, but most states have lifted the ban, and adventurous gardeners can now enjoy the mouthwateringly sweet, muscatlike flavor of a perfectly ripe, freshly picked gooseberry.

Gooseberries are generally classified as either culinary or dessert varieties. Culinary fruit is sour but when cooked with added sugar makes wonderful jams, jellies, and pies. Dessert fruit is sweet enough to eat straight from the bush. Some varieties offer the best of both worlds: pick half the berries when they are young and use them for cooking, then let the other half ripen and eat them freshly picked. The berries themselves may be green, yellow, or red, and smooth or slightly hairy, and their dimensions can vary greatly.

Most gooseberries grow very vigorously and need regular pruning to keep them under control, although if you train them as cordons against a wall or fence, you'll be able to fit two or three different varieties into a limited space.

Which types to grow

■ **Bushes** Probably the easiest kind to grow, although they can reach 6 ft (2 m) in height and spread.
■ **Cordon** Needs regular pruning but economical on space and the fruit is easy to pick.
■ **Standard** Grown on a long leg and will need stakes at either side for support.
■ **Fan** Less common, but ideal for a sheltered, sunny fence or wall.

Must-grow gooseberries

1 'Greenfinch'
Culinary/dessert
Bushes don't grow too large, so this is a good choice if space is limited. Less prone to mildew and leaf spot than most other varieties. Good flavor.
■ **Harvest** July

2 'Lancashire Lad'
Culinary/dessert
This traditional 19th-century variety with dark red berries has a loyal following. Some resistance to mildew but needs fertile soil.
■ **Harvest** July–Aug

3 'Leveller'
Culinary/dessert
Large yellow berries with a superb flavor; often grown competitively. However, it fruits heavily only if grown in fertile, well-drained soil and is susceptible to mildew.
■ **Harvest** July–Aug

4 'Hinnonmaki Red'
Culinary/dessert
Sometimes called 'Hino Red', this variety is very hardy, easy to grow, and also resistant to mildew. The red berries are sweet and aromatic.
■ **Harvest** July

5 'Hinnonmaki Yellow'
Culinary/dessert
Like the red, the yellow variety originally comes from Finland. It too can withstand cold winters and is resistant to mildew. The fruit is sweet and aromatic, with a slight apricot flavor.
■ **Harvest** July

6 'Careless'
Culinary/dessert
One of the earliest of the green varieties, 'Careless' is a traditional berry that dates back to the 19th century. The flavor is good and crops are heavy, though it is prone to mildew.
■ **Harvest** July

6

9

7 'Invicta'
Culinary/dessert
Bushes grow strongly and produce bumper crops of firm, smooth-skinned fruit ideal for cooking and preserving. Good mildew resistance.
■ **Harvest** June–July

8 'Langley Gage'
Dessert
A sweet, aromatic, old-fashioned variety that can be eaten straight off the bush when fully ripe. Worth seeking out from specialty nurseries.
■ **Harvest** July–Aug

9 'Whinham's Industry'
Culinary/dessert
A traditional variety first bred in northern England. It grows well in most conditions, although it is prone to mildew. Use green berries for cooking or eat raw when they ripen to dark red.
■ **Harvest** July

'Captivator' (not illustrated)
Dessert
A European–American hybrid producing good crops of berries sweet enough to eat raw when fully ripe. This almost thornless variety is mildew-resistant.
■ **Harvest** July–Aug

'Martlet' (not illustrated)
Culinary/dessert
A new, mildew-resistant variety with high yields of smooth, sweet, red berries that can be eaten raw or cooked.
■ **Harvest** July–Aug

'Remarka' (not illustrated)
Culinary/dessert
Early-ripening red variety with good flavor and some resistance to mildew.
■ **Harvest** July

'Pax' (not illustrated)
Culinary/dessert
A recently introduced red variety with large, tasty berries and fewer thorns. Easy to grow and fairly resistant to mildew.
■ **Harvest** July

'Xenia' (not illustrated)
Culinary/dessert
A new variety from Switzerland. Large, red, sweet berries ripen very early. Strong-growing and mildew-resistant.
■ **Harvest** June

Growing gooseberries

Gooseberries are not hard to grow. Tolerant of most weather and soil conditions, they are natural survivors. The only places they won't grow well are in desert areas of the Southwest and in the hot Central Valley of California. However, there's a big difference between a plant that produces a handful of small berries and one that is laden with a bumper crop of ripe, juicy, delicious fruit. The secret lies in a little tender loving care: feeding, watering, mulching, and pruning, plus nets to keep off birds and a watchful eye for mildew and imported currantworm.

PLANTING A GOOSEBERRY BUSH

Gooseberry bushes grow either on a short, single "leg" from which lateral branches spread out, or as stooled bushes, in which case the branches all emerge in a cluster straight from the rootball. Bushes with a leg should have a clean main stem, without any shoots or side branches, to a height of 4–6 in (10–15 cm) above soil level. Standard bushes, which grow on a leg 2–3 ft (60–90 cm) high, need staking for support.

1 Dig a hole deep enough and wide enough to accommodate the plant's roots comfortably. Add some well-rotted compost or manure and work it into the soil. Make a small mound of soil in the center of the hole and gently spread the roots over it. Check the depth to ensure that the old nursery soil mark on the stem is level with the surface of your soil.

2 Carefully fill the hole with soil, firming it down around the roots as you go. Water generously and at regular intervals over the next few weeks. For initial pruning, see page 226. Spread an organic mulch around the plant to help retain moisture and suppress weeds.

The year at a glance

	spring			summer			fall			winter		
	E	M	L	E	M	L	E	M	L	E	M	L
plant bare-root	▬											▬
plant container	▬											
winter-prune	▬								▬	▬	▬	▬
summer-prune				▬	▬							
harvest						▬	▬					

Choosing plants

Gooseberries are sold as either bare-root or container-grown plants. If you buy them from specialty nurseries, they will probably be bare-root. Gooseberries are self-fertile.

When to plant

■ BARE-ROOT Plant bare-root plants as early in spring as possible. Newly planted gooseberries can withstand temperatures as low as 20°F (–7°C) and still establish themselves well.
■ CONTAINER-GROWN Although container-grown plants can be planted at other times of year, early spring is still the best time.

Where to plant

Gooseberries are cool-climate plants. They are happy in partial shade but appreciate being sheltered from the wind. Avoid frost pockets: although gooseberries are hardy and will survive severe winters, new leaves and flowers appear early in spring and can be vulnerable to frost damage.

Soil type

Gooseberries are fairly tolerant and don't mind soil that is a little alkaline. However, a slightly acidic pH of 6–6.5 is ideal. They dislike being waterlogged and will grow more vigorously and produce heavier crops if your soil is well-drained and if you have added plenty of well-rotted compost or manure to it.

Planting distances

- BUSHES 4–5 ft (1.2–1.5 m) apart.
- CORDONS 12–18 in (30–45 cm) apart.
- ROW SPACING 5 ft (1.5 m) apart.

Growing in containers

It is possible to grow gooseberries in containers although, because their roots spread widely, they may be happier in the ground. A standard or a double cordon supported with a stake is a better option than a bush. Choose a container with a

minimum diameter of 12 in (30 cm) and fill it with multipurpose, soil-based potting medium mixed with some sand or gravel to improve drainage. Feed with a high-potash fertilizer in spring, and above all keep the pot well-watered.

Routine care

- WATERING Gooseberries need plenty of water throughout their growing season. Take special care to water regularly and often when the weather is hot and dry or the skins of the fruits may split as they swell.
- FEEDING Gooseberries need potassium. You should be able to supply them with as much as they require by sprinkling potassium sulfate over the

soil at a rate of about ½ oz/sq yd (15 g/sq m) in early spring. At the same time, add a general fertilizer such as blood, fish, and bone. Avoid high-nitrogen fertilizers: the leaf growth that they stimulate invites mildew.

■ MULCHING After fertilizing, spread mulch around the plants to help keep down weeds. Pull out by hand any weeds that do appear; using a hoe risks damaging the roots of the gooseberries.

■ NETTING Use nets to keep off birds. Some songbirds will eat the fruit buds in winter, and blackbirds and others will eat the berries in summer.

■ FROST PROTECTION Gooseberries flower early in the year and may need protection with floating row cover overnight if there is a hard frost.

Harvesting and storing

Gooseberries will grow larger if you thin out the crop. Start picking alternate berries from late spring onward, using them for cooking and leaving the remaining fruit to swell up and ripen fully as the summer progresses.

Ripe dessert gooseberries are best eaten soon after picking, when the flavor and sweetness are at their height. However, they will keep in the refrigerator for ten days or so, and they freeze well.

Yield

Yields can vary widely, not just from variety to variety and even from bush to bush but also from one year to the next, depending on the weather. With luck, these are roughly the kinds of quantities you can expect:

■ BUSH 7–10 lb (3.5–4.5 kg).

■ CORDON 2–3 lb (1–1.5 kg).

Harvest gooseberries by going over each bush two or three times searching for berries that are just slightly soft and therefore ready for picking. Leave a short length of stalk attached to prevent the skins from tearing.

JOSTABERRIES AND WORCESTERBERRIES

The jostaberry is a cross between a gooseberry and a black currant, originally developed in Germany. The Worcesterberry is actually a native species of *Ribes*—*Ribes divaricatum*. They are both grown in the same way as gooseberries.

■ **Jostaberries** (far left) bear purple-black fruits that are larger than black currants but a little smaller than gooseberries. The taste combines elements of both, and the berries can be cooked or eaten raw when fully ripe. The plants are vigorous, resistant to most pests and diseases, and mercifully free of sharp thorns.

■ **Worcesterberries** (left) are used for making jam in the United Kingdom, but here they're sold as plants for a wildlife garden. They may be sold as coast black gooseberry. The smooth-skinned fruits start off green and turn red-black as they ripen. They are unlikely to become sweet enough to eat raw. Beware—these plants are armed with vicious spines.

Season by season

Late winter
◼ Winter-prune established gooseberries.

Early spring
◼ Plant bare-root gooseberries as soon as the ground is workable.
◼ Apply potassium sulfate and a blended fertilizer around existing plants.
◼ Buds begin to burst and new young leaves start to appear.
◼ Last chance for winter pruning of established plants.
◼ Prune newly planted gooseberries.

Mid-spring
◼ Blossoms open. Be ready to protect against frost.
◼ Mulch around plants to suppress weeds.
◼ If necessary, spray against plant bugs after blossoms have fallen.

Late spring
◼ Fruitlets form and begin to swell.
◼ Start thinning out unripe fruits by picking every other berry to use for cooking.
◼ Weed and water regularly.
◼ Inspect the center of bushes for larvae of imported currantworm. Pick them off and destroy them.

Early summer
◼ Harvest early-season fruits.
◼ Summer-prune now or in midsummer.
◼ Watch for any signs of American gooseberry mildew, leaf spot, or dieback.

Midsummer
◼ Harvest mid-season fruits.
◼ Complete summer pruning now.

Late summer
◼ Harvest late-season fruits.

Mid-fall
◼ Take cuttings to propagate new plants.

Late fall
◼ Winter pruning can start now, though it may be better left until late winter or early spring.

Pruning and training gooseberries

The main aim of pruning gooseberries is first to create an open, uncrowded structure so that light and air can circulate freely, thus reducing the risk of disease, and second—because gooseberries fruit on older wood—to keep cutting back stems and sideshoots to encourage them to be productive. Gooseberries, red currants, and white currants are all pruned in the same way.

Pruning a gooseberry bush

For the first two or three years of their lives, newly planted gooseberries need formative pruning to train them into the shape required.

1st winter pruning
LATE WINTER–EARLY SPRING

- Whatever time of year you plant, begin pruning in late winter or early spring.
- Select 4–5 main stems and cut each back by a half or three-quarters of its length—unless the job has already been done by the plant nursery. Cut to a bud that faces outward and upward, in the direction you want the stem to grow.
- Remove all other stems, especially any that are crowding the center, and, if the bush is growing on a short leg, any shoots lower than 4–6 in (10–15 cm) above ground.

2nd winter pruning
LATE WINTER–EARLY SPRING

- Cut each of the main stems back by about a quarter or a half of the growth they put on last year.
- Select enough new shoots to give a total of 8–10 strong, healthy, equally spaced stems and prune those back by a quarter, too.
- Cut back any unwanted new shoots to 4 buds or about 2 in (5 cm).

Winter pruning an established bush
LATE FALL–EARLY SPRING

- If the plant is overgrown, prune out up to a quarter of the oldest branches and any tangled growth from the center by cutting the stems down to the base.
- Shorten long stems by cutting them back by about half of the previous year's growth. For upright bushes, cut to an outward-facing bud. For arching bushes with stems prone to drooping, cut to an inward-facing one.
- Prune crowded growth and any suckers from around the base. If the bush is growing on a short leg, make sure it is clear.
- If the plant is not overgrown, simply tip-prune main stems and cut back hard any new sideshoots to 1–4 buds.

Summer pruning an established bush
EARLY–MIDSUMMER

- Prune all new sideshoots so that only 5 leaves remain on each.

Pruning a gooseberry cordon

Cordons require a regular routine of both summer and winter pruning in order to maintain their shape. Pruning them hard and regularly should produce good crops, and the neat, decorative form of the plant will also make for easy access when it's time to harvest the berries.

(from top to bottom) **With established bushes,** shorten any long stems in late winter using sharp pruners. **Prune these stems** to an outward-facing bud. **Weak stems** and suckers should be removed from the base of the bush, as well as any overcrowded growth, to leave the center clear.

1st winter pruning
ON PLANTING

- Plant in late fall or early spring and prune right away—unless the nursery has already done so.
- Prune the main leader by a half of the previous summer's growth.
- Cut back all sideshoots to just 1 or 2 buds.

1st summer pruning
EARLY–MIDSUMMER

- Prune all new sideshoots so that they have only 5 leaves left.

Winter pruning an established cordon
LATE WINTER–EARLY SPRING

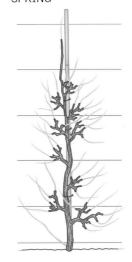

- Prune the main leader by a quarter of last summer's new growth. Cut to a bud facing in the opposite direction from last year's. Continue tying in the leader as it grows. When it reaches the top of the cane, cut it off to just 1 new bud each year.
- Prune back all sideshoots to 1 or 2 buds in order to keep generating new fruiting spurs.
- Remove any shoots that grow at the base of the stem.

Summer pruning an established cordon
MIDSUMMER

- Prune all new sideshoots so that only 5 leaves remain.

What can go wrong

Buds and blossoms

New buds stripped by birds
Birds are a continual nuisance. Some songbirds eat buds during winter, and will come back in summer to take the fruit.
■ See **Birds** (p.335).

Blossoms die
Although gooseberries are hardy, they blossom early in the year and there is always a danger that a severe frost will scorch young leaves and damage or destroy flowers.
■ See **Frost** (p.316).

Leaves

1 Leaves turn brown and fall off
This may be the first sign of gooseberry dieback, usually caused by a form of the fungus botrytis. As the infection takes hold, entire branches die off, and unless you cut them out and destroy them promptly you may lose the plant completely.
■ See **Gooseberry dieback** (p.328).

2 Curled, distorted leaves
Gooseberry aphids hatch in spring from eggs that have overwintered on the bushes. The small aphids will be visible feeding on new shoots. Leaves that they have infested appear curled and twisted.
■ See **Aphids** (p.334).

3 Leaves being eaten
The most likely culprits are the caterpillarlike larvae of the imported currantworm. They have pale green bodies up to ¾ in (20 mm) long, often covered with small black spots, and a black head. In the case of a bad attack, a whole bush can be stripped in a few days. Look for tiny, pale green eggs underneath the leaves.
■ See **Imported currantworm** (p.336).

4 White or gray powdery covering
This is most likely to be American gooseberry mildew, a fungal disease that regularly attacks gooseberries, though some varieties are more resistant than others. New shoots are affected first, then the leaves and berries. As the infection worsens, the powdery coating turns brown.
■ See **American gooseberry mildew** (p.324).

Brown spots on leaves
Small, irregular brown spots surrounded by yellow patches appear first on older leaves at the bottom of the plant. Affected leaves die and the disease spreads upward to attack new growth. The cause is fungal leaf spot.
■ See **Fungal leaf spot** (p.327).

Brown, curled edges on leaves

Leaves that are curled and scorched yellow or brown at the edges may be an indication of potassium deficiency, especially if there are also purple–brown spots on the undersides.
■ See **Potassium deficiency** (p.321).

Leaves turn yellow between veins

A deficiency of iron or manganese can cause a distinctive yellowing of the leaves. These elements are likely to be present in the soil but high alkalinity (a pH of more than 7.0) is probably preventing the plants from absorbing them—a disorder known as lime-induced chlorosis.
■ See **Iron deficiency** (p.320) or **Manganese deficiency** (p.321).

Orange or red blisters on leaves

Blisters or pustules, which are more likely to appear after a dry spring, are caused by a fungal infection called gooseberry rust or cluster cup rust. They may spread to fruit and stems.
■ See **Gooseberry rust** (p.328).

Small holes in leaves

Tiny red-brown spots and holes with tattered brown edges are signs of plant bugs. The insects feed on the sap in young leaves, infecting and killing the plant tissue with their saliva. They are difficult to see and may have departed by the time you spot the damage.
■ See **Plant bugs** (p.335).

Fruit

5 Dried, shriveled fruit

Severe attacks of gooseberry dieback affect both fruit and leaves, causing berries to dry out and shrivel up.
■ See **Gooseberry dieback** (p.328).

6 Cracked skin

Scars and cracks in the skin of the fruit may be caused by birds, or may be evidence of attack by plant bugs, especially if leaves are also holed and tattered.
■ See **Birds** (p.335) or **Plant bugs** (p.335).

7 Brown, feltlike patches

The brown covering is a fungal growth caused by American gooseberry mildew. Strictly speaking, the berries are still edible, but they will probably be stunted, lacking in flavor, and distinctly unappetizing. Cut out and destroy all affected parts of the plant. Prune regularly to encourage air circulation and reduce damp, humid conditions.
■ See **American gooseberry mildew** (p.324).

Fluffy, gray mold

Affected fruits become covered with gray-white or gray-brown mold and may start to rot. Botrytis is to blame—the same fungus that can also cause gooseberry dieback.
■ See **Botrytis** (p.326).

Red currants and white currants

Like gooseberries, currants were once a popular fruit, but they became unpopular in the early 20th century due to fears that they would spread white pine blister rust, a serious disease of pine trees. Now that we've come to realize that most red and white currants are resistant to this disease, most of the bans against growing them have been lifted.

Once established, these currants are very productive, and neither bushes nor cordons require a lot of attention: some fertilizer every spring, a simple prune twice a year, in summer and in winter, a bit of weeding and watering, and protection from hungry birds.

Of the red and white varieties, red currants have the tarter, more acidic flavor. White currants, which are in fact a creamy yellow or even a faintly flushed pale pink, may look less glamorous and jewel-like, but they tend to be naturally sweeter. Even sweeter still are the recently introduced pink currants, which can be eaten straight from the bush.

Fully ripe fruit may be sweet enough to eat raw, but for cooking and for making jelly, harvest the berries when they are slightly unripe and still retain some acidity. If you want to store fresh currants for as long as possible, pick them when they're dry, not when they're wet.

Which forms to grow

■ **Bushes** are the easiest form to grow and produce the most fruit, though they can reach 6 ft (2 m) in height and spread.
■ **Standard** A good choice for growing in a container.
■ **Cordon** Needs regular pruning but economical on space and the berries are easy to pick.
■ **Fan** Less common but worth considering for a sheltered wall or fence.

Must-grow red & white currants

1 'White Versailles'
White currant
Popular, long-established, and widely available with early-fruiting, sweet, pale yellow berries that are perfect for eating raw when fully ripe.
■ **Harvest** early July

2 'Stanza'
Red currant
A late-flowering variety, so a good choice for regions prone to early frost. The dark red fruit have a tart but good flavor.
■ **Harvest** late July

3 'Rovada'
Red currant
This modern Dutch variety can produce extremely heavy yields of bright red, attractive berries on long strigs.
■ **Harvest** late July–August

4 'Red Lake'
Red currant
Widely grown, reliable, disease-resistant, and heavy-fruiting. Like 'Rovada', the fruit are on long strigs but ripen earlier.
■ **Harvest** late July

5 'Blanka'
White currant
Sometimes spelled 'Blanca', a new variety that may challenge 'White Versailles'. The creamy yellow-white fruit are equally sweet but more abundant and ripen slightly later.
■ **Harvest** late July–August

6 'Jonkheer van Tets'
Red currant
Popular, tried-and-tested, Dutch variety that ripens early and produces high yields of excellent fruit. Vigorous, so if space is limited, this is a good choice for cordons.
■ **Harvest** early July

'Junifer' (not illustrated)
Red currant
A recently introduced French variety, it is one of the earliest and heaviest-fruiting.
■ **Harvest** early July

Growing red and white currants

Although red and white currants are closely related to black currants, they are in fact grown much more like gooseberries. These cool-climate plants do well in northern regions and will happily tolerate partial shade, though the berries will ripen more quickly and taste sweeter with the help of some summer sunshine.

The year at a glance

	spring			summer			fall			winter		
	E	M	L	E	M	L	E	M	L	E	M	L
plant bare-root	■											
plant container	■											
winter prune	■										■	
summer prune					■							
harvest					■	■						

Choosing plants

Red and white currants are sold as either bare-root or container-grown plants. Buying them from a specialty nursery will give you a wider choice.

When to plant

■ BARE-ROOT Plant bare-root plants as early in spring as possible.
■ CONTAINER-GROWN Although container-grown plants can be planted at other times of year, early spring is still the best time.

Where to plant

Choose a sheltered site, out of strong winds, but avoid frost pockets and incorporate well-rotted organic matter into the soil before planting. Red currants are hardy enough to survive most winters and although they blossom fairly early in spring, the flowers are reasonably frost-resistant—more so than black currants. They are one of the few fruits that will grow against a north-facing wall, although they ripen earlier in sunshine, provided they don't get too hot. Red and white currants generally don't grow well in areas with hot summers. Try planting them in partial shade or on a north-facing slope.

PLANTING A RED CURRANT BUSH

Red and white currant bushes grow best on a short "leg" from which lateral branches or stems spread out. The leg should be free of any sideshoots to a height of 4–6 in (10–15 cm) above soil level. Standard bushes grow on a longer leg, 2–3 ft (60–90 cm) high.

1 Check the depth of your planting hole to ensure that the old nursery soil mark on the main stem is level with the surface of your soil.

2 Work some well-rotted compost or manure into the soil around the roots, taking care not to damage them.

3 Carefully fill the hole with soil, firming it down around the roots as you go.

4 Water generously now (and at regular intervals over the next few weeks), then spread organic mulch around the plant to keep moisture in.

Soil type

Red and white currants do best in fertile soil with a pH of 6.5–7. However, it must be free-draining: they really dislike being waterlogged.

Planting distances

- BUSHES 5 ft (1.5 m) apart.
- SINGLE CORDONS 15–18 in (38–45 cm) apart.
- ROW SPACING 5 ft (1.5 m) apart.

Growing in containers

Currants grow well in containers because they are quite shallow-rooted and don't seem to mind the restriction. Use a container with a minimum diameter of 12 in (30 cm) filled with all-purpose soil-based potting mix blended with some sand or gravel to improve drainage. Feed with a general blended fertilizer in spring, and make sure you water regularly, especially when the weather is dry.

Routine care

- WATERING Water regularly and often when the weather is hot and dry. Don't let plants dry out.
- FEEDING In early spring, apply a general fertilizer such as blood, fish, and bone, and, to ensure a good supply of potassium, sprinkle potassium sulfate over the soil at a rate of about ½ oz/sq yd (15 g/sq m). Be wary of high-nitrogen fertilizers:

the vigorous leaf growth may invite mildew.

- MULCHING After feeding, water the ground well and spread mulch around the plants to help keep down weeds. Pull out any weeds that do emerge.
- NETTING If necessary, use nets to keep off birds—both in winter when they will eat the buds and in summer as the fruits color and ripen. A fruit cage is recommended.
- FROST PROTECTION Plants are hardy but may need floating row cover on frosty nights.

Harvesting and storing

Fruit is usually ready for picking in July and August. The currants don't all ripen at once, so you'll have to go over the plant several times. It's a lot easier to cut entire trusses (or "strigs") than it is to pick individual currants. You can then eat the perfectly ripe ones raw, and use the less ripe, firmer ones for cooking or preserving. Ripe currants won't keep for long, even in the refrigerator, but they freeze well.

Yield

Yields can vary from variety to variety and from year to year, depending on the weather, but you should be able to expect:

- BUSH 9–11 lb (4–5 kg).
- CORDON 2.2 lb (1 kg).

(far left to right) **Single, double, or triple cordons** are an economical way of getting a lot of fruit from a relatively small space. They need regular pruning and tying in. **Tie in cordons** to 5- or 6-ft (1.5–1.8-m) bamboo canes supported by a post-and-wire structure or secured against a wall or fence. You'll need at least two horizontal wires, one at a height of 2 ft (60 cm) and the other at 4 ft (1.2 m). **A fruit cage** or nets are the only sure way of protecting fruit from birds. **Testing for ripeness** is easy with red currants, which are ready to pick when plump and bright scarlet. It's harder to tell with white currants, as their color change is more subtle; taste is the best test.

Season by season

Late winter
- Winter-prune both newly planted and established currants.
- New buds should be visibly swelling.

Early spring
- Plant bare-root currants as soon as the ground can be worked.
- Apply potassium sulfate and a blended fertilizer.
- New young leaves and flowers start to appear. Protect against frost if necessary.
- Mulch around plants to suppress weeds.
- Last chance for winter pruning.

Mid-spring
- Blossoms are fully open, and pollinating insects should be at work.
- If necessary, spray against plant bugs after blossoms have fallen.

Late spring
- Fruitlets form and begin to swell.
- Weed and water regularly.

Early summer
- Summer-prune this month and next.
- Watch for any signs of leaf spot or gray mold.
- Inspect bushes for signs of currant borer damage and cut off and destroy infested stems.

Midsummer
- Harvest early and mid-season fruits.
- Complete summer pruning by mid-month.

Late summer
- Harvest late-season fruits.

Mid-fall
- Take cuttings to propagate new plants.

(left to right) **New buds** form at the base of last year's stems. **Long strings** of tiny flowers appear, usually in mid spring. Plants are self-fertile and pollination should take place without the need for a partner. **Taste berries** for ripeness before picking.

Pruning and training red and white currants

Prune red currants and white currants in the same way as gooseberries (see pp.226–27). They fruit on buds that form at the base of last year's new shoots and also on older spurs. Both bushes and cordons need to be pruned hard every winter to encourage the formation of spurs, and again in the summer to cut back the new growth on sideshoots.

(top to bottom) **In summer,** shorten the new sideshoots so the plant concentrates its energy back on the main stem. **From late fall,** cut back the shoots you shortened in summer to one bud.

Winter-pruning an established bush

Prune between late fall and early spring. If the center of the bush is overgrown and crowded, aim to open it up to let in light and air. Remove any old, unproductive, or crossing stems, and cut back sideshoots to encourage the development of the short spurs that will bear the currants.

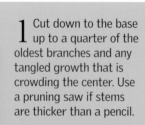

1 Cut down to the base up to a quarter of the oldest branches and any tangled growth that is crowding the center. Use a pruning saw if stems are thicker than a pencil.

2 Cut out any weak, low-growing stems from around the base of the bush. If the bush is growing on a short leg, leave it clear.

3 Remove about half of the previous year's growth from the end of each main stem, cutting just above an outward-facing bud.

4 Prune back sideshoots to just one bud, which will encourage the spurs to produce new growth, flowers, and then fruit.

Pruning an established cordon

Cordons need pruning in both summer and winter. In early or midsummer, prune new sideshoots back to just 5 leaves. In late fall or early spring, cut back the main leader to leave just one bud of last year's growth, and prune all sideshoots to one or two buds to keep generating new fruiting spurs.

What can go wrong

Buds and blossoms

New buds stripped by birds
Birds eat buds in winter, and return in summer for the fruit.
■ See **Birds** (p.335).

Blossoms die
Currants flower early and frost can harm blossoms and young leaves.
■ See **Frost** (p. 316).

Leaves and stems

1 Leaves being eaten
The most likely culprits are imported currantworms, which are sawfly larvae.
■ See **Imported currantworm** (p.336).

2 Pink spots on stems and branches
Small, pink or orange pustules on stems and branches that have died back indicate coral spot, a type of fungal canker disease. The fungus enters the plants through wounds, so to avoid it, treat plants carefully and don't leave stubs when pruning. Remove stems that show symptoms. No other control is needed.

3 Entire stems die
Leaves turning brown and whole stems dying may be a sign of gooseberry dieback, which can also affect currants. It is usually caused by a fungus (Botrytis or Eutypa).
■ See **Gooseberry dieback** (p.328).

4 Curled, blistered leaves
Currant aphids are pale yellow and should be easily visible feeding on new shoots. Leaves that they have infested appear twisted and develop red or yellow blisters. Other types of aphids may also attack the leaves.
■ See **Currant aphids** (p.336).

5 Brown spots on leaves
Small, irregular brown spots surrounded by yellow patches appear on leaves, which may then die.
■ See **Fungal leaf spot** (p.327).

Small holes in leaves
Tiny red-brown spots and holes with tattered brown edges may be signs of plant bug damage.
■ See **Plant bugs** (p.335).

Fruit

Fluffy, gray mold
Affected fruit become covered with gray-white or gray-brown mold, their skins may split, and they may start to rot.
■ See **Botrytis** (p.326).

Black currants

Black currants are tough, self-reliant plants, but they fell from popularity nearly a century ago because they are alternate hosts for a serious disease of white pines—white pine blister rust. Some states still have restrictions on the planting of black currants, so check with your local extension service before buying.

Black currants are cool-weather plants, and if you have the right climate conditions for them they'll go on for year after year even if neglected. But put in just a bit of extra effort and it will certainly be repaid. If you weed, feed, and water them, and if you learn to prune them properly so that the plant is continually producing new healthy growth on which the following year's fruit will be carried, then you'll get bigger, better fruit, and a lot more of them.

In recent years, modern varieties (those whose names begin with 'Ben') have been bred to resist frost damage, mildew, and other pests and diseases. There has been a move, too, toward developing larger, sweeter berries—not as intensely flavored for cooking, but perfect for picking and eating fresh, straight from the bush.

Ripe black currants will keep for a few days provided they are firm when picked, and can be made into delicious jams, jellies, and juices. The fruit is very popular in the UK because of its high vitamin C content, and black currants are widely grown commercially.

Which types to grow

■ **Bushes** Black currants are always grown as "stooled" bushes, which means that all the stems emerge directly from ground level instead of branching out from a single trunk or leg. Bushes can reach a height and spread of up to 6 ft (2 m).

Must-grow black currants

1 'Ebony'
Perhaps the sweetest of all varieties, as well as one of the earliest. Its larger-than-average berries are perhaps the best for eating fresh, straight from the bush.
■ **Harvest** early to mid-July

2 'Ben Lomond'
Launched in 1975, this was the first of the specially bred Scottish black currants with the prefix 'Ben'. It was crossed with Scandinavian varieties to delay flowering and thus be less prone to frost damage.
■ **Harvest** late July

3 'Ben Sarek'
Compact, smaller-than-average bushes that can be planted slightly closer together or squeezed into limited spaces. Yields can be so high that fully laden branches may droop and require support with canes and string. Reasonable frost- and disease-resistance.
■ **Harvest** mid to late July

4 'Big Ben'
A new variety that can be eaten fresh or used for cooking. Its huge berries can be twice the average size, and have a good sugar/acid balance.
■ **Harvest** from mid-July

5 'Ben Connan'
Produces an early crop of large berries that are sweet and juicy. Some resistance to frost, mildew, and leaf spot.
■ **Harvest** from mid-July

6 'Baldwin'
A long-established variety with medium-sized berries that are fairly tart in flavor and best for cooking. Growth is compact and the fruit are not usually prone to splitting.
■ **Harvest** late July

'Titania' (not illustrated)
A variety that originates from Scandinavia. Good frost and mildew resistance. Tall, productive bushes produce high yields of large berries.
■ **Harvest** late July

Growing black currants

Black currants are cool-climate plants and grow well in northern regions, provided you give them a sunny location and protect them from hard frost when in bloom. They don't stay productive forever, so it's wise to think about replacing established bushes after eight to ten years.

The year at a glance

	spring			summer			fall			winter		
	E	M	L	E	M	L	E	M	L	E	M	L
plant bare-root	▬						▬	▬				
plant container	▬	▬					▬	▬	▬			
winter-prune	▬							▬	▬	▬		
summer-prune					▬							
harvest					▬	▬						

Choosing plants

Black currants are sold as either bare-root or container-grown plants. Buy certified disease-free, two-year-old plants. Specialty nurseries offer a wider choice of varieties than most garden centers.

When to plant

■ BARE-ROOT Plant in the fall or early spring. Mulch fall-plantings well to prevent frost-heaving.
■ CONTAINER-GROWN Plant at any time soil conditions allow—fall is ideal. Avoid hot, dry summer months.

Where to plant

Choose a sheltered site, out of strong winds, but avoid frost pockets: black currants are hardy enough to survive most winters, but they flower early in spring and are vulnerable to frost damage.

Soil type

Black currants are tolerant of most soils, though a pH of 6.5–7 is ideal. They are hungry, thirsty plants, and appreciate rich, fertile soil that has had plenty of organic matter added to it to help provide the nutrients and retain the moisture they need.

PLANTING A BLACK CURRANT BUSH

Plant deeply—at least 2 in (5 cm) deeper than the previous nursery soil marks on the stems—to encourage new, underground stems.

1 Dig a hole deep enough and wide enough to accommodate the plant's roots. If you haven't already done so, add some well-rotted compost or manure and work it into the soil.

2 Check the depth to ensure that the old nursery soil marks on the stems will sit 2 in (5 cm) below the surface of your soil.

3 Carefully fill the hole with soil, ensuring that there are no air pockets among the roots.

4 Firm down the soil. Water generously and, if possible, mulch around the plant. Prune newly planted bushes immediately (see p.244).

Planting distances
- BUSHES 5 ft (1.5 m) apart.
- ROW SPACING 5 ft (1.5 m) apart.

Growing in containers
Black currant bushes usually do well in containers, and bringing them in undercover at night to protect them from frost is particularly helpful. Plant them in a pot with a diameter of 12–18 in (30–45 cm) filled with all-purpose soil-based potting mix blended with some sand or gravel to improve drainage. Feed with a general blended fertilizer in spring, and water regularly, especially in dry weather. Be prepared to repot at least once every three years, replacing some of the old potting medium with fresh.

Routine care
- WATERING Black currants need a lot of water, especially when the fruits are starting to fatten up. Water regularly and often and try not to splash water on the stems to prevent fungal infections.
- FEEDING In early spring, apply a general fertilizer and, to boost nitrogen, sprinkle ammonium sulfate over the soil—about ¾ oz/sq yd (25 g/sq m).
- MULCHING After feeding, water the ground well and spread a thick organic mulch around the plants. Pull rather than hoe out any weeds.
- NETTING You will have to use nets to keep off birds—certainly in summer as the fruits color and ripen. A fruit cage is recommended.
- FROST PROTECTION Plants are hardy but may need to be covered with floating row cover if there is a danger of frost when they are in flower.

Harvesting and storing
Depending on the variety, fruits are usually ready for picking from mid- to late summer. Traditional, old-fashioned black currants ripen first at the top of the "strig," so you must pick individual currants as they become ready to harvest. Modern varieties, however, are bred to ripen simultaneously, so you can snip off an entire strig at once. Ripe black currants won't keep for long—no more than a few days in a sealed container in the refrigerator—but they can be frozen successfully.

Yield
Yields can vary from variety to variety and from year to year, but from an average bush you should expect 10–12 lb (4.5–5.5 kg) of fruit.

(below, left to right) **After feeding,** water the ground well and spread thick organic mulch around the plants to conserve moisture and keep down weeds. **Support heavy-fruiting varieties** as they grow with bamboo canes and thick string. **Black currants** are ready to pick when plump and shiny blue-black. Try to get the timing just right, as the longer they are left on the bush, the sweeter they taste.

Season by season

(left to right) **Buds break** in late winter. **Tiny flowers** are very vulnerable to frost damage. **Green fruitlets** don't need thinning. (below) **Bushes** are hardy and withstand very low temperatures.

Late winter
- Winter-prune established bushes.

Early spring
- New young leaves and flowers start to appear. Protect against frost if necessary.
- Feed with ammonium sulfate and a general fertilizer.
- Mulch around plants to suppress weeds.
- Plant bare-root black currants as soon as the ground can be worked.
- Last chance for winter pruning.

Mid-spring
- Blossoms are fully open, and pollinating insects should be at work.

Late spring
- Fruitlets form and begin to swell.
- Weed and water regularly.
- Inspect bushes for imported currantworms (see p.336) and destroy any you find.

Early summer
- Watch for any signs of leaf spot or mildew.
- Continue weeding and watering as fruits ripen.
- Net against birds.

Midsummer
- Harvest early- and mid-season fruits.
- Give established bushes a summer prune if they are overcrowded and the fruit is shaded.

Late summer
- Harvest mid- and late-season fruits.

Mid-fall
- Take cuttings to propagate new plants.
- New bare-root currants start to become available from specialty nurseries.
- Plant bushes now or in late fall.

Late fall
- Prune new bushes after planting.
- Winter-prune established bushes between now and early spring.

Pruning and training black currants

Black currants fruit mainly on lengths of stem that grew the previous summer—in other words, on one-year-old wood. New growth put on in the current year will fruit next year. Stems three years old or older are less productive and should therefore be cut out. So, the aim of pruning is, in effect, to renew the whole bush every three or four years.

Pruning a newly planted black currrant

The most important function of pruning now is to encourage the roots to establish, ready for the emergence of strong new growth in the spring. So, as soon as you've planted a new bush you should prune the stems almost to the base. This might sound a little bit harsh but actually it will get the bush off to the right start.

1st winter pruning
OCTOBER–MARCH

BARE-ROOT
- If planting in December–March, cut all stems back to about 1 in (2.5 cm) above the level of the soil. Only 1 or 2 buds should remain on each stem.

CONTAINER-GROWN
- No need to prune, provided the established root system is intact during planting.

2nd winter pruning
NOVEMBER–MARCH

- Very little pruning is required. If any of the new stems are weak or if they are growing parallel with the ground, cut them out entirely.

Pruning an established black currant

An established, overgrown bush may need opening up to let in light and air. You should also remove some older, dark-colored stems, so they can be replaced by newer, paler, fruit-bearing ones. You can leave this job until fall or winter, or start it as early as July to allow sunlight to reach ripening fruits.

Summer/winter pruning
JULY and NOVEMBER–MARCH
- Cut to one bud above ground level as many as one-third of the dark, three-year-old or older stems.
- Remove any weak, crossing, damaged, or diseased stems, as well as any growing too close to ground.
- Leave healthy, one- and two-year-old stems untouched; they will bear fruit next year.

Cut out up to a third of old, unproductive wood in winter. This will open up the bush, prevent overcrowding, and make it easier to pick the fruits when they ripen next summer.

What can go wrong

Buds and blossoms

Blossoms die
Black currants flower early in spring and frost can destroy flowers and scorch young leaves.
■ See **Frost** (p.316).

Leaves and stems

1 White or gray powdery mold on leaves
This is an indication of American gooseberry mildew. Leaves are usually affected first, then the fruit.
■ See **American gooseberry mildew** (p.324).

2 Curled, blistered leaves
Leaves that appear twisted and develop red or yellow blisters are usually infested with currant aphids. The insects are pale yellow and should be visible feeding on new shoots.
■ See **Currant aphids** (p.335).

3 Sticky leaves covered in aphids
Aphids can cover upper surfaces of leaves with sticky honeydew, which may develop into gray mold. The aphids can be found on the undersides of the leaves.
■ See **Aphids** (p.334).

4 Entire stems die
If leaves turn brown and whole stems die, suspect gooseberry dieback, which can also affect currants. The usual cause is a fungus (Botrytis or Eutypa).
■ See **Gooseberry dieback** (p.328).

5 Yellow leaves with green veins
This probably indicates lack of iron or manganese. Called lime-induced chlorosis, it is common in alkaline soil with a high pH.
■ See **Iron deficiency** (p.320) or **Manganese deficiency** (p.321).

Brown spots on leaves
Anthracnose and other fungal diseases can cause small, irregular brown spots surrounded by yellow patches appear on leaves, which may then die.
■ See **Fungal leaf spot** (p.328).

Small holes in leaves
Tiny red-brown spots and holes with tattered brown edges may be signs of tarnished plant bug or lygus bug damage.
■ See **Plant bugs** (p.335).

Leaves being eaten
The most likely culprits are imported currantworms, which are actually sawfly larvae.
■ See **Imported currantworms** (p.336).

Fruit

Fluffy, gray or brown mold
Affected fruit become covered with mold and start to rot.
■ See **Botrytis** (p.326) or **American gooseberry mildew** (p.324).

Berries stripped by birds
Birds find the ripening fruit irresistible.
■ See **Birds** (p.335).

Blueberries

Delicious and highly nutritious, blueberries are a natural choice for home gardeners. There are three main types of blueberries: highbush, lowbush, and rabbiteye. Gardeners in the northern half of the US can grow lowbush blueberries, which are reputed to be the tastiest, or highbush types, which grow up to 6 feet tall and are very productive. Half-high blueberries are hybrids of lowbush and highbush types, growing 3–4 ft (1–1.25 m) tall, and are easy for home gardeners to manage. In hot-summer and mild-winter areas, rabbiteye blueberries are the best choice, though they do need a short winter chilling period to induce the plants to break dormancy.

As long as you grow them in the acidic soil they require, blueberries are fairly trouble-free. There are a few insect pests to combat, and Southern gardeners will need to watch plants for disease.

If their wonderful, sweet, juicy flavor were not reason enough to grow them, blueberries also have a reputation as a "superfood," because they are very high in the antioxidants that are claimed to help combat the aging process and improve memory and coordination.

Leave blueberries to ripen fully—making sure they come away easily from the stalk—if you want them to be sweet enough to eat raw. Pick over the bushes several times, since the berries don't all ripen at once. Blueberries keep for longer than most soft fruits and also freeze well.

Which types to grow

■ **Bushes** Highbush and rabbiteye blueberries are pruned as informal, upright bushes; formal training methods don't work well. Lowbush blueberries are low, spreading plants that need only simple pruning to remove old growth.

Must-grow blueberries

1 'Berkeley'
Tall bushes producing generous crops of large, pale powder-blue berries. Fruit are less likely to split than some other varieties.
■ **Harvest** August

2 'Spartan'
Flowers late but fruits early, so ideal for areas where frost may be a problem. Large, pale-blue berries with good flavor.
■ **Harvest** July

3 'Earliblue'
Thought to be one of the earliest fruiting of all the varieties, its large, pale-blue, sweet berries may be ready to pick in mid-July.
■ **Harvest** July

4 'Coville'
Heavy crops of large berries with a slightly tart flavor. Named after the 19th-century American botanist who pioneered domestic blueberry growing.
■ **Harvest** August

5 'Jersey'
A hardy variety that is good for cooler regions. Medium to large juicy berries with a sweet flavor. Not self-fertile, so plant with a partner.
■ **Harvest** August

6 'Bluetta'
Compact, smaller than normal bushes and early fruiting. Plenty of medium-sized, high-quality fruit.
■ **Harvest** July

7 'Brigitta'
Tall, upright variety bred in Australia. Pale-blue berries are firm and crisp, and store well in the refrigerator.
■ **Harvest** August–September

8 'Herbert'
If 'Earliblue' is the earliest to ripen, then 'Herbert' has earned an equal reputation as the best-tasting berry. Large fruit with a wonderful flavor.
■ **Harvest** August

9 'Chandler'
Huge blue-black berries that when ripe may be almost as large as cherries. The harvest period is long and may last for up to six weeks.
■ **Harvest** August–September

10 'Bluecrop'
Popular, widely grown variety with vigorous, upright growth, producing large berries with a good flavor. Make sure berries are ripe before picking.
■ **Harvest** July–August

11 'Top Hat'
A dwarf variety, even smaller than 'Sunshine Blue': average height and spread may be as little as 16–24 in (40–60 cm). Perfect for containers and tight spaces. Medium-sized, purple berries with excellent flavor.
■ **Harvest** July–August

'Duke' (not illustrated)
Mild-tasting, medium-sized berries that store well. Attactive yellow-orange leaf color in fall. This variety may not be easy to find, but it is still prized because it flowers late and fruits early.
■ **Harvest** July

'Ozarkblue' (not illustrated)
A so-called Southern highbush blueberry that will survive cold winters but tolerate hotter summers than most other varieties. A good choice for warmer regions.
■ **Harvest** August–September

'Pinkberry' or 'Pink Lemonade' (not illustrated)
Two names for an unusual, recently introduced pink form of blueberry. The berries deepen in color from pale pink to bright rose pink as they ripen, and are sweeter than regular blueberries.
■ **Harvest** July–August

'Sunshine Blue' (not illustrated)
Compact bushes that are smaller than most, rarely growing more than 3 ft (1 m) tall. Good for small gardens and for container growing. Distinctive red buds and bright pink flowers.
■ **Harvest** August

Growing blueberries

Blueberries are very easy to grow. In fact, they're among the easiest of all soft fruits. That said, you must grow them in the very acidic soil that they need in order to thrive. They then require a minimum of care, no training, and only a little, simple pruning. New, young plants can seem slow to get going but, once established, they are productive and long-lived. They can last for twenty years or more—indeed, they may even outlast you.

The year at a glance

	spring			summer			fall			winter		
	E	M	L	E	M	L	E	M	L	E	M	L
plant												
prune												
harvest												

Choosing plants

Blueberries can be bought as bare-root or container-grown plants. If possible, buy certified disease-free, two- or three-year-old plants in containers. They will establish more quickly than bare-root plants.

Flowering and pollination

Many blueberries are what's called partially self-fertile, which means that they are theoretically capable of setting fruit from their own pollen. However, it's safer to plant more than one (ideally, a minimum of three different varieties) so that they cross-pollinate each other.

When to plant

■ PLANTING IN THE GROUND Plant either bare-root or container grown plants in fall or spring. Do not attempt to plant if the ground is frozen or waterlogged.

■ PLANTING IN CONTAINERS Container-grown plants can be purchased and potted up at any time during the growing season, though the best time for potting them on into a new container is in spring. Avoid repotting in hot, dry summer conditions.

Where to plant

Choose a sheltered site, out of strong winds. Most blueberries are very hardy and relatively resistant to frost damage, although those that come into flower very early in the spring are most at risk, and may

Not all blueberry varieties flower at the same time. Some begin in early spring; others flower in late spring. To guarantee cross-pollination, it's best to plant varieties that will blossom more or less simultaneously.

PLANTING A BLUEBERRY BUSH

Only attempt to grow blueberries in acidic soil. If yours is naturally neutral or alkaline, consider creating a raised bed filled with soil that you can ensure has the correct level of acidity. Prepare the ground several months in advance by digging in composted sawdust, composted pine bark, or acidic potting mix.

1 Mark out your planting position, allowing a space of up to 5 ft (1.5 m) all around.

2 Give the plant a good soaking with rainwater, and remove it from its container.

3 Dig a hole deep enough and wide enough to accommodate the plant's rootball, with an additional 4 in (10 cm) all around. Check the depth to ensure that the top of the rootball is level with or slightly below the surface of your soil.

4 Carefully firm down the soil, ensuring that there are no air pockets among the roots.

5 Water generously, preferably with rainwater and not with hard city or well water, unless it is your only option.

6 Spread a mulch of composted sawdust, leafmold, or pine bark around the plant.

need protection. In summer, all blueberries like plenty of sunshine but most will tolerate partial shade for a few hours a day.

Soil type

The nature of the soil is the most important aspect of growing blueberries. They will grow only in very acidic soils, those with a pH of 4–5.5. If you are successful with rhododendrons, azaleas, camellias, heathers, and other acid-loving plants, then you'll probably succeed with blueberries, too. If not, then employ raised beds or containers, where it is easier to manage the acidity of the soil.

Neutral or slightly alkaline soils were once acidified by adding peat. Eco-friendly alternatives include composted sawdust, composted pine bark or needles, sulfur dust or chips, and acidic potting mix. Beware: some peat substitutes are too alkaline. Blueberries also need free-draining soil. They won't do well in heavy clay soils prone to waterlogging.

Planting distances

■ HIGHBUSH and RABBITEYE 4–5 ft (1.2–1.5 m) apart in rows 7–9 ft (2–2.5 m) apart.
■ LOWBUSH 1 ft (30 cm) apart in rows 3–5 ft (1–1.5 m) apart.

Routine care

■ WATERING Blueberries need a lot of water. Water regularly and often, using rainwater if possible. If using tap water is unavoidable, you may need to apply additional quantities of acidic mulch or use special acidic fertilizer in order to maintain the low pH level.

■ FEEDING In spring, after pruning, apply a lime- and calcium-free general fertilizer. Don't use tomato or other general vegetable fertilizers. For an additional boost of nitrogen, you might also sprinkle ammonium sulfate over the soil at a rate of about ½ oz/sq yd (15 g/sq m).

■ MULCHING A thick organic mulch spread around the plants after feeding will help retain moisture and keep down weeds. Use only acidic material: composted sawdust, chipped or composted pine bark, pine needles, or leafmold. Avoid farmyard manure and ordinary compost.

■ NETTING You will have to use nets to keep off birds—certainly in summer as the fruits color and ripen. A fruit cage is recommended.

■ FROST PROTECTION Plants are hardy but early-flowering varieties may need to be protected with floating row cover if there is a danger of frost once buds have burst.

Harvesting and storing

Blueberries have a relatively long harvest period. Early varieties should be ready to pick in July; late varieties may last into early September. The berries don't all ripen at the same time, so you may have to go over each bush several times looking for the ones that are ripe.

Blueberries keep for longer than most soft fruits—for a week or more in the refrigerator. They also freeze particularly well.

Yield

Yields depend on the age of the bush, the variety, and of course the weather, but you should expect 3.3–5.5 lb (1.5–2.5 kg) from a four-year-old bush and up to 11 lb (5 kg) or even more from a fully established, mature bush.

GROWING BLUEBERRIES IN CONTAINERS

Blueberries usually do well grown in tubs or containers, particularly if you take care to maintain the soil at the right level of acidity. The trick is to use special acidic potting mix formulated for other acid-loving plants such as rhododendrons and camellias. Blend the potting mix with coarse grit to improve drainage, and mulch the surface with acidic, organic material. Feed with a lime-free general fertilizer in spring, and water regularly, especially in dry weather. Blueberries should never be allowed to dry out, nor should the container be allowed to sit in water.

Start off young plants in a pot with a diameter of 12–14 in (30–35 cm). Check the rootball and be prepared to pot on to a larger container every couple of years. Remember that in open ground, highbush blueberries can grow 6 feet tall and rabbiteyes can reach up to 15 feet tall. So for containers, half-high blueberries are the best choice.

PROPAGATING BLUEBERRIES

You can propagate blueberries from softwood cuttings taken in midsummer. Always insert them into acidic potting mix.

1 Select a healthy shoot and cut it off just above a leaf joint so you have a cutting 4 in (10 cm) long.

2 Make holes with a dibber in a small pot of potting mix and insert cuttings around the edge. Water, and put the pot in a propagator.

(right) **Don't pick the berries** as soon as they turn blue. Wait until they develop a powdery white bloom on their skins and turn slightly soft. They should pull away easily between your finger and thumb, leaving the stalk behind.

Season by season

(above, left to right) **Buds** are already beginning to burst in late winter. **Bell-like flowers** appear early in spring and may need protection from frost. **Small fruit** begin to form as soon as the blossoms start to drop. From now on, keep watering with rainwater. (right) **Berries** ripen in stages rather than all at once.

Late winter
■ Prune blueberry bushes now or in early spring.
■ Apply dormant oil to control aphids or scales if they have been a problem in past seasons.

Early spring
■ Complete any winter pruning now.
■ On early-flowering varieties, young leaves and blossoms start to appear.
■ Protect against frost if necessary.
■ Spread an acidic mulch around plants.

Mid-spring
■ On most bushes, blossoms are fully open, attracting pollinating insects.
■ Pot on blueberries in containers if necessary.
■ Plant new bushes now; remove flowers so plants channel resources into establishing a root system.
■ Feed with a lime-free general fertilizer.

Late spring
■ Late-flowering varieties are in flower now.
■ As blossoms drop, small fruitlets form and swell.
■ Weed and water regularly.
■ Continue to remove blossoms from new bushes.

■ If you've had past problems with blueberry maggots, cover bushes with floating row cover once fruit has set.

Early summer
■ Continue weeding and watering as fruit ripens.
■ Net against birds.

Midsummer
■ Harvest early- and mid-season fruit.
■ Take softwood cuttings to propagate new plants.

Late summer
■ Harvest mid- and late-season fruit.

Early fall
■ There may still be a few late-season fruit left for picking.

Fall
■ Rake back mulch before leaves fall. After leaves have fallen, re-spread the mulch over the fallen leaves and add a layer of fresh mulch on top. This helps to prevent future disease problems.

Pruning blueberries

Most of the fruit is produced on stems that are between one and three years old. In addition, young new stems that shoot up from the soil in the current summer, from midsummer onward, may produce a second crop of fruit at the end of the season. These berries may even be larger than the first crop. Wood that is older than three years won't fruit as well or as plentifully as newer wood. Prune it out gradually.

Pruning highbush and rabbiteye blueberries

Blueberries are always pruned in the winter, when the plants are in their dormant phase. You can do it at any time between late fall and early spring. If you do wait until spring, the fruit buds will have fattened up visibly. You'll then be able to see which stems are going to fruit heavily and should therefore be left untouched.

1st and 2nd winter pruning
LATE FALL–EARLY SPRING

- Very little pruning is required in the first 2 years after planting.
- Remove any damaged or diseased stems.
- Thin any obviously weak or crossing stems from the center of the bush.
- Prune out any thin stems growing parallel with or too close to ground.

Winter pruning an established bush
LATE FALL–EARLY SPRING

- If the bush has become overgrown, aim to open up its center to let in light and air.
- Remove any dead, damaged, or diseased stems.
- Cut 1 or 2 of the oldest, thickest, least productive stems right down to the base. Aim to leave 4 to 6 main stems.
- Remove any lateral shoots growing too close to the base of the main stems.
- Tip-prune the twiggy ends of the stems that produced fruit last year. Always cut back to a strong sideshoot or to a bud that is facing upward.
- Don't prune out more than a quarter of the bush at once.

(top to bottom) **Use loppers** to cut old, unproductive stems down to the base in winter. **Prune out** any diseased or damaged stems, cutting back to a strong, healthy shoot.

What can go wrong

Leaves and stems

1 Scorching on edges of leaves
Leaves turning brown and curling at the edges, and the tips of new shoots dying back, are the classic signs of drought. If not lacking moisture, the plant may be in need of potassium.
■ See **Potassium deficiency** (p.321).

2 Small, brown, shell-like insects on stems
Scale insects are sometimes found on plant stems.
■ See **Scale insects** (p.340).

3 Multicolored, mottled patches on leaves
Irregular pale green, yellow, and red markings are often signs of one of the several viruses that can attack blueberries. They may also be a symptom of a lack of magnesium.
■ See **Blueberry virus** (p.326) or **Magnesium deficiency** (p.321).

Yellow leaves with green veins
Lime-induced chlorosis may be a sign that the soil is too alkaline and plants are unable to take up sufficient iron and manganese.
■ See **Iron deficiency** (p.320) or **Manganese deficiency** (p.321).

Dead brown leaves remain on stems
Clusters of leaves turning brown, dying off, and failing to drop may look like "flags" against normal green foliage. When they finally do fall, the dead stem is likely to have turned almost black.
■ See **Blueberry stem blight** (p.325).

Skeletonlike leaves
Japanese beetles feed on leaf tissue, but not on leaf veins.
■ See **Japanese beetles** (p.336).

Fruit

4 Berries eaten
Birds are very partial to the ripening fruit and begin eating the berries as soon as they start to change color from green to blue. Any damaged fruits also attract wasps and flies.
■ See **Birds** (p.334) and **Wasps** (p.341).

Fluffy, gray or brown mold
In wet summers or on sites where conditions are damp and humid, fruit may become covered with mold and start to rot, sometimes after harvesting. Flowers, leaves, and stems may also be affected. The cause is likely to be the fungal infection Botrytis.
■ See **Botrytis** (p.326).

Mushy berries
Blueberry maggots are fly larvae that feed inside the berries, ruining the harvest.
■ See **Blueberry maggots** (p.335).

Shriveled berries
Cherry fruitworm caterpillars feed on fruit and produce webbing as protection. If the shriveled berries are hard and gray in color, the cause may be a fungal disease called mummy berry.
■ See **Cherry fruitworm** (p.335) and **Mummy berry** (p.328).

Cranberries and lingonberries

Natural habitat for cranberries is peat-rich bogs. They are low-growing, sprawling, evergreen plants that are not hard for Northern gardeners to grow, provided that they can re-create the right growing conditions. Southern gardeners, however, are not likely to succeed with these crops.

Wild cranberries found in Europe and Japan are a different species: they are slightly smaller, and tend not to be grown commercially.

Cranberries ripen in the fall, later than blueberries. Although the deep-red fruits look appetizing, they are far too tart to be eaten raw and, after the addition of generous quantities of sugar, are usually used for juices, jellies, muffins, and the cranberry sauce without which a Thanksgiving or Christmas turkey would be almost unthinkable.

Ripe cranberries can stay on the bush, so pick them as you need them. Frost will, however, damage the berries, so harvest before temperatures dip below freezing.

Growing cranberries

Cranberries are not hard to grow if you can give them the conditions they need. If you can't, you should probably not bother. The two most important things are acidic soil and plenty of water—in other words, the sort of environment that mimics their natural habitat.

The year at a glance

	spring			summer			fall			winter		
	E	M	L	E	M	L	E	M	L	E	M	L
plant	▬	▬	▬									
trim	▬											
harvest cranberries							▬	▬	▬			
harvest lingonberries				▬	▬	▬						

Planting cranberries

Because they have such specific requirements, cranberries are usually best grown in containers or in specially constructed beds. They are sold as container-grown rather than bare-root plants. Unlike blueberries, they are self-fertile, so you don't need more than one plant to guarantee pollination.

When to plant

Plant cranberries and lingonberries in the spring after the danger of hard freezes has passed.

Must-grow cranberries

1 'Pilgrim'
One of the most popular and widely grown varieties—rightly so, because plants are heavy bearers and the berries are among the largest. They are dark red and can grow to the size of cherries.

2 'Early Black'
Not actually black but rather a rich, dark red-purple. This variety produces generous crops of medium-sized berries that are ready for picking earlier than most other varieties—perhaps even in August. Originally from Massachusetts.

ALSO TRY

'Franklin'
A cross between 'Early Black' and another long-established U.S. cranberry, 'Howes', this compact variety is ideal for container-growing. It fruits slightly more heavily than 'Early Black' and ripens almost as early.

'CN'
A vigorous, spreading variety that produces heavy crops of large, juicy red berries. It is widely grown commercially.

Where to plant
Choose a sunny site, but not an enclosed, south-facing one that gets too hot. Cranberries do best in a raised or sunken bed where you can control the acidity of the soil and the drainage.

Soil type
Cranberries, like blueberries, will only grow in very acidic soils, those with a pH of 4–5.5 or even lower. And they need the right balance between being constantly moist yet not becoming waterlogged.

Planting distances
- PLANTS 12 in (30 cm) apart.
- ROW SPACING 12 in (30 cm) apart.

Growing in containers
Use a pot or container with a diameter of at least 15–18 in (38–45 cm), and fill it with a mix of acidic potting mix and coarse, lime-free grit to improve drainage. Stand the pot in a nonporous dish or tray and keep it topped off with rainwater so that the soil never dries out.

Growing in special beds
Cranberries can be grown in either raised or sunken beds filled with acidic soil to a depth of 6–8 in (15–20 cm). If possible, when

(left to right) **Cranberry flowers** are tiny and appear in early summer, by which time insect pollinators are plentiful. **A specially built bed** made from an old ceramic sink, set into the ground, is ideal for growing cranberries. Fill it with acidic potting mix and keep the soil moist.

constructing the bed, line it with plastic that has been perforated with plenty of drainage holes. Fill with acidic potting mix or a suitably light, low-pH soil. Cover the surface with a layer of lime-free grit or sand to act as a mulch. Once established, plants will spread to form a matlike ground cover.

Routine care

■ WATERING Cranberries need a lot of water and must be kept constantly moist, using rainwater if possible.

■ FEEDING Not usually necessary, but if crops are disappointing, try applying a little liquid, lime-free general fertilizer in mid-spring.

■ MULCHING A topdressing of grit or sand will help retain moisture and keep down weeds.

Harvesting and storing

Cranberries usually start to ripen at the end of September, but there is no need to pick them right away unless frost is expected. They will happily stay on the bush for another month or two as long as temperatures stay above freezing. You will almost certainly collect your cranberries by hand, though when grown commercially they are harvested by flooding entire fields so that the berries float. They can then be "combed" from the plants by machine.

Cranberries store well—for as long as two or three months in a refrigerator. They also freeze well.

Pruning

Cranberries don't really need pruning as such, though they benefit from an annual trim in spring to remove any straggly, untidy stems or runners and to encourage bushy growth.

What can go wrong

Diseases and disorders are rare, although if the soil is not acidic enough, plants may suffer from lime-induced chlorosis (see p.320). Few pests seem to target cranberries, and neither birds nor slugs find them to their taste.

GROWING LINGONBERRIES

Like cranberries, lingonberries grow as low, spreading, evergreen bushes. They have pale pink and white flowers that appear in May or June, and they usually produce two harvests of small red berries, the first at the end of July and the second in September. Lingonberries also need acidic soil and are therefore best grown in containers filled with special acidic potting mix. They don't need quite such boggy conditions as cranberries, but they must nevertheless be kept well watered.

Must-try unusual berries

These berries push the boundaries of what is usually defined as grow-your-own fruit. If you are curious and have the space, give them a try.

1 Goji berry

Originating in the foothills of the Himalayas, goji berries are among today's fashionable superfoods owing to their very high concentrations of minerals, vitamins, and antioxidants. The plants are very hardy, and will survive severe winters as well as hot, dry summers. Grow them in a sheltered, sunny spot with plenty of room. Once established, purple-and-white flowers are followed by small, red berries in fall. The berries are usually eaten dried, like raisins, or used in juices.

2 Aronia

In the wild, aronia berries or chokeberries grow in damp, acidic soil, often near the edges of woodlands. In gardens, they are grown as ornamental shrubs for their white or pink flowers and vibrant fall leaf color. The small, red-currant-sized fruit of the red, black, and purple chokeberry are edible and can be used for juices and jams. They are very high in antioxidants.

3 Garden huckleberry

Wild huckleberries (*Gaylussacia dumosa*), like blueberries, grow wild in acid, boggy soils, often at high altitudes. The garden huckleberry is unrelated and, although a member of the deadly nightshade family, it is edible, not poisonous. Sow seeds in pots indoors in late spring and grow much like tomatoes or eggplants. Pick the berries when they turn black, and use in tarts and jams.

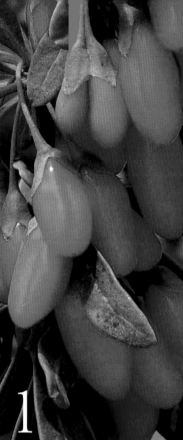

1

5

6

4 Honeyberry

The honeyberry is in fact an edible form of honeysuckle. Native to northern Europe, Asia, and North America, it grows to a height of 3–6 ft (1–2 m) and produces purple-blue berries from early summer onward. The fruits taste rather like wild blueberries. Honeyberries are worth tracking down from specialty nurseries and are easy to grow, but you'll need to buy at least two as they need a companion for successful pollination. Honeyberries are extremely hardy, drought-resistant, and, unlike blueberries, they don't need acidic soil.

5 Oregon grape

Despite its name, this isn't a grape but actually a type of mahonia (*Mahonia aquifolium*), and often grown as a decorative garden shrub. The Oregon grape produces yellow flowers in spring and small blue-black berries that ripen in July or August. They can be eaten raw but are usually cooked, sweetened, and made into preserves.

6 Bilberry

In Europe and northern Asia, bilberries are traditionally a wild food. Known in the UK as whortleberries or whinberries, in Scotland as blaeberries, and in France as *myrtilles*, they grow in acidic, boggy soil, often on high moorlands. They taste like blueberries but are smaller, with purple flesh and juice. Unfortunately, they are difficult to buy commercially and very hard to grow. Confusingly, in North America, the so-called bog bilberry is actually a form of huckleberry.

7 European elderberry

Strictly speaking, European elderberry is a tree fruit rather than a soft fruit, and one that is not often cultivated. However, if you have plenty of space, it's worth planting, and an annual winter-prune should keep it from becoming too large. Harvest the sweet-smelling flowers for making soft drinks, and use the berries in pies, tarts, jams, jellies, or homemade wine.

Grape Vines

A backyard grape vine is a fun project that will yield sweet results—if you grow dessert grapes—or if you're adventurous, you can try growing your own wine grapes. Grapes grow well in most areas, although gardeners in the Southeast may need to stick with muscadines. And gardeners in the North or at high altitudes may need to grow grapes in a greenhouse or hoophouse.

Pruning a grape vine has the reputation of being a dark art. The various different techniques are rich in complexity and make for strong opinions. Yet, in all honesty, it's only as hard as you want to make it. There's nothing wrong with growing a vine informally, allowing it to scramble up over a trellis or arbor. You'll almost certainly get some grapes, though perhaps not as many as you might hope for. If you want to train grapes more formally, you can investigate the two-arm or four-arm Kniffen systems. Or you can prune grapes as they are grown in Europe or in some commercial vineyards—by cordon pruning or using the guyot system. Both are easier to learn than you might think.

Grapes may ripen slightly unevenly, depending on how much sun they receive. Wait until they are all ready, then cut off the entire bunch with a sharp pair of pruners.

Must-grow grapes

1 **'Buckland Sweetwater'**
Dessert
Usually fruits early and reliably if watered regularly and fertilized from time to time. Pick the grapes as soon as they turn amber-gold.
- **Color** white-amber
- **Harvest** September–October

2 **'Dornfelder'**
Wine and dessert
A hybrid German variety that can be eaten fresh or used to make red wine. It is one of the few red wine grapes suitable for cool temperate climates.
- **Color** purple-red
- **Harvest** early October

3 **'Brandt'**
Dessert
This is an attractive, easygoing vine that doesn't need complex pruning and is therefore a good choice for training over an arbor or up a wall. The grapes are perhaps not the largest, but they have a good, sweet flavor nevertheless.
- **Color** purple
- **Harvest** mid-October

4 **'Müller-Thurgau'**
Wine and dessert
This is a perennially popular grape for home winemaking. It is easy to grow, should ripen in most sheltered spots, and usually produces a good crop.
- **Color** pale yellow-green
- **Harvest** mid-October

5 **'Flame'**
Dessert
A red seedless grape often sold in supermarkets. Much better homegrown.
- **Color** red
- **Harvest** September–early October

6 **'Lakemont'**
Dessert
A relatively modern, white seedless grape that can be grown outdoors in a warm, sheltered location. It has a wonderful, sweet muscat flavor.
- **Color** gold-yellow
- **Harvest** September–early October

7 'Perlette'
Dessert
A French grape that produces good crops of sweet, juicy, seedless grapes.
- **Color** yellow-green
- **Harvest** late September

8 'Muscat of Alexandria'
Dessert
Not the easiest of grapes to grow, as ideally the fruit need a long period on the vine in order to ripen fully. Definitely worth trying, though, because its flavor is so outstanding.
- **Color** gold-yellow
- **Harvest** November–December

9 'Black Hamburgh'
Dessert
Also known as 'Schiava Grossa' and 'Trollinger', this is a long-established, popular grape. It is sweet and juicy, with a good flavor, and is easy to grow.
- **Color** purple-black
- **Harvest** September–October

'Concord' (not illustrated)
Dessert and juice
The best-known slipskin grape. Purple, seeded fruit that do best with a long, hot growing season.
- **Color** purple
- **Harvest** September

'Canadice' (not illustrated)
Dessert
A very hardy seedless grape that bears large clusters of sweet fruit. Resists black rot but can be susceptible to mildew.
- **Color** red
- **Harvest** August–September

'Interlaken' (not illustrated)
Dessert
Very sweet, meaty, seedless berries. The loose clusters are also good for drying to make raisins. Quite hardy and disease-resistant.
- **Color** white
- **Harvest** mid- to late August

'Himrod' (not illustrated)
Dessert
Thompson Seedless is one of the parents of this excellent variety, which bears large loose clusters. Vines do well in a wide variety of soils.
- **Color** amber
- **Harvest** August

Muscadine grapes (not illustrated)
Dessert, juice, wine
Good for Southern gardens because of their heat and disease tolerance; not hardy enough for the North. Many varieties are available. Some are self-fertile; some have male and female flowers on separate plants. Vines can grow extremely large over time if not kept trained.
- **Color** black
- **Harvest** August–September, depending on variety

'Regent' (not illustrated)
Wine and dessert
Originally bred in Germany for growing in cool temperate climates, this is a red-wine grape that fruits heavily and is disease-resistant. When fully ripe, the grapes are sweet enough to eat fresh.
- **Color** blue-black
- **Harvest** early October

Growing grapes outdoors

In order to fruit successfully, grapes need the following: a cold spell during the winter (though not so cold that they are killed off), warmth in spring when they flower and set fruit, and heat and sunshine in summer to ripen the grapes. In areas with very cold winters, your choices of varieties are more limited, and you may need to lay the vines on the ground for the winter and bury them or mulch them to protect them from the cold.

The year at a glance—outdoors

	spring			summer			fall			winter		
	E	M	L	E	M	L	E	M	L	E	M	L
plant bare-root	■											
plant container	■	■	■	■	■	■						
summer prune		■	■	■	■	■						
winter prune									■	■	■	
harvest							■	■				

Flowering and pollination

Most grapes are self-fertile, and are pollinated by the wind rather than by bees or other insects.

Choosing grape vines

Young plants are available bare-root from some specialty nurseries, but they are more commonly supplied container-grown. They are likely to have been either grown from cuttings or grafted onto disease-resistant rootstocks.

When to plant

■ BARE-ROOT Plant in early spring before the buds on the dormant vines have begun to swell.
■ CONTAINER-GROWN In theory, you may plant at any time during the growing season, but

For top-quality plants visit a specialty supplier, who will also be able to offer advice about suitable varieties for your yard.

springtime, after danger of frost is past, is best. Avoid summer months if it is hot and dry.

Where to plant
Grapes need full sun. If you're going to train them on post-and-wire supports, choose a south-, southwest-, or southeast-facing slope, somewhere protected from strong winds, and orient the rows north to south. Alternatively, grow them against a sunny, sheltered wall or fence. In both cases, avoid frost pockets.

Soil type
The roots of grape vines penetrate deep into the ground and spread widely, so they are able to survive in most soils, including extremely dry and stony ground. Soils with a pH in the range of 6.0–7.5 should be suitable. The few sites on which they will struggle are thin, shallow soils and heavy, poorly drained ones prone to waterlogging. In soils that are very rich, vines may produce too much foliage and too few grapes.

How to plant
Prepare the site a month or two in advance by weeding carefully and digging in plenty of well-rotted compost or manure. Construct

(above) **Grapes grown outside** require two good summers in a row: the first so new shoots ripen and buds form, the second to ensure fruit sets and ripens.

(below) **Prune a new dormant vine** at spring planting, cutting it down to a strong, healthy bud about 12 inches above ground level. If planting an actively growing vine, wait until winter to prune.

Cut away some of the foliage from time to time during the summer so that air can circulate freely and sun can get to the ripening bunches of grapes.

a post-and-wire support for cordon (see p.276) or guyot (see p.278) vines. If you're growing your vine against a wall or fence, attach the necessary wires.

Dig a hole and plant the vine so that the old nursery soil mark on the stem is level with the surface of your soil. Insert a cane or thin stake into the hole and tie the vine to it for support. If the vine is completely dormant, prune it immediately (see p.269).

Planting distances outdoors
- CORDONS 3–4 ft (1–1.2 m) apart.
- SINGLE GUYOTS 3 ft (1 m) apart.
- DOUBLE GUYOTS 5–6 ft (1.5–2 m) apart.

Routine care
WATERING Water both newly planted vines and those grown against walls regularly throughout the spring and summer.
- FEEDING Be careful not to overfeed grapes, or growth will be too rampant. In the summer, feed dessert grapes with a diluted, high-potassium liquid fertilizer every couple of weeks. If signs of magnesium deficiency appear (see p.321), spray with a solution of Epsom salts.
- MULCHING Remove weeds and mulch lightly with compost around the base of well-trained vines in late winter.
- NETTING Birds can be a problem in summer as fruit ripens, and nets may be necessary.
- THINNING Dessert grapes usually fruit better if thinned (see p.272), although it's not necessary with grapes grown for winemaking. Removing some of the leaves in summer will help ripen the grapes.

Harvesting and storing
For the best flavor and maximum sweetness, it's important to leave grapes on the vine until they are absolutely ripe. They may not actually reach that point, however, until several weeks after they've developed their full color. The only foolproof method is to taste them. When they're ready, cut off the whole bunch using sharp scissors or pruners (see p.273). If they were dry when picked, grapes will keep in a cool place for a few days, but they're far better eaten right away.

Yield
It's difficult to generalize about yields. The heaviness of the crop varies according to many factors, including how the vine is grown, trained, and pruned. An established cordon may produce two or three bunches of wine grapes, but perhaps only one bunch of dessert grapes, per lateral. A guyot-trained vine may produce twice as many. It really depends on how many flower trusses you leave in place to develop.

Growing grapes under cover

In harsh-winter areas, growing vines under cover opens up a much wider choice of varieties, including grapes that need higher temperatures and a longer growing season than you could ever offer them outdoors. There are a number of options. The simplest is to grow vines in containers and move them indoors or out, according to the weather and the season. The second is an unheated greenhouse, conservatory, hoophouse, or even a porch. And the third is a heated greenhouse, where you have complete control over the microclimate.

The year at a glance—indoors

	spring			summer			fall			winter		
	E	M	L	E	M	L	E	M	L	E	M	L
plant bare-root	▣									▣	▣	
plant container	▣	▣	▣							▣	▣	▣
summer-prune		▣	▣	▣	▣	▣						
winter-prune									▣	▣	▣	
harvest							▣	▣	▣			

Grapes grown in greenhouses or conservatories need a support system of strong, horizontal wires to take the weight of the sideshoots that bear the fruit. It's also important to provide plenty of ventilation.

Flowering and pollination

Although grapes are usually self-fertile, outdoor-grown vines are pollinated by the wind, so those grown under cover may need a little help. Once the flowers are open, give the vines a gentle shake or gently cup your hand and run it over them to help transfer pollen. This method is more likely to be successful in the middle of the day, when the atmosphere is warm and dry.

Planting under cover

Indoors, grapes are usually grown as cordons (see p.276). The way in which they are trained will depend on the design of your greenhouse or conservatory. In the case of a south-facing lean-to, the vine can be attached either to the back wall or to wires strung across the front, closer to the glass. In a tall greenhouse, the vine can be trained up into the roof space, leaving room for other plants beneath. In all cases, it's important not to crowd the vine. Good air circulation is vital.

When to plant

■ BARE-ROOT November–March, when vines are dormant. The best time is November or December, since your new vine will be dormant and you will be able to prune it back as soon as it is in the ground, without causing the cut to weep sap.
■ CONTAINER-GROWN In theory, you may plant at any time of year, although November or December are best, for the same reason.

(top to bottom) **Thinning bunches** of dessert grapes encourages the fruits that remain to develop their full size and flavor. Use sharp, long-nosed scissors and remove first any diseased grapes, then the smallest, and finally some from the middle. In all, reduce the size of the bunch by about a third.

Where to plant

You have two choices. The first is to plant your vine in a specially prepared soil bed inside the greenhouse. The second is to plant it directly into the soil outside, then train it through a hole in the wall so that it grows and fruits under cover. What are the pros and cons? Planting inside gives you more control and is probably better for a heated greenhouse, but it can involve more work. You must ensure that the soil is kept in top condition, that the bed has good drainage, and that the vine is regularly watered. Without rainfall, the only moisture it will receive is the watering you provide. Planting outdoors is easier, but it will take longer for the soil to warm up in spring, so tender vines will not get off to such an early start.

Soil type

For an indoor soil bed, use a loam-based planting mix. For outdoor soil requirements, see page 269.

How to plant

Before planting, put up a system of strong, horizontal wire supports spaced 10–12 in (25–30 cm) apart. Make sure they are at least 12 in (30 cm) away from the wall or glass, in order to avoid sun scorch and to allow air to circulate.

Plant the vine so that the old nursery soil mark on the stem is level with the surface of your soil and tie it to a cane for support, at least initially. In late fall or early winter, prune it immediately (see p.269). Otherwise, wait until fall.

Planting distances under cover

It's unlikely that the average-sized greenhouse will be large enough for more than one vine, although it can of course be trained as either a single or multiple cordon. If you have more space, plant cordons 3–4 ft (1–1.2 m) apart.

Routine care

■ HEATING AND VENTILATING Open vents between November and January to give vines the period of winter chill they need while dormant. In a heated greenhouse, gradually increase the temperature from late winter onward in order to stimulate vines into growth. An unheated greenhouse should begin to warm up from early spring onward. Open and shut vents as required in order to keep air circulating freely, and don't let spring temperatures fall below 40°F (5°C) at night or rise above 68°F (20°C) during the day.

■ WATERING Water regularly during the growing season if the vine is planted inside. Ease off as the grapes ripen, and avoid any sudden overwatering that may cause skins to split.

■ FEEDING For vines planted outside, see p.270. Vines planted inside may need more frequent liquid feeding—perhaps once a week between flowering and the grapes starting to color. They also need a topdressing of fresh potting mix each fall or winter.

■ MULCHING In early spring, after the first good watering of the year, mulch around the base of the vine with well-rotted compost or manure.

■ THINNING Greenhouse grapes grow larger and are healthier if thinned (see opposite). It's a fiddly job, and one you may have to do more than once, but it's worthwhile for dessert grapes. For wine grapes, it's not necessary.

■ SCRAPING BARK In winter, use a blunt knife to scrape away any old, loose bark. It harbors pests, such as mealybugs (see p.337) and spider mites (see p.339. If necessary, spray with a suitable insecticide.

Harvesting and storing

As with grapes grown outdoors, it's important to leave fruit on the vine until it's absolutely ripe. In the case of late-season dessert varieties, this "finishing" or "holding" period may last several weeks, meaning that grapes in a heated greenhouse can be harvested as late as early winter.

Yield

Yields vary according to variety, method of training, and growing conditions. As a rough guide, you might expect 10 bunches of grapes per 12 ft (4 m) of cordon. A single bunch can weigh about 1 lb (450 g).

Pick dessert grapes by cutting off the whole bunch, suspending it from a 3–4-in- (8–10-cm-) wide "handle" of lateral stem at the top. Try not to touch dessert grapes with your fingers or you'll spoil the bloom on the surface.

GROWING IN CONTAINERS

Container-grown grapes can live indoors or out. Indeed, you can easily give them the best of both worlds if you move them outside into the garden or onto a deck during winter, when they need a spell of cold, and then bring them back under cover at other times of the year when they need warmth.

A standard is the form most commonly grown in pots. One-year-old vines can be started off in pots as small as 7 in (19 cm) in diameter. In the fall of the following year, pot them on into 12–15-in (30–38-cm) pots. Use loam-based potting mix blended with some sand or gravel to improve drainage. Feed with a general liquid fertilizer in spring and summer, and keep the pot well-watered. Each winter, topdress with fresh soil and pot on to a larger container only when necessary.

An established standard vine should have a clear stem of about 3–4 ft (1–1.2 m) topped with a "head" of fruiting spurs. Restrict fruiting to just one bunch of grapes per spur, by pruning them as you would those on a cordon (see p.277).

Season by season

(left to right) **Buds** burst and leaves unfurl as spring temperatures rise. **Flowers** bloom from tight clusters of tiny buds. **Fruitlets** set and begin to swell.

Midwinter
■ Untie established cordons and let the central leader or "rod" hang down to stimulate new growth.

Late winter
■ Winter-prune established cordons now or in early spring.
■ Close greenhouse vents once the winter chill period is over, and start to increase the temperature in heated greenhouses.
■ Apply a general compound fertilizer around indoor and outdoor vines.

Early spring
■ Plant bare-root vines before they come out of dormancy.
■ Re-tie cordons that have been allowed to hang horizontally.
■ Weed and also mulch indoor and outdoor vines.

Mid-spring
■ Temperatures in unheated greenhouses should be rising now.
■ Plant young container-grown vines now or in late spring.
■ Prune established cordons now or in late spring, thinning to two shoots on each spur.

Late spring
■ Flowers usually open now.
■ Begin weeding and watering regularly.
■ Give vines a regular liquid feed while grapes are developing, between now and late summer.

Early summer
■ Thin bunches of dessert grapes.
■ On established cordons, start pruning back laterals and pinching out unwanted growth.
■ Begin to tie in new vertical shoots on guyot vines and remove unwanted growth.

Late summer
■ Net outdoor vines against birds.
■ Prune out excessive foliage to let sun and air reach ripening grapes.

Early fall
■ Start harvesting early-season grapes.

Mid-fall
■ Harvest mid- and late-season grapes.

Late fall
■ Late-season grapes grown under cover may still be ripening on the vine.
■ After harvesting, open greenhouse vents to give vines their necessary period of winter chill.
■ On guyot vines, remove all the growth that fruited this year, and prune and tie in the three main shoots required for next year.

Early winter
■ Top-dress greenhouse vines with fresh potting mix.
■ Scrape away loose bark from the base of vines to expose pests.

Pruning and training grapes

Pruning is essential. Without it, vines very quickly grow out of control and you'll end up with a straggly plant that is all foliage and little or no fruit. The cordon and guyot methods are the most commonly used. Both will keep vines neat and orderly, as well as encouraging the new growth that will fruit in the current year. All major pruning is carried out in winter when vines are dormant; otherwise they weep sap so freely they may actually be weakened. Only minor pinching out is done in summer.

Post-and-wire supports

Outdoors, both cordon and guyot systems need a structure of sturdy post-and-wire supports. Use 3 x 3 in (8 x 8 cm) wooden posts each 8 ft (2.5 m) in length. Drive them into the ground to a depth of 24 in (60 cm) at intervals of 12–16 ft (4–5 m), and brace the posts at either end of the row with diagonal struts. Stretch horizontal lengths of heavy-gauge galvanized wire between them: single wires at 16 in (40 cm) and 2 ft (60 cm) from the ground, and double wires at 3 ft (90 cm), 4 ft (1.2 m), and 5 ft (1.5 m).

Indoors, in a greenhouse or sunroom, attach single horizontal wires to the wall or frame of the building, spacing them 10–12 in (25–30 cm) apart and at least 12 in (30 cm) away from walls or windows.

This cordon-trained indoor vine is putting on healthy new growth in spring. The flower trusses, which are visible toward the top of the vine, will bear fruit during the coming summer.

Pruning a single cordon vine

The method shown here is most often used for greenhouse grapes, though it is also widely employed outdoors. Growth consists of a single upright stem (the cordon) from which horizontal, fruit-bearing laterals shoot out left and right, like arms. It is sometimes known as the "rod-and-spur" system, because the central cordon is termed the rod and because the laterals grow from spurs that form on it. The laterals are pruned back and grow afresh each year.

1st winter pruning
LATE FALL–EARLY WINTER

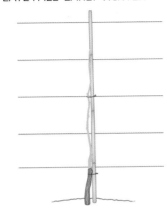

- If you planted in late fall or early winter, cut down the leader to a strong, healthy bud about 12 in (30 cm) above ground level.
- If you planted any later, leave the vine to grow or it will weep sap.

1st summer pruning
LATE SPRING–LATE SUMMER

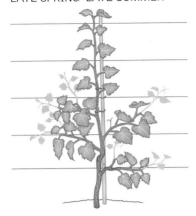

- Keep pruning to a minimum. Let the central leader grow. It may reach a height of 10 ft (3 m) or more. Tie it in to a cane or thin stake.
- Cut back all laterals growing directly from the leader so that they have only 5–6 leaves left.
- Pinch out any new sideshoots growing from the laterals to just 1 leaf.

2nd winter pruning
LATE FALL–EARLY WINTER

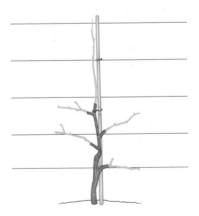

- Prune when the vine enters dormancy—as soon as the leaves have fallen.
- Cut back the central leader by about two-thirds of the growth it put on last year. Only brown stem that has ripened should remain.
- Prune laterals back to 1–2 healthy-looking buds.

2nd summer pruning
LATE SPRING–LATE SUMMER

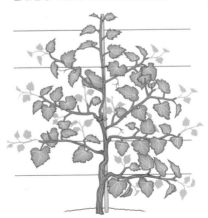

- It's best not to let the vine produce any grapes this year, so pinch out any flowers that form.
- Tie in the central leader as it grows.
- Cut back all laterals to 5–6 leaves.
- Pinch out sideshoots growing from the laterals to just 1 leaf.

3rd winter pruning
LATE FALL–EARLY WINTER

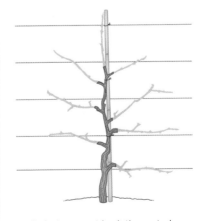

- As last year, cut back the central leader by about one-half or two-thirds of the growth it made last year. Remove wood that is still green, leaving only brown, ripened stem remaining.
- Prune laterals back to 1–2 healthy-looking buds.

Spring pruning an established cordon
MID–LATE SPRING

Summer pruning an established cordon
EARLY–MIDSUMMER

Winter pruning an established cordon
LATE FALL
and EARLY-MIDWINTER

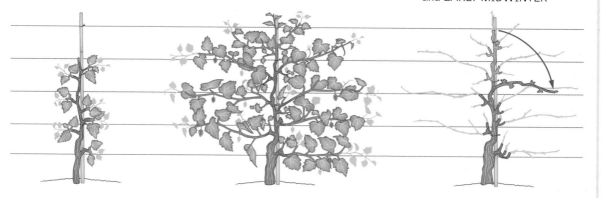

- In spring, new shoots will emerge from the spurs on the central leader.
- Remove all except 2 shoots from each spur. The 1st (the strongest) will form the lateral that bears this year's fruit. The 2nd is for backup, in case the 1st is damaged or dies.
- Once the 1st new lateral is growing strongly, pinch back the 2nd to just 2 leaves.

- Tie in the central leader as it grows.
- Cut back all laterals without flower trusses to 5–6 leaves.
- Cut back laterals with flower trusses to 2 leaves beyond the farthest truss and tie them in to horizontal wires.
- Remove surplus flower trusses. Leave just 1 per lateral for dessert grapes, and 1 per 12 in (30 cm) for wine grapes.
- Pinch out sideshoots growing from the laterals to just 1 leaf.

- Prune back the laterals that fruited last summer to 1–2 healthy-looking buds.
- Thin out old, congested spurs by removing surplus wood with a pruning saw.
- Cut back the central leader to a bud facing in the opposite direction from last year's. It should be just below the topmost wire.
- In late winter, before growth begins, release the top half of the central leader so that it bends over horizontally. Tie it loosely to one side. Doing this ensures that new shoots form on all the spurs, not just the upper ones.
- In spring, when shoots start to emerge, lift the central leader back into position and re-tie it.

In spring, restrict sideshoots to two per spur. Once you can tell which is the stronger, start training it horizontally, then remove the weaker one, along with any other new growth.

Pruning a double guyot vine

The method shown here is most often used for grapes grown outdoors, supported on posts and wires. It's also the system you're likely to see in commercial vineyards. It differs from the cordon method in that there is no tall, single upright stem. Instead, each year just three shoots are grown from a short, stubby trunk or leg. Two are trained horizontally as arms, one to the left and one to the right. From these two arms, shoots grow vertically to carry the current summer's fruit. The third, central shoot is cut back hard. Its job during the summer is not to bear fruit at all but to produce the three main shoots required for the following year.

1st winter pruning
NOVEMBER–DECEMBER

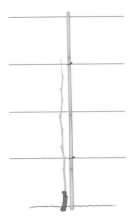

- If you planted in November or December, cut down the leader to a strong, healthy bud about 6 in (15 cm) above ground level.
- If you planted any later, leave it to grow on or it will weep sap.

1st summer pruning
MAY–AUGUST

- Keep pruning to a minimum. Let the central leader grow, and tie it in to a cane or thin stake as it does so.
- Cut off completely any strong laterals growing upward in competition with the leader.
- Prune back all other laterals so that they have only 5–6 leaves left.

2nd winter pruning
NOVEMBER–DECEMBER

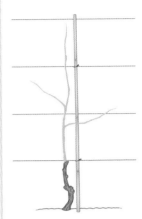

- Prune as soon as the leaves have fallen, when the vine enters its dormant period.
- Cut back the central leader to about 15 in (38 cm) above ground level—just below the bottom wire. Ensure at least 3 strong, healthy buds remain.

Winter pruning an established guyot
NOVEMBER–DECEMBER

- Untie and remove completely the two horizontal arms, together with all their vertical shoots. Having fruited in the summer they are no longer required.
- Of the 3 remaining shoots, cut back the central one to 3–4 buds in preparation for the following year.
- Prune back the other 2 shoots to about 2 ft (60 cm), with 8–12 buds on each.
- Gently bend them down either side of the main stem and tie them in place so they will produce vertical shoots next summer.

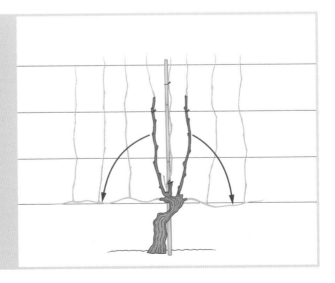

2nd summer pruning
MAY–AUGUST

- 3 strong shoots should grow from the buds you left last winter.
- As they grow, gather them together with string and tie them loosely to the cane or stake.
- Repeatedly pinch out all other new shoots growing from the base or leg of the vine.

3rd winter pruning
NOVEMBER–DECEMBER

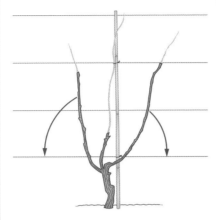

- Cut back the central shoot to 3–4 strong, healthy buds. Growth from these buds should form the 3 main shoots for the year after next.
- Prune back the other 2 shoots to a length of about 2 ft (60 cm). Each should have 8–12 strong, healthy buds.
- Gently bend these shoots down in an arc on either side of the main stem and tie them to the lowest horizontal wire. New shoots will grow vertically from them during the summer.

3rd summer pruning
MAY–AUGUST

- As shoots grow vertically from the two horizontal arms, thread them between the double wires or tie them in. Remove the growing tips when they reach the top wire, and pinch out completely any small new sideshoots.
- As last year, 3 strong new shoots should grow from the buds you left on the central stem last winter. If there are more than 3 remove them.
- As the 3 central shoots grow, tie them in. Remove any flowers and pinch out sideshoots to just 1 leaf.

Summer pruning an established guyot
MAY–AUGUST

- Thread or tie in vertical shoots. Remove the growing tips when they reach the top wire, and pinch out completely any new sideshoots.
- Restrict bunches of grapes to 1 per 12 in (30 cm).
- Remove any more than 3 new shoots growing from last winter's central stem. As they grow, tie them in, remove any flowers, and pinch out any young sideshoots they produce to just 1 leaf.

What can go wrong

Leaves, shoots, and stems

1 Leaves mottled and bronzed
Spider mites can cause upper surfaces of leaves to become speckled or mottled with pale yellow-bronze spots, then dry up and die. Fine silk webbing may also be visible.
■ See **Spider mites** (p.340).

2 Blisters and feltlike patches on leaves
Blistering on the upper surface of leaves and hairy, feltlike patches that turn from white through yellow to brown—usually on the undersides but sometimes above as well—could be caused by the larvae of the grape blister gall midge as they feed inside the leaf. The galls may look alarming, but do not cause any significant harm to the plant. You can handpick and destroy the leaves to reduce the occurrence of galls in the future; no other control is needed.

3 Yellow leaves with green veins
Gradual yellowing of the leaves is usually a sign of a mineral deficiency in the soil. When the margins of leaves are affected (as shown here), a shortage of magnesium is likely. If the yellowing is all over and the veins stand out prominently in green, it may be due to a lack of iron or manganese.
■ See **Common mineral deficiencies** (pp.320–21).

4 Small, white, wax-covered insects on stems
Mealybugs feed on sap that they suck from stems and branches. They are more of a problem on vines grown under cover.
■ See **Mealybugs** (p.337).

5 Leaves curled and distorted
Leaves that curl up at the edges and are twisted or stunted may be a symptom of accidental contamination by hormonal weedkiller—to which grape vines are particularly sensitive. Plants are seriously damaged only rarely; they should recover the following year, and fruit is still safe to eat.

6 Roots eaten
Strawberry root weevil larvae feed on plant roots; they can seriously damage young plants, especially in containers.
■ See **Strawberry root weevils** (p.340).

7 Small, brown, shell-like insects on stems
Scale insects may be found on stems and branches, especially in greenhouses. They are elliptical and have a domed shell.
■ See **Scale insects** (p.340).

White powdery coating on leaves
Gray-white powdery mildew appears on the leaves and can develop into dark blotchy patches. Fruit can be affected too. The cause is a fungus, which tends to be worse in hot, humid conditions.
■ See **Powdery mildew** (p.329).

Yellow blotches on leaves with mildew beneath

Pale green or yellow blotches appear on upper surfaces of leaves with corresponding patches of gray-white mildew below. Leaves may dry up and die. Infected fruit may shrivel.
■ See **Downy mildew** (p.327).

Galls on leaves and roots

Pink or yellow, round galls form on leaves and roots. Inside can be found tiny insects called phylloxera that feed on sap, rather like aphids. Most grapes grown these days are resistant to them.
■ See **Grape phylloxera** (p.336).

Leaves sticky with honeydew

An infestation of whiteflies can cover foliage in sticky honeydew and often patches of black, sooty mold too.
■ See **Whiteflies** (p.341).

Skeletonlike leaves

Japanese beetles feed on leaf tissue, but do not eat the leaf veins.
■ See **Japanese beetles** (p.336).

Fruit

8 Fruit shrinks and fails to ripen

A proportion of grapes in the bunch do not ripen properly—black grapes may turn red, and green ones are translucent. They wither and taste unpleasant.
■ See **Waterberry** (p.331).

9 Fruit rots on the vine

Furry gray–brown mold on the skin of grapes is a sign of botrytis. If grapes develop purple-brown spots and then shrivel up, the cause is likely black rot.
■ See **Botrytis** (p.326) and **Black rot** (p.325).

10 Powdery coating and splits in fruit

Grapes develop a covering of gray-white powdery mold. Later, the mildew turns brown, and grapes become leathery, harden, and split open.
■ See **Powdery mildew** (p.329).

Fruit eaten or stripped

Birds, wasps, and other insects feed on ripening grapes, making holes in the skin, aggravating existing ones, or even stealing the fruits entirely.
■ See **Birds** (p.335) and **Wasps** (p.341).

Berries split open

The larvae of grape berry moths feed on flowers as well as the flesh and seeds of developing grapes. After berries split, they may rot.
■ See **Grape berry moth** (p.336).

Tender and Unusual Fruit

This chapter includes a range of fruits from warm temperate, tropical, or subtropical climates. Many of them require high temperatures, high humidity, and consistently high levels of sunlight. Even those that are not so demanding need hot summers and mild winters. Admittedly, a few are hardy enough to survive all but the coldest of winters, but the principal challenge for the fruit grower isn't simply keeping them alive, but coaxing them into flowering and producing fruit. In Canada and most parts of the U.S., many won't. Even if they could, flowers and new shoots may be killed by spring frost, and ripening fruit may damaged by fall frost.

Unless you live in Florida or California, the only worthwhile strategy is to grow these fruits in a greenhouse, a conservatory, or a hoophouse, where the microclimate can be controlled precisely. Plants can also be grown in containers and moved in and out as the weather dictates. A few may still prove impossible—but, hopefully, you'll have fun trying.

A full-sized mandarin tree such as this one may thrive outdoors in a warm, frost-free climate, but in cooler regions it must be grown in a large greenhouse or hoophouse to fruit so generously.

Citrus fruits

Let's be honest: unless you live in southern California or Florida, you're unlikely to face a glut of homegrown citrus fruit. Citrus trees are subtropical plants that need a lot of heat and light and won't tolerate frost. Having said that, don't rule them out. Take inspiration from the gardeners of northern Europe, where there is a long tradition of growing citrus fruit in greenhouses—it's where the name "orangery" comes from. And there are all sorts of techniques for coaxing a crop from trees grown partly outdoors and partly indoors.

The citrus family includes a wide range of different fruits—including oranges, lemons, limes, grapefruit, pummelos, citrons, mandarins, tangerines, clementines, satsumas, kumquats, and more. The way in which they are classified is complex, and names can be confusing. There are plenty of hybrids, too, such as the mandarinquat (mandarin/kumquat), tangor (tangerine/orange), and tangelo (tangerine/pummelo).

Kumquats resemble oranges but are smaller and slightly more elongated in shape. Unlike oranges, ripe kumquats can be eaten whole, including the skin, though the flesh can be rather tart. All citrus trees make attractive plants for a sheltered yard and work well in pots.

Which types to grow

- **Bushes** Suitable outdoors only for warm climates.
- **Dwarf bushes and dwarf standards** The best choice for growing in a container under cover.

Must-grow citrus fruit

1 'Calamondin'
Thought to be a cross between a mandarin and a kumquat, 'Calamondin' is widely available as a dwarf container-grown tree for growing indoors. Outdoors in hot climates it grows into a large tree. The fruit are small, rounded, and when completely ripe may be sweet enough to eat raw. Otherwise, use for marmalade or cooking.

2 'Buddha's Hand' citron
Not an easy plant to grow since it needs high temperatures, but it's worth trying purely for its bizarre, alien-looking fruit. Each "finger" is a separate segment of fruit, individually covered with skin. Although inedible, this fruit is traditionally prized in East Asia for its wonderful fragrance.

3 Lime
Although we think of limes as green-skinned, that's purely because they are usually harvested and sold before they are ripe. Given time, they turn yellow, like lemons. There are two main types: West Indian (also known as Mexican or Key lime) and Persian, which is slightly hardier and more compact.
■ **Varieties to try** 'Tahiti', 'Bearss'.

4 Mandarin
Cross-breeding and hybridization of mandarins has been taking place for centuries and there are scores of different varieties—including satsumas (which originated in Japan), tangerines (named after Tangier in Morocco), tangors (mandarin-orange hybrids), and clementines (probably the best choice for cool, temperate climates).
■ **Varieties to try** Mandarin 'Fortune', 'Nova'; Clementine 'De Nules', 'Fina'; Tangerine 'Dancy'; Tangor 'Ortanique'; Satsuma 'Okitsu', 'Owari'.

5 Kaffir lime
Grow this for its leaves. They have a lovely, distinctive fragrance and are a key ingredient in Thai cooking. The knobby fruit look intriguing but are in fact almost inedible, and are more likely

to be used in shampoos, insecticides, and air fresheners than in the kitchen. Alternative names include keiffer, k-lime and 'Makrut' lime.

6 Grapefruit
These are among the largest of citrus fruits and take the longest to ripen—up to 18 months from flowering. They need a lot of heat and are not easy to ripen in cool temperate climates. They are heavy, too, and only fairly large trees with strong branches will support them.
■ **Varieties to try** 'Marsh', 'Star Ruby' (or 'Sunrise'). New Zealand grapefruits—crossed with pummelos—require less heat. Try 'Golden Special', 'Wheeny'.

7 Kumquat
Smaller than most citrus fruits, oval-shaped kumquats are juicy, thin-skinned, and when ripe can be eaten raw, as well as being used for cooking. The trees are hardier, too. Botanically speaking, kumquats are classified separately from other citrus fruits, but are regularly crossed with them to produce hybrids, such as limequats and orangequats.
■ **Varieties to try** 'Nagami', 'Eustis', limequat.

8 Lemon
The fastest-growing of the citrus fruits, this is also the one most likely to need pruning to keep it tidy. Most lemons flower more than once a year, and so may carry fruit that will ripen at different times. Pick them when they are full-size and fully colored.
■ **Varieties to try** 'Garey's Eureka', 'Lisbon', 'Meyer', 'Variegated Eureka', 'Verna', 'Villafranca'.

9 Orange
Oranges are classified as either sour or sweet. Sour oranges, of which 'Seville' is probably the best known, are used for making crystallized fruit, drinks, and marmalades. Sweet oranges require more heat to ripen fully. They include navel oranges, which feature a little hole at the end of the fruit (the so-called navel), and blood oranges, which have pink or red flesh.
■ **Varieties to try** 'Salustiana', 'Valencia'; Blood orange 'Moro', 'Sanguinelli'; Navel orange 'Navelina', 'Lane Late', 'Washington'; Sour orange 'Chinotto', 'Seville'.

6

Growing citrus fruit

Citrus trees need a consistently warm, sunny climate. Their natural habitat provides them with year-round temperatures that rarely drop below about 60°F (15°C) and an optimum 60–70 percent humidity. Elsewhere, they may be able to survive short periods of cold, but they are likely to be damaged, perhaps even killed, by frost. They are very difficult, then, to grow outdoors in many areas. They can, however, be grown indoors or in a home greenhouse— at least during the times of the year when they need protection.

When buying a young container-grown tree, look for a healthy plant with plenty of shiny, deep green leaves. Avoid plants with bare stems where leaves have dropped, and check for signs of scale insects or mealy bugs; they are difficult to eradicate. Mature plants in pots will fruit well, given the right conditions.

Flowering and pollination

Although citrus trees usually flower in spring, blossoms can appear at any time of year, provided conditions are warm and moist, and the tree is not dormant. Once set, the fruit takes a long time to ripen—a minimum of about six months, and in the case of grapefruits up to 18 months—so it's not unusual to see both fruit and blossoms on trees at the same time. Almost all citrus are self-fertile, so a single tree can be grown on its own.

Choosing trees

Don't be tempted to grow citrus from seed. It's perfectly possible but it takes too long. Instead, buy container-grown, two- or three-year-old plants from a nursery or garden center that can guarantee they are virus-free. For trees whose permanent home will be in containers, choose plants that have been grafted on to dwarfing rootstocks, and if possible buy named varieties.

When to plant

Outdoors, spring is the best season to plant. It's also the best time to pot up or repot container-grown trees, but don't pot them on too often or plant them in containers that are too large.

Where to grow

Trees planted outdoors need a sunny, sheltered site where there is no danger of frost. If grown permanently indoors, they need a position where they receive plenty of light, especially during summer, coupled with good ventilation. Trees in containers can be moved outdoors onto a warm, sunny deck or patio in summer, and brought into a heated greenhouse or sunroom during winter. Beware: bringing them indoors for the winter is tricky. The chances are that it will be too hot, too dry, and too dark. If you have no alternative, turn the heat down to no higher than 60°F (15°C), keep the air humid by misting or spraying, and make sure the plants are close to large, bright windows.

Soil type

Citrus trees are tolerant, though they grow best in reasonably fertile, free-draining soil with a slightly acidic pH in the range 6.0–7.0. For containers, use a loam-based potting mix or a commercial mix formulated especially for citrus.

Routine care

■ TEMPERATURE CONTROL Citrus trees hate sudden changes in temperature and may respond by dropping their leaves. This doesn't necessarily mean that they've died, and they will probably regrow the following spring, but the shock is not good for the plants. Try to acclimatize them gradually to any kind of change in their growing conditions.

■ FROST PROTECTION Container-grown trees need to be covered or moved indoors if there is any risk of frost. If the tree freezes, it will die.

■ WATERING Outdoors, water regularly during spring and summer, to avoid flower or fruit drop. Plants growing in pots should be soaked thoroughly, to the point where the soil is fully saturated and water drains freely out of the base—but don't let the pot sit in water or the roots may rot. Let the soil almost dry out before you water again. In winter, when trees are dormant or semidormant, you can water a lot less frequently. Getting the balance right is tricky: as many, if not more, citrus plants die from overwatering as from underwatering.

■ FEEDING Outdoors, use a general blended fertilizer two or three times a year between early spring and early fall. For container-grown plants, use special citrus fertilizer. There are two different types: one for winter, and one for summer.

■ MULCHING Outdoors, a layer of mulch around the base of the tree will help retain moisture in the soil and reduce weed growth.

Citrus blossoms are strongly fragrant and if grown under cover are capable of perfuming a whole greenhouse or sunroom.

■ THINNING FRUIT Large, freestanding trees growing outdoors do not need thinning, but don't allow plants in pots to carry more fruit than they are able to support. Remove some if the crop becomes too heavy.

Harvesting and storing

Fruits need plentiful sunlight and high temperatures and humidity in order to ripen fully. The only sure way to tell if fruits such as sweet oranges and mandarins are ripe is to taste them. Timing is less critical with lemons, limes, and other sour citrus fruits. Pick and use them when they are fully colored and no longer seem to be growing larger.

Fruits should keep for a few weeks in a refrigerator, fewer if left at room temperature. If you're not ready to use them right away, it's better to leave them on the tree until you are.

Yield

Yields are hard to quantify as they vary according to the type of fruit, how the tree is being grown, and the climatic conditions. From an average-sized, container-grown tree in a cool temperate region, you might expect 10–20 fruits per year. Large, container-grown trees ten or more years old may produce up to 100 fruits per year.

Pruning and training citrus fruit

Unlike most other fruit trees, citrus trees require very little pruning. When trees are young, remove any low-growing lateral shoots in order to keep the main trunk clear, and cut out any overly vigorous shoots that grow vertically upward in the center of the tree; they are called water shoots and are unlikely to fruit. Thereafter, prune back to a healthy bud any dead, damaged, or diseased growth as soon as you spot it. Watch out for sharp thorns.

Pruning a citrus bush

Full-size trees can be grown outdoors only in warm, frost-free climates. The bush form is the most common. Trees have a short main trunk or central leader, then an open-centered crown made up of a handful of laterals that form the main framework of branches.

Pruning is best carried out before new spring growth starts, but in warm climates you can prune at any time of year. It's difficult to say how long the early stages of shaping a young tree will take; it depends on how quickly the tree grows.

Outdoors in warm temperate or subtropical climates, lemon trees (seen here) can grow up to 20 ft (6 m) tall. Grapefruits can reach 30 ft (10 m) or more, while limes tend to be smaller.

1st pruning

LATE WINTER–EARLY SPRING in cool climates

ANY TIME of YEAR in warm climates

- Newly planted trees should comprise just a single main stem. They do not need staking.
- When the stem reaches 3–4 ft (90–120 cm) high, prune it back to about 2 ft (60 cm). Cut just above a leaf.
- Pinch out any shoots sprouting from the rootstock, below the graft union.

2nd pruning

LATE WINTER–EARLY SPRING in cool climates

ANY TIME of YEAR in warm climates

- Laterals will have formed below your last pruning cut.
- Choose the 3 or 4 strongest and best placed, and prune each back to about 12 in (30 cm) from the main stem.
- Pinch out new shoots growing low down on the main stem, below the laterals.

Subsequent pruning

LATE FALL–EARLY SPRING in cool climates

ANY TIME of YEAR in warm climates

- Laterals will now be starting to form the main branch leaders.
- Cut them back by one-third of the growth they put on since you last pruned them.
- Tip-prune sublaterals or sideshoots by 3–4 leaves.
- Open up any crowded growth in the center.
- Pinch out new shoots growing from the main stem.

Pruning an established citrus bush

LATE FALL–EARLY SPRING in cool climates

ANY TIME of YEAR in warm climates

- While trees are still relatively young, tip-prune main branch leaders if they become too long.
- Prune out any shoots growing into the crown of the tree, in order to keep a fairly open center.
- After harvesting the fruits, cut the shoots that bore them back to a healthy sideshoot that does not have any fruit.
- Once trees are mature, restrict pruning to the removal of any dead, damaged, or diseased growth, and any suckers that grow from the rootstock itself.

Pruning a potted citrus tree

The standard or half-standard form is probably the best choice for citrus grown in containers. It's not difficult to train a young plant—though you should be patient; don't remove too much growth at once. The aim is to create a clean, straight main stem and a bushy, rounded crown. You will need to stake the tree until its roots are well established and its trunk is able to support its own weight.

1st pruning

LATE WINTER–EARLY SPRING in cool climates
ANY TIME of YEAR in warm climates

2nd year pruning

LATE WINTER–EARLY SPRING in cool climates
ANY TIME of YEAR warm climates

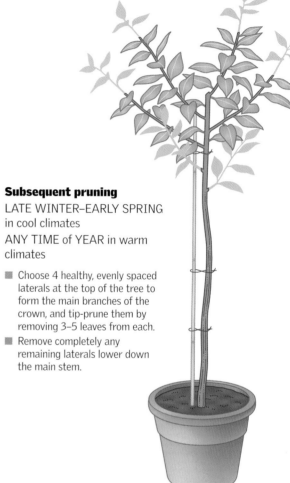

Subsequent pruning

LATE WINTER–EARLY SPRING in cool climates
ANY TIME of YEAR in warm climates

- Choose 4 healthy, evenly spaced laterals at the top of the tree to form the main branches of the crown, and tip-prune them by removing 3–5 leaves from each.
- Remove completely any remaining laterals lower down the main stem.

- Start with a young plant that has a strong, straight, single main stem.
- Tie it in to a vertical cane or stake.
- Prune back each lateral or sideshoot by about one-third.

- Once the tree is tall enough, cut off the central leader or main stem, pruning just above a bud.
- Remove completely the laterals that you pruned last time.
- Leave untouched any new laterals or sideshoots that have appeared above them.
- There is no need to remove single leaves that appear on the main stem. They will drop off naturally.

Pruning an established citrus standard

LATE WINTER–EARLY SPRING in cool climates,
ANY TIME of YEAR in warm climates

- Once established, trees should require very little pruning.
- Tip-prune laterals if they get too long, in order to retain a rounded shape to the crown.
- Remove any shoots that appear on the main stem.
- Cut out any dead, damaged, or diseased growth.

What can go wrong

1 Small, brown, shell-like insects on stems
Scale insects may be found on stems and branches, especially in greenhouses or indoors.
■ See **Scale insects** (p.339).

2 Small, white, wax-covered insects on stems
Mealybugs feed on sap that they suck from stems and branches.
■ See **Mealybugs** (p.337).

3 Leaves are mottled and yellowed
If upper surfaces of leaves become speckled or mottled with pale yellow-bronze markings, then dry up and die, the cause may be spider mites. In severe cases, you may see fine silk webbing.
■ See **Spider mites** (p.339).

Leaves are curled and sticky
Both aphids and whiteflies feeding on sap on the undersides of leaves cause them to curl up and become misshapen. Foliage may be sticky with honeydew, on which gray mold may grow.
■ See **Aphids** (p.334) and **Whiteflies** (p.341).

Leaves are yellowed or silvered with black specks
The discoloration is likely to be caused by sap-sucking insects called thrips. The black specks are their excrement.
■ See **Thrips** (p.340).

Leaves drop unexpectedly
A number of things can cause leaves (and sometimes flowers) to fall. Sudden changes in temperature or humidity, overwatering, and underwatering are the most likely causes. Leaves may regrow in time.
■ See **Routine care** (p.289).

Leaves and stems wilt and die back
Citrus trees planted in poorly drained soil are very prone to fungal infections that cause rot—as are container-grown plants that are overwatered or allowed to stand in water.
■ See **Foot and root rots** (p.327).

Dark brown patches on skin of fruit
These spots are a symptom of scab, a fungal disease.
■ See **Scab** (p.330).

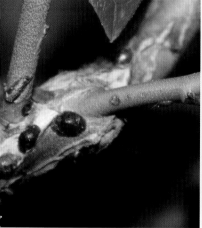

Melons

There are hundreds, if not thousands, of different melons in cultivation around the world, many of which are notoriously difficult to classify and name with any consistency. However, the main distinction is between watermelons and other types of melons. What we call melons usually have pale green, yellow, or orange flesh that is dense, meltingly sweet, and wonderfully aromatic. They include cantaloupes, muskmelons, and yellow or green, thicker-skinned winter melons, such as honeydews. Watermelons are usually larger and have red or pink flesh that is crisper and juicer.

Melons are tropical or subtropical plants and need high temperatures and high humidity to grow properly. In the southern half of the country, melons will grow well in most areas. However, if you have short or cool summers, you may need to grow them in a cold frame or greenhouse, or use black plastic and row covers. Recent years have seen the introduction of new cantaloupe varieties bred to tolerate cooler outdoor conditions. Even so, they're unlikely to ripen fully unless they enjoy a good spell of hot, sunny summer weather.

When melons are about the size of grapefruit, support them in nets or string bags. The heavy fruit contain a lot of water and may split and spoil if they ripen and fall to the ground.

Must-grow melons

1 'Charentais'
These melons are referred to as either a named variety or a type. They are cantaloupes and originate from France, where they are widely grown for their sweet, scented, dark-orange flesh.

2 Cantaloupe melons
Most are round or slightly flattened with ridged gray-green or pale yellow-brown skin that may or may not have lacy, netlike patterning. The flesh is pale green, orange, or pink. The best choice for cool climates.
■ **Varieties to try** 'Amber Nectar' (or 'Castella'), 'Antalya', 'Emir', 'Hearts of Gold', 'Sweetheart'.

3 Winter melons
This group includes honeydew and casaba melons. They usually start to ripen as temperatures begin to fall. Oval with yellow or green skins, their flesh is sweet, but they aren't as fragrant as cantaloupes and muskmelons.
■ **Varieties to try** 'Honeydew Green Flesh', 'Jade Lady', 'Rocky Ford'.

4 Muskmelons
Their smooth yellow, green, or pale brown skins have distinctive netlike markings, and the flesh is usually orange or pink and very sweet. A heated greenhouse is vital in cool climates.
■ **Varieties to try** 'Blenheim Orange', 'Hale's Best Jumbo', 'Hero of Lockinge'.

5 'Ogen'
Reputedly named after the kibbutz in Israel where the prototype was first bred, several slightly different forms of 'Ogen' exist. Most have smooth, slightly netted skins, turning from light green to yellow when ripe. The flesh is pale green.

6 Watermelons
These need the warmest, most humid climate. Given the right growing conditions, they can be enormous—up to 100 lb (45 kg) in weight. Flesh is red, pink, or orange, crisp, and juicy.
■ **Varieties to try** 'Blacktail Mountain', 'Charleston Grey', 'Sugar Baby'.

Growing melons

Melons are annuals and need to be started from seed each year. They're usually available as potted seedlings at garden centers, but you'll get a much wider choice if you buy seeds and raise them yourself. Sow the seeds in pots indoors and plant them out when the soil is warm enough. When you grow melons depends on your climate: outdoors in the garden, under row covers or in cold frames, or in a greenhouse or hoophouse.

The year at a glance

	spring			summer			fall			winter		
	E	M	L	E	M	L	E	M	L	E	M	L
sow seeds	▬	▬	▬									▬
plant greenhouse		▬	▬	▬								
plant outdoors			▬									
harvest greenhouse				▬	▬	▬	▬					
harvest outdoors					▬	▬	▬					

When to sow and plant

For plants that will be grown outdoors, sow seeds in pots in April and germinate them indoors or under cover. They should be ready to plant out in May or June, when the soil is warm and frosts are over. For plants to be grown in a heated greenhouse, you can sow earlier—in February and March for crops in June and July. And in an unheated greenhouse, sow in May or June for crops in September and October.

Melons need heat to get them off to a good start. Seeds are unlikely to germinate at all if the

SOWING MELON SEEDS

Germination can be hit-and-miss, so it's always best to sow seeds in pots and keep them warm until seedlings appear. You can then plant them out when conditions are favorable.

1 Sow seeds into damp potting mix at a depth of about ½ in (1 cm), two or three to a pot.

2 Put a clear plastic bag over each pot and secure it with a rubber band.

3 Place the pots indoors on a sunny windowsill, each in its individual propagation tent.

4 Once seedlings have emerged—in a week to ten days—move the plants outdoors during the day to harden them off.

temperature is below 64°F (18°C). Thereafter, 77–86°F (25–30°C) is ideal, though some varieties will tolerate cooler conditions.

Where to plant

Outdoors, choose a sheltered, sunny site. In cool climates, you'll need a warm sun trap and a long, hot summer. You may also need to protect plants with cloches. Even a mild frost will kill them.

Melons can be grown in cold frames filled with a pre-prepared mix of good soil and well-rotted compost or manure. Mound up the soil slightly and plant seedlings at the top to prevent waterlogging.

In greenhouses, melons can be planted either directly into borders or in growing bags. Plant them in small mounds in the soil to ensure they don't get waterlogged, or use special collars to help keep water off the stems (see left).

Soil type

Melons like deep, fertile soil with a pH of 6.5–7. It should be free-draining but constantly moist, with plenty of organic material incorporated before planting.

Fit a collar around the stem so you can water the surrounding soil without wetting the plant. This reduces the risk of rots. Special terra-cotta collars are available but improvised plastic ones work just as well.

GROWING MELONS IN A COLD FRAME

In truth, most traditional cold frames used for growing melons outdoors in cool temperate climates are too small. You'll be lucky to get more than one plant in each. However, the large portable cold frames shown here are similar to low plastic tunnels, and offer a lot more space.

1 Prepare the ground with a mulch of well-rotted compost or manure. Clear a number of planting holes in the soil and water thoroughly.

2 Cover the area that will form the base of the frame with black plastic.

3 Cut holes in the plastic above the pre-prepared planting holes.

4 Plant pot-grown melons through the holes in the plastic. The plastic retains moisture, inhibits weeds, and keeps the growing melons dry and clean.

Planting distances

- OUTDOORS IN OPEN GROUND 3 ft (1 m) apart.
- IN A GREENHOUSE single cordons 16 in (40 cm), double cordons 24 in (60 cm) apart.

Flowering and pollination

When grown outdoors in warm climates, insects usually pollinate melons quite readily. If you can time the opening and closing of the lid or window on a cold frame to coincide with a spell of warm weather, and the moment when the flowers are all fully open, they may do the same. If not, plants will need pollinating by hand. Melons grown in a greenhouse certainly require it.

Melons are self-fertile. They produce both male and female flowers, which will pollinate one another. They are not difficult to tell apart. Use a soft, dry brush to collect pollen from the male flowers and transfer it to the female ones. Alternatively, remove a male flower, pick off the petals, and push it carefully into the center of each of the female flowers. Repeat every day for a week or so.

Routine care

- WATERING Regular watering is important once plants have become established. The soil must remain constantly moist—not too wet, not too dry. Water carefully, since splashing the stems can cause them to rot.
- FEEDING Once fruit have formed, feed weekly with a liquid tomato fertilizer. Stop when the fruit are almost ripe.
- VENTILATION Melons need the right mix of high humidity and good ventilation. As long as it's not too cold, take particular care to open cold-frame lids and greenhouse windows when the flowers

(clockwise from top left) **Female flowers** have a rounded swelling at the base of their petals. It is where the fruit will develop if fertilization takes place. **Male flowers** are slender and straight, without any visible bulge. They are always the first to appear. **Greenhouse melons** sown and planted at different times will give you an early and a late crop. The main stems are trained up canes, with the laterals or sideshoots supported on horizontal wires.

Cut back shoots to two leaves beyond the melon you want to grow and ripen.

(below, left to right) **Tie in to horizontal wires** the lateral shoots that grow from either side of the main stem or cordon, using flexible plant ties. **Pinch out** any tendrils that grow from the shoots. Now that you've tied them in, they're not needed for support and simply divert energy from developing fruit.

are ready for pollination and at the end of the growing season, when the fruit are ripening. That's when the plants need a dry atmosphere. At other times, spray or damp down to raise the humidity. If necessary, paint or shade panes of glass to prevent sun scorch.

Pruning and training

Melons are vines and so naturally trail or climb. Outdoor melons and those grown in cold frames are usually left to sprawl over the ground. Greenhouse melons, however, need training to help them climb. The usual technique is to construct a support system from canes and wires, and to train them vertically up toward the roof of the greenhouse.

Melons don't really need pruning, but you may find that it's a good idea to limit their growth. For outdoor and cold-frame melons, pinch out the tip of the main stem once five leaves have appeared, and do the same for greenhouse melons once the main stem reaches a height of about 5–6 ft (1.5–2 m). This encourages the growth of the sideshoots that will form the main laterals. Traditional wisdom has it that melons grown outdoors or in a cold frame should be allowed only four laterals or main shoots each, and greenhouse melons no more than six. Once these have formed, you should pinch out the growing tip of each lateral when it has five leaves.

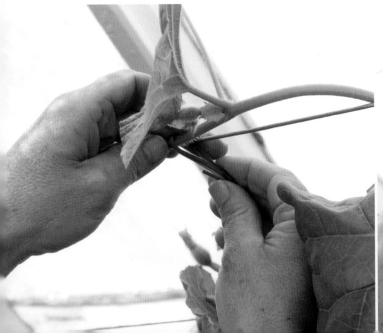

This will stimulate the growth of sublaterals or sideshoots on which flowers appear. If pollination is successful, fruit will begin to develop. When they reach the size of golf balls, choose the healthiest looking melon on each lateral, pinch out the shoot two leaves beyond it, and remove all other flowers and fruit. You should now have a maximum of either four or six melons per plant. If you have fewer, that's fine. In fact, plants with only one or two are likely to produce larger fruit.

Harvesting and storing

Leave melons on the vine for as long as possible to ripen. The longer you leave them, the sweeter and more aromatic they will become. But leave them too long, and they will start to rot—if they don't fall off first. Telltale signs include slight cracking at the end attached to the stalk, softening at the other end, and a gradually intensifying fragrance. As the optimal moment approaches, apply a gentle squeeze-and-sniff test a couple of times a day.

You can store melons in the refrigerator, but don't serve them too cold or they won't release their full aroma.

Yield

- ◼ OUTDOOR MELONS maximum 4 per plant.
- ◼ GREENHOUSE MELONS maximum 6 per plant.

Support ripening melons with nets or string bags. Otherwise the heavy fruits will snap the stems they are growing on, or fall to the ground and become bruised and damaged.

WHAT CAN GO WRONG

Leaves are curled and sticky
See **Aphids** (p.334) and **Whiteflies** (p.341).

Mottled yellow leaves, purple spots on leaf undersides
◼ See **Downy mildew** (p.327).

Holes in leaves
Cucumber beetles chew on leaves and blossoms, and their feeding can spread viruses. Cover young plants with row covers to prevent damage; spray plants with kaolin clay to repel the beetles. Hand-pick beetles; spray with pyrethrins.

Leaves develop pale green patches, then wilt and die
Squash bugs suck sap from plants, eventually killing leaves and weakening the plants. Hand-pick or spray with neem. Protect plants with row covers when possible to prevent damage.

Leaves with brown blotches or spots
Various fungal and bacterial diseases cause these symptoms, including anthracnose, angular leaf spot, and scab. Some may be controlled by copper sprays. Plant resistant cultivars when available.

Plants wilt suddenly
Squash vine borers tunnel inside vines, causing sudden wilting and sometimes killing plants. Cover stem bases with aluminum foil to prevent adults from laying eggs. Slit vines and kill the borers inside. Fusarium and bacterial wilt can also cause wilt; destroy infected plants.

Kiwifruit

Despite the name "kiwi," these fruit are not actually native to New Zealand. Their original name, Chinese gooseberry, gives a much better indication of where they first came from: eastern Asia. However, New Zealanders renamed them, marketed them aggressively, and began to export them to the rest of the world.

The plants are not hard to grow. In fact, they are very vigorous, and left to their own devices they can grow 28 ft (9 m) or more. But unless you can give them the right growing conditions, it's not so easy to get them to fruit.

(top to bottom) **Kiwifruit** are about the size of chicken eggs, with brown, slightly furry skins. Inside, the flesh is bright green with a mass of small, edible, black seeds. **Hardy varieties** have been bred that are virtually hairless. The skins are very smooth and you don't need to peel the fruit before eating them.

Growing kiwifruit

Kiwifruit are deciduous vines and will survive very mild winters, but most U.S. gardeners would be better off growing hardy kiwi instead of the tender type. The spring shoots and blossoms of tender kiwi are easily damaged by even a slight frost. The fruit need a sunny site and a hot summer if they are to ripen properly. You should probably attempt kiwifruit only if you are able to grow dessert grapes outdoors. They are, unfortunately, too large for a greenhouse.

The year at a glance

	spring			summer			fall			winter		
	E	M	L	E	M	L	E	M	L	E	M	L
plant	▬						▬	▬	▬			
summer-prune				▬	▬	▬						
winter-prune							▬	▬	▬	▬	▬	▬
harvest							▬					

Choosing a variety

Some kiwifruit are self-fertile and will pollinate themselves. Others are not, and bear only male flowers or only female flowers. A female kiwifruit must be planted with a male or self-fertile partner in order to produce fruit.

'Jenny' is the best-known modern, self-fertile variety. Among traditional, non-self-fertile kiwifruit, the most widely available female plants are 'Hayward' and 'Bruno'. 'Tomuri' is a good choice as a male partner.

So-called hardy kiwifruit are slightly different from the regular type. The fruits are smaller and can be eaten whole, including the skin, like grapes. Varieties include 'Issai' and 'Ananasnaya'.

When and where to plant

Plant in late fall or early spring during the period of winter dormancy. Kiwifruit grow best in a warm, sheltered corner or against a south-facing wall, away from any danger of frost pockets.

Soil type

Kiwifruit need fertile, free-draining soil with a pH of about 6.5–7.

(top to bottom) **New growth** is very vulnerable to spring frost, and tender young shoots and buds are easily damaged. Protect with row cover if necessary. **Kiwifruit flowers** are white or cream in color, fragrant, and can measure up to 1½ in (4 cm) in diameter. They may be either male or female.

Planting distances

10–16 ft (3–5 m) apart.

Routine care

■ WATERING Water generously and regularly throughout the growing season. Ease off in the fall.
■ FEEDING Apply a general compound fertilizer in early spring, before growth starts.
■ MULCHING In spring, after feeding, spread a layer of organic mulch around the base of the plants.

Pruning and training

Kiwifruit are so vigorous that unless you train and prune them regularly, you'll end up with a knotted mass of vines with too much foliage and not enough fruit. There are two approaches to training: one formal, the other informal. Both need strong support systems, because established vines become very heavy.

The formal method is to grow the plants as espaliers, with a vertical central stem from which laterals spread out left and right, supported on horizontal wires about 18 in (45 cm) apart. The laterals will produce sublaterals or sideshoots. You can develop these into fruiting spurs if you pinch them back to between five and seven leaves beyond the final fruit during the summer. Then prune them again in winter, this time to two buds beyond the point where the final fruit grew until you picked it. The espalier system is best for self-fertile varieties, where you are growing just one plant.

The informal method allows the vines to scramble up over an arbor or trellis, though it helps if you can train laterals along overhead wires or wooden struts once they reach the top. As with an espalier, pinch out growing tips in summer, and in winter cut back last year's growth in order to develop a system of fruiting spurs. If you are growing varieties that are not self-fertile, plant a male and female together, in the same planting hole if necessary.

Harvesting and storing

Kiwifruit may not ripen until October. However, in some areas you may have to pick them earlier, before they are damaged by the first frost. They will continue to ripen indoors, gradually becoming softer. In fact, stored in a cool dry place, they should keep for a couple of months or more.

Yield

It takes a long time for a kiwifruit to reach its full fruiting potential—up to seven years in some cases. At that point, a single vine may produce 22–33 lb (10–15 kg) of fruit.

What can go wrong

Very few pests and diseases seem to trouble kiwifruit. Drought or irregular watering may cause leaves to fall, and small, underdeveloped fruit are usually a sign of a poor summer—too cold and not enough sunshine.

A kiwi vine climbs up a homemade arbor built from sturdy wooden poles supporting a metal frame.

Cape gooseberries

Cape gooseberries, also known as husk cherries and ground cherries, get their name from the Cape of Good Hope, at the southern tip of Africa, where they were widely grown in the 19th century. They are also known as *Physalis*, which is their botanical name. They are part of the same plant family as tomatoes, eggplant, and potatoes, and their closest relatives are the tomatillo, which is also edible, and the ornamental garden plant Chinese lantern, which is not.

Cape gooseberries are small, round, orange fruit that grow inside a papery shell or husk, and have a distinctive tart-sweet flavor that, to some, is an acquired taste. They need a warm climate to produce fruit reliably. However, if you can grow tomatoes and eggplant successfully in your garden, it's worth giving Cape gooseberries a try.

Fruits ripen in stages from late summer onward and, like Chinese lanterns (*Physalis alkekengi*), they are encased in a similar, though less colorful, papery husk. You can leave fruit on the plant until deep yellow and fully ripe, as birds don't seem to find them very palatable, but pick them before the first frost.

Growing Cape gooseberries

Cape gooseberries are perennials, but they are not hardy and won't survive cold winters. It's therefore best to treat them as annuals and grow them afresh from seed every year. They need much the same growing conditions as tomatoes. There are no named varieties.

The year at a glance

	spring			summer			fall			winter		
	E	M	L	E	M	L	E	M	L	E	M	L
sow indoors	▬											
plant undercover		▬	▬									
plant outdoors		▬	▬									
harvest				▬	▬	▬						

When and where to sow

Sow indoors in mid-spring. Use seed flats or pots filled with standard seed-starting mix and sow at a depth of ¼ in (½ cm). Either cover and place on a sunny windowsill or use a heated propagator. Germination requires a steady minimum temperature of about 64°F (18°C).

When and where to plant

If you have a sunny, sheltered site, plant out seedlings directly into the ground in late spring or early summer. If not, grow them in containers or plant them in a greenhouse border where they can be trained up canes or stakes.

Soil type

Cape gooseberries need fertile, well-drained soil with a slightly acidic pH of about 6.5.

Planting distances

- PLANTS 30 in (75 cm) apart.
- ROW SPACING 3–4 ft (1–1.2 m) apart.

Growing in containers

Transplant seedlings into a pot or container with a diameter of at least 12–15 in (30–38 cm), and fill it with potting mix blended with a little sand or coarse grit to improve drainage. Containers can be brought under cover in cold weather and moved onto a warm deck or balcony during summer.

Routine care

- WATERING Water regularly, but don't overdo it or you'll end up with too much foliage. Plants don't like being waterlogged.
- FEEDING Feed once or twice with tomato fertilizer when the fruit start to form.
- PINCHING OUT If the plant seems reluctant to

PLANTING CAPE GOOSEBERRIES

Prepare your planting site in advance by removing any weeds, digging in some well-rotted organic matter, and raking over the surface of the soil to break up any lumps. Harden off indoor-raised seedlings before planting them out.

1 Dig a hole that will comfortably accommodate the rootball of the pot-grown seedling. Draw the soil around it, firm it down, and water it in thoroughly.

2 Protect with a cloche if the wind is still cold or if there is any risk of overnight frost.

(above, left to right) **Flowers** may keep appearing until quite late in the summer, so it's not unusual to see both fruit and flowers on a single branch at the same time. **Cape gooseberries** are ready to pick when the green husks have dried out and turned a pale brown color, and the fruit inside are bright orange-yellow. They get sweeter as they ripen—although they will always have a sharp tang. (below). **Unfold** and discard the inedible papery husks to eat the fruit raw or, if you have a good crop, make jelly.

produce flowers, pinch out the growing tips.

■ STAKING Plants can grow quite tall, and may need staking and tying loosely with string.

Harvesting and storing

As they ripen, the outer husks or lanterns enclosing the fruit become papery and pale brown. Inside, the fruit themselves turn an ever-deepening yellow-orange and their flavor intensifies. In the case of plants grown outdoors, it's often a race to see if the fruit will ripen before the arrival of the first frost. If you have to pick them before they are fully ripe, don't worry; they will go on ripening somewhere dry and sunny indoors. Even ripe fruit can be stored in their husks for several weeks.

What can go wrong

Cape gooseberries are mercifully trouble-free. Outdoors, aphids (see p.334) can be problematic. Under cover, the usual greenhouse pests and diseases may strike, including whiteflies (see p.341) and powdery mildew (see p.329).

Other tender and unusual fruit

These plants are not for everyone. If you live in a cool temperate region, remember that they are a long way from home. Their natural habitat may be either dry scrub and semidesert, or hot, humid, subtropical and tropical climates, so growing them indoors or in a greenhouse will be your only option.

Avocados

Avocados are fun to grow, although whether or not you can persuade them to produce any fruit is another matter entirely. Their native habitat in tropical Central America provides them with consistent high temperatures and high humidity. In cool climates they will grow under cover but need heat to stand any chance of fruiting.

■ HOW TO GROW Avocados can be grown from seed. Remove the stone, soak it in hot water, and plant it in a small pot filled with potting mix. Slicing off the top and dipping it in fungicide sometimes speeds up germination, but you may still have to wait weeks or even months for a shoot to appear. It's easier to buy ready-grown plants grafted onto special disease-resistant rootstocks. You may need more than one to guarantee cross-pollination. Avocados grown under cover need temperatures of 68–86°F (20–30°C), 70 percent humidity, and regular watering and feeding. Even then, insufficient sunlight and days that are too short may mean that they never fruit.

Bananas

Wild bananas came originally from southeast Asia, although they are now grown in most tropical regions of the world. In spite of the fact that they are tree-sized, they are not trees at all; they are in fact large stalks or shoots that sprout from underground rhizomes.

■ HOW TO GROW One look at the conditions required to grow a banana that produces fruit will give you an immediate idea of what chance you have: a steady temperature of about 80°F (27°C) during the day and 68°F (20°C) at night, constant humidity of at least 50 percent, and around twelve hours of bright light every day. Even if you think you can provide this in a greenhouse or hoophouse, bear in mind that banana plants are very large: they can quickly grow to 25 ft (8 m) in height. Except in the tropics, this is one for the dedicated enthusiast.

Loquats

Also known as Japanese medlars or plums, loquats are orange-yellow fruits about the size of apricots,

with soft, aromatic flesh that may be sweet or sour depending on its ripeness. The trees are evergreen and originate in China, though they are now widely grown in regions with subtropical or Mediterranean climates. Unusually, they flower in the fall and bear fruit in the spring—so they need mild winters if they are to avoid frost damage.

■ HOW TO GROW Loquats are tolerant, fairly hardy, and easy to grow, though in cool temperate climates they may not ever flower or set fruit unless grown under cover. In warm climates, plant in fall in a sunny, sheltered spot. Avoid frost pockets. Water and feed young trees during the growing season. Harvest the fruit when they have softened slightly and are fully ripe.

Mangos

Like avocados, growing mangos is something you're more likely to do out of curiosity than as a serious attempt to produce fruit. They are tropical plants native to India and southeast Asia, and will fruit only in similarly hot climates. Even the hardiest varieties need average temperatures of about 77°F (25°C) and very high light intensity. Frost will almost certainly kill them.

■ HOW TO GROW It's possible to grow a mango from seed, if you remove the husk before planting, but once the seed has germinated, it will probably produce a tree that is far too vigorous and won't bear fruit. Instead, buy a young tree grafted onto a dwarfing rootstock. Outdoors, mangos need a sheltered site in full sun, and watering in dry spells.

Under cover, they need heat, light, and—except when in flower—high humidity. During the growing season, water with room-temperature rainwater and feed with liquid tomato fertilizer.

Olives

Unless you live in a hot, dry area of California or Arizona, it's not easy to grow your own olives. Even if you get fruit to ripen, they need to be cured in salt or lye (sodium hydroxide) to remove excessive bitterness, and then stored in oil or brine. And you'd need a small orchard to produce enough to make oil. However, the gnarled, long-lived, evergreen trees are extremely attractive, and in areas with reasonably warm winters, they are worth growing purely for ornamental reasons.

■ HOW TO GROW Plant in free-draining soil in a sheltered, sunny location. In cooler areas, grow trees in containers so that you can bring them under cover in winter. Most varieties are self-fertile, though all are more likely to flower and set fruit if pollinated by a partner. Accustomed to dry, infertile conditions, mature olives will tolerate periods without much water and do not need

(below, far left to right) **Avocados** will struggle to ripen in cool, temperate climates, but you can still enjoy their fragrant flowers. **Bananas** are best grown under cover, but even small varieties are fairly tall. **Loquat** trees may bear fruit if grown under glass. **Mangos** are very big trees, so choose a dwarf variety. **Olives** are popular trees and often grown as standards in containers.

feeding. Prune them in spring, cutting back old growth and encouraging plenty of new sideshoots, on which fruit should be borne the following year.

Papayas

Papayas are tropical fruit that look a little like melons. They originally came from Central America, although they are now grown widely around the world. Confusingly, they are sometimes also called pawpaws, but they are not the same species as our native pawpaw (see right).

■ HOW TO GROW Outdoors, papayas will grow and fruit successfully in hot, sunny, humid conditions. Frost, cold winds, and waterlogged soil will damage, if not kill, them. Pollination is a challenge, too. Some plants bear both male and female flowers, and will self-pollinate. Others are strictly single-sex, with flowers that are either all male or all female. Worse still, next year they may swap gender. To preempt such transsexual behavior, the safest thing is to plant several trees as neighbors. In cool climates, papayas must be grown in a tall heated greenhouse or hoophouse.

Passion fruit

Of this large family of evergreen vines, purple granadilla is the passion fruit usually grown for its fruit. They are oval and about the size of small plums, with wrinkled purple or yellow skins and yellow-orange flesh. The pulpy, aromatic seeds can be scooped straight from the fruit.

■ HOW TO GROW Passion fruit need frost-free winters and average temperatures of 68–75°F (20–24°C) during the growing season. They may be happy in the corner of a sunny patio or against a south-facing wall, but if not, grow them under cover. Propagate seeds indoors and plant out in May or June (in the same way as melons, see p.297). Train the vines up wires or a trellis. Water plentifully and feed with tomato fertilizer. In winter, cut back last year's sideshoots to within two buds of the main stems; they won't fruit again, so you are aiming to encourage new growth that will.

Pawpaws

Also known as prairie bananas and custard bananas, pawpaws grow wild throughout the eastern United States. This native fruit will grow well in all parts of the United States except colder parts of New England and the upper Midwest and coastal areas with cool summers. When they are ripe, the yellow-green fruit have a creamy flesh with a mild tropical-fruit flavor resembling bananas, mangos, and citrus. But don't eat them when they are unripe because they can cause stomach upsets.

■ HOW TO GROW Plant during the dormant season, in late fall or early spring. Choose a sheltered site with deep, fertile, free-draining soil. Some varieties are self-fertile, but others may need pollinating by hand. Feed and water regularly, especially in the spring and early summer. Harvest in September or October.

Pepinos

The pepino is a little like a small melon. The fruit are yellow, cream, or green, with juicy, orange-yellow flesh that tastes like a combination of melon, pear, and cucumber. For that reason, they are sometimes known as melon pears. They come from the Andes in South America, and are members of the same family as potatoes and tomatoes.

■ HOW TO GROW Grow pepinos from seed in the same way as tomatoes or peppers. Sow in pots in late winter, either indoors on a sunny windowsill or in a propagator. In cool temperate climates, transplant them into containers. They can be put outside once all danger of frost is over and stay there until the fall, when you should bring them under cover to ripen. Support, pinch out, water, and feed them as you would tomato plants.

Persimmons

Japanese persimmons, as their name suggests, are native to Japan, China, and other parts of Asia. They are large trees and can be grown in cool climates, although they are vulnerable to frost in spring, and need warm temperatures in fall if the fruit are to ripen. Depending on the variety, fruit are either astringent (they are high in tannin and too bitter to eat until softened or cooked) or non-astringent (they are sweet enough to eat raw when ripe). American persimmons are hardier but tend to produce small, astringent fruit.

■ HOW TO GROW Choose a sunny, sheltered site and plant in fertile, free-draining soil. Avoid frost pockets. Water if there is any danger of the tree drying out. Persimmons can be grown under cover, although they will need very large containers.

Pineapple

Pineapple originate from Central America. It was Christopher Columbus who brought the first fruit back to Europe at the end of the 15th century. They need subtropical or tropical growing conditions: high temperatures, high humidity, rich soil, and lots of light.

■ HOW TO GROW In cool temperate regions, the only way to grow pineapple is in containers in a greenhouse or hoophouse—a large one, since they can eventually reach 12 ft (4 m) in height. The easiest way to start is with a ripe, store-bought pineapple. Cut off the top, along with about ½ in (1 cm) of the flesh—not too much or it will rot. Stand the crown in a flat dish for a week or so to dry out, maintaining a minimum temperature of about 64°F (18°C). Plant it in a 12-in (30-cm) pot, so that the base of the leaves is at soil level. Now, water regularly, don't let the temperature fall below 68°F (20°C) or rise above 90°F (32°C), feed with liquid tomato fertilizer in spring and summer, keep

(far left to right) **Papayas** are small trees that resemble palms. **Passion fruit** have beautiful flowers as well as delicious fruit with edible seeds. **Pawpaws** are native to North America and unrelated to tropical papayas. **Pepinos** resemble small melons. **Persimmons** store well if you keep a short length of stalk attached. **Pineapple** fruit at the end of a central flower spike.

humidity and light levels high, and don't allow the plant to stand in a draft. It may be several years before you get even a modest-sized fruit.

Pineapple guavas

Also known as feijoa, from its botanical name, the pineapple guava is a native of high altitude parts of subtropical South America. However, it is also happy enough in many cool temperate regions, where it is often grown as an ornamental garden plant. In order to grow pineapple guava for its fruit, the plant needs long, hot summers, and may require protection to ensure not only that late spring frost doesn't destroy the flowers, but also that early fall frost doesn't damage fruit that have not yet ripened.

■ HOW TO GROW Pineapple guavas can be grown from seed but it's easier and faster to buy a young container-grown plant. Plant in a warm, sunny, sheltered spot or in pots that can be brought under cover during winter and when there is a risk of frost. Water regularly throughout the spring and summer. Prune lightly after harvesting.

Pineapple guavas are green-skinned, egg-sized fruit with sweet, aromatic flesh with a pineapple-mint flavor. The flowers are edible, too.

Pomegranates

Pomegranates originate from southwest Asia and are therefore happiest growing in hot, arid conditions. Don't attempt them unless you can give them the right kind of microclimate. In cool temperate regions, your only chance is to try them in containers under glass—although bear in mind that they do not like high levels of humidity.

■ HOW TO GROW Pomegranates can be grown from seed, but it's better to start with a plant raised from a cutting. For container growing, use a 8–9-in (21–24-cm) pot filled with potting mix blended with grit to improve drainage. Water regularly but not excessively in spring and summer, and less often in winter. Feed with liquid tomato fertilizer during the growing season. Maintain a minimum temperature of 50°F (10°C), ensuring that the plants get as much heat and light as possible in summer. To grow trees in the open, plant in a sunny, sheltered site. Although self-fertile, crops are better if trees have a partner for cross-pollination. Prune in winter or early spring during the dormant period.

Prickly pears

Prickly pears are cacti, and their natural home is in the arid areas of the southwestern U.S., Central and South America, and the Mediterranean. The purple or red fruit, which grow on the ends of the cactus's pads, are edible—provided that the spines are meticulously removed first. They are sometimes known as cactus figs or Indian figs.

■ HOW TO GROW In cool temperate regions, prickly pears can be grown only in greenhouses or conservatories. They need a consistent temperature of 64–77°F (18–25°C) and may not survive if it falls below 50°F (10°C) for anything more than short periods. Soil should be sandy and free-draining,

and the air should be kept dry, not humid. Beyond that, the plants have very few requirements. But be patient; they may take several years before they fruit—and don't be tempted to touch them without wearing gloves.

Strawberry guavas

The strawberry guava comes from the same family as the evergreen garden shrub myrtle. It originates from tropical Central and South America, where it can grow to 16 ft (5 m) in height. There is also a yellow-skinned variety commonly known as lemon guava. So-called tropical or apple guavas are closely related, but the fruit are larger and the plants less tolerant of low temperatures.

■ HOW TO GROW To grow strawberry guavas outdoors, you'll need a sunny, sheltered, frost-free site, with consistent daytime temperatures of 75–86°F (24–30°C) throughout the summer. In cool temperate zones, it's wiser to grow the plants in containers, bringing them under cover when necessary. Hand-pollinate, and water and feed regularly in the growing season. In warm climates, guavas may flower continuously, and fruit ripen all year round. In cooler climates, fruit should be ready to harvest between October and December.

Tamarillos

Also known as tree tomatoes, tamarillos come from the same family as tomatoes and eggplant. These fruit are subtropical natives of South America, and are egg-shaped with green skins that slowly turn red, orange, or yellow. They are sweet enough to eat raw only when fully ripe. The skin is unpalatable.

■ HOW TO GROW Tamarillos need lots of sunshine, high temperatures, high humidity, and a sheltered site. They won't tolerate frost. Plant in rich, free-draining soil but take care to water plentifully during dry spells. In cool climates, grow them in containers under cover.

(below, far left to right) **Pineapple guavas** are small trees with dark green, leathery foliage. **Pomegranates**, which grow on small trees in their native habitat, need a hot summer to ripen. **Prickly pears** are hardier than many other cacti and delicious to eat, but the spines can seriously irritate the skin. **Strawberry guavas** are traditionally cooked and made into jelly. **Tamarillos** grow on shrubby trees in Peru and Brazil, where they ripen reliably. In cooler regions, they are unappetizing raw and much better eaten cooked.

Fruit Doctor

Ask any fruit grower and chances are they'll claim to suffer more than their fair share of pests and diseases. Why? The answer is probably twofold. First, fruit trees, bushes, and canes last a lot longer than other food crops. In contrast, most vegetables are annuals—there one year and gone the next. So, unless they're grown year after year in the same spot, they are less likely to build up persistent infections or colonies of soil-dwelling insects. With fruit, such problems have time to accumulate. Second, there's the maturing fruit itself. Few things in the garden attract wasps, flies, birds, and other wildlife as powerfully as sweet, ripe fruit. It's as irresistible to them as it is to you.

Nets and fences are the ultimate defense against birds and animals. And ensuring good hygiene and providing the right growing conditions are the best way to guarantee healthy plants. Beyond that, it's worth learning as much as you can about what you're up against. This chapter catalogs the pests, parasites, diseases, and disorders that most commonly attack fruit, and its aim is to arm you with the information you need to keep them at bay.

Diagnosis isn't difficult here. Brown rot has completely spoiled these cherries. Remove and destroy them right away or the fungal spores will spread rapidly and infect other parts of the tree.

What's wrong?

When things go wrong, the cause of the problem is likely to be one of three things: a plant disease; an attack by a pest or parasite; or a disorder triggered by the wrong growing conditions. Attacks by animals, birds, and most insects are the easiest to diagnose. If your fruit bushes are crawling with aphids or birds are feasting on your strawberries, then the culprits are there in front of your eyes. Similarly, it should be obvious if your plants have suffered from frost, drought, or sun scorch. However, there's a wide range of fungal, bacterial, and viral diseases, nutritional disorders, and infestations by microscopic mites too tiny to see with the naked eye, that are somewhat harder to diagnose.

Disease or disorder?

Plants that are suffering often display very similar visible symptoms whether they are under attack by pests or suffering from a disease or disorder. Wilting of blossoms and new shoots, leaf curling and distortion, and yellowing of foliage are all common early warning signs that something is wrong. Often, such symptoms look like disease but aren't. They are simply the plant's response to being put under stress—perhaps by frost, underwatering, or a lack of certain nutrients. Don't make a diagnosis too hastily. And, most importantly, don't resort to chemicals unless you're sure you have no alternative.

(below, left to right) **Frost damage** occurs when the temperature falls below freezing, causing sap within plant cells to expand and rupture the cell walls. Blossoms and young shoots quickly wilt and die back. **Watering** plants in containers is vital during hot weather. They dry out more quickly than those in open ground. **Soaker hoses** and drip irrigation systems water the soil, not the foliage, and are a good investment.

Good or bad growing conditions?

No plant will thrive unless you can give it the right growing conditions. As a fruit grower, this should be your mantra. After all, your primary aim is to grow plants that produce as large a crop of perfect, healthy fruit as possible. A tree or bush that survives but produces poorly is pointless.

Lack of water, exposure to strong winds or frost, insufficient light, waterlogged soil, and nutrient deficiencies are all examples of poor growing conditions. Getting things right should be your number one priority—plants that are in good health are much better able to resist disease and attack by pests and parasites.

Remember that many of us try to grow fruit in a climatic zone that is not the same as the plant's native habitat. In cool temperate regions, it will always be a challenge to grow (and ripen) peaches, nectarines, apricots, figs, melons, and grapes outdoors. And even attempting tropical and subtropical crops, such as avocados, mangos, papayas, and bananas, requires a heated greenhouse and meticulous control of the microclimate. It's not just a question of temperature, although that is crucial; it's also a matter of humidity, light intensity, and the number of daylight hours.

Friend or foe?

When it comes to wildlife, there's a fine line between what's welcome and what isn't. Birds can be valuable allies, since they keep down the insect population by eating grubs and caterpillars. But they may be one of your worst enemies, too—they can strip fruit bushes and strawberry beds in just a matter of hours. Insects are the same. Some are positively beneficial—bees, hoverflies, ladybugs, and lacewings, for example. Others are extremely destructive, tunneling into ripening fruit and feeding voraciously on plant tissue.

Interestingly, it is possible to use insect against insect. Biological controls involve the deliberate introduction of predatory mites or parasitic wasps to kill specific pests, such as whiteflies or spider mites. Using nematodes (microscopic worms) to target Japanese beetle grubs, or live bacteria to infect certain caterpillars, utilizes the same strategy.

(below, left to right) **Ladybugs** are most definitely friends. Both adults and larvae feast on aphids. **Greenhouses** provide microclimates that extend the range of plants you can grow—but may also provide the perfect conditions for insect pests. **Beer traps** are an eco-friendly and effective way of keeping wasps away from ripening fruit.

Healthy soil

The soil in which you plant your fruit trees and bushes is vitally important. If it is fertile and has good structure, chances are that the plants will grow well, stay healthy, and produce good crops. Soils differ widely. Some are light and sandy, others are heavy and claylike. Some are acidic, others are alkaline. And some are rich in nutrients, others are thin and poor.

Soil structure

All soils consist of minute particles of weathered rock, mixed with water and organic matter from rotted-down remains of plants and animals. It is the size of the particles that largely determines the nature of the soil. Sandy soils are made up of fairly large particles, so they are usually light and gritty to the touch. Clay soils are made up of much smaller particles, so they tend to be dense and heavy, more like dough or pastry. The more organic matter the soil contains, the better its structure. It makes clay soils more free-draining and lessens the risk of their becoming compacted or waterlogged. And organic matter makes sandy soils more water-retentive, and counteracts any loss of fertility that may occur when nutrients are washed out by rain.

Soil acidity and alkalinity

All soils have a pH value. It's a measurement of how acidic or alkaline they are. Soils with a low pH are acidic, and those with a high pH are alkaline. It's rarely a big issue, since most fruit are fairly tolerant, if anything preferring neutral or perhaps slightly acidic soils. The exceptions are blueberries and cranberries: they grow well only in acidic soils.

■ ACIDIC SOILS are low in calcium. It is fairly easy to make them more alkaline by adding lime (calcium carbonate) or a lime-rich material, such as mushroom compost.

ACIDIC OR ALKALINE?

1–5	very acidic
6	acidic
6.5	slightly acidic
7	neutral
7.5	slightly alkaline
8	alkaline
9–14	very alkaline

Measuring soil pH is done using a simple test kit. Add soil to the solution in the test tube, shake well, then match the resulting color against the pH chart provided.

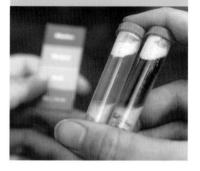

(below left to right) **Clay soil** is sticky when wet and can be rolled into a ball. **Sandy soil** is light, feels gritty, and the particles don't stick together. **To reduce soil acidity,** spread powdered lime over the soil and rake it evenly. Wear gloves and a face mask, and avoid windy days.

■ ALKALINE SOILS are high in calcium, and are often found in limestone areas. They can trigger a nutrient disorder called lime-induced chlorosis (see p.320). Alkaline soils can be made more acidic by adding composted sawdust, composted pine bark or needles, sulfur dust or chips, or loam-based acidic potting mix.

Feeding your soil

Generous crops of fruit year after year make heavy demands on the soil. They take out a lot of nutrients. It should come as no surprise that some of that goodness needs to be put back. Feeding your soil will keep it healthy, fertile, and productive. There are two methods. The first is to add organic material in the form of compost or manure. The second is to use fertilizers—either organic or synthetic, whichever you prefer.

Composts and manures

These are natural organic materials made up of decomposed or rotted plant matter and animal waste. When dug into the soil before planting, they improve its structure by breaking up compacted masses so that air can circulate, and roots can grow deeply and spread widely. They improve drainage, too. Clay soils drain more freely, while sandy soils retain moisture for longer.

Farmyard and stable manures are ideal soil improvers, if you can find a source for them. They usually comprise straw and animal dung, sometimes with wood shavings or sawdust as well. Leave them to rot down for at least six months before using them. Garden and household compost is decayed plant matter that has been broken down by tiny microorganisms. You can buy it, but it's easy to make your own.

Once trees and perennial fruit are established, it's best to add composts and manures as a surface mulch. In time, worms will do the work for you and draw it down into the soil.

Fertilizers

These provide a more concentrated, quick-acting source of nutrients than manures and composts. They are usually sold in liquid, powder, granule, or pelleted form, and may be organic or synthetic. Organic fertilizers are derived entirely from plant or animal material. They include bonemeal, dried blood, alfalfa meal, soy meal, fish meal, and kelp extracts. Synthetic fertilizers are extracted from minerals or are produced using industrial-scale chemical processes.

Key nutrients

All fertilizers contain at least one of the three key elements that plants need from the soil: nitrogen (N, added in the form of nitrates), phosphorus (P, added in the form of phosphates), and potassium (K, added in the form of potash). Many contain a mixture of all three. Some also include calcium, magnesium, and sulfur, as well as trace elements such as boron, copper, iron, manganese, and molybdenum.

(top to bottom) **Spread well-rotted compost** or manure around the plants, taking care not to pile it up against the trunk or stem. Mulching after watering will increase moisture retention. **Farmyard manure** improves soil structure and adds back valuable nutrients. **Garden compost** piles rot down to produce rich, fertile material that should be dark and crumbly, just like soil.

Common nutrient deficiencies

If plants are denied their necessary nutrients, they fail to grow properly and show signs of malnutrition, just like humans. Often, the cause is not that the minerals are actually missing from the soil but that chemical imbalances prevent plants from absorbing them properly—perhaps due to lack of water or because the soil is too acidic or too alkaline.

Boron deficiency

Boron is washed out of light soils by heavy rain. Low levels occur in very dry or recently limed soils.

■ **Symptoms** Shoots may die back and leaves yellow. Apples and pears may be distorted and develop corklike patches; strawberries are small and pale, and leaves are distorted with yellow tips.

■ **Treatment** Mix borax with horticultural sand and rake it into the soil, if possible before you plant.

Calcium deficiency

Calcium levels are low in acidic soils. Even where there is sufficient calcium, plants may be unable to absorb it if the ground is very dry.

■ **Symptoms** Apples develop **bitter pit** (see p.325). Sometimes the flesh becomes "glassy" and semitransparent.

■ **Treatment** Add powdered lime to soil and rake it in to increase the pH level. Prevent soil from drying out by watering regularly and applying a mulch to retain moisture.

Iron deficiency (lime-induced chlorosis)

It's rare to find soil that is truly short of iron. What tends to happen is that the high levels of calcium in recently limed or very alkaline soils prevent plants from absorbing the iron that is available. For this reason, the disorder is also known as lime-induced chlorosis. It usually goes hand-in-hand with manganese deficiency.

■ **Symptoms** Leaves yellow, starting at the edges then spreading in between the veins, which remain green. Finally, the entire leaf may turn brown and wither. New leaves are affected first. Symptoms are similar to those of both manganese and magnesium deficiency. Tree fruit, such as apples, pears, and peaches, and soft fruit, such as strawberries, raspberries, and blueberries, can be badly affected.

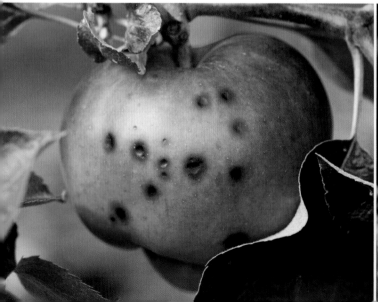

Treatment Acidifying the soil may help, but it is best to buy special chelated or sequestered iron mixtures, which provide iron in a form that plants are able to absorb.

Magnesium deficiency

Heavy rain will readily wash magnesium out of light soils. Levels may also be low in acidic soils or when high-potash fertilizers have been used to increase the amounts of potassium.

Symptoms Leaves turn yellow between the veins and around the edges because there is insufficient magnesium to produce green chlorophyll. The yellow areas may turn red, purple, or brown. Unlike iron and manganese deficiency, old leaves are affected first.

Treatment Apply Epsom salts (magnesium sulfate) as a foliar spray or spread it over the soil.

Manganese deficiency

Insufficient manganese is most common in acidic, peaty soils or in poorly drained, sandy soils.

Symptoms Almost identical to those of iron deficiency, with which it is often associated.

Treatment Avoid adding too much lime to soils where the problem has been identified. Spray affected plants with manganese sulfate solution.

Nitrogen deficiency

Soils without much organic matter are those most likely to have insufficient nitrogen. So, too, are soils in containers. Periods of heavy rain, which wash out nutrients, make the problem worse.

Symptoms Leaves are pale green or yellow due to insufficient chlorophyll. Some may even turn pink, red, or purple. Older leaves near the base of the plant are the worst affected. Plants are generally smaller and more spindly than they should be.

Treatment Add lots of well-rotted compost, manure, or other organic material, or some high-nitrogen fertilizer.

Potassium deficiency

This is most likely to occur in light, sandy soils.

Symptoms Potassium is part of the process by which plants absorb water and photosynthesize. Without enough potassium, leaves curl, turn yellow, scorch at the edges, and may have purple-brown spots underneath. Flowering is poor, fruit are small, and plants may be more vulnerable to disease.

Treatment Add potassium sulfate fertilizer. Composted bracken or comfrey will help restore levels, too.

(below, far left to right) **Bitter pit** in apples is a sign of lack of calcium, often caused by dry conditions. **Chlorosis** is caused by iron or manganese deficiency and produces distinctive yellowing of the leaves in between the veins. **Magnesium deficiency** can show as yellow leaf markings, particularly at the margins. **Potassium deficiency** typically causes leaves to turn brown, scorch, and curl upward at the edges.

Diseases and disorders

Most diseases that commonly afflict fruit are caused by one of three things: a fungus, a virus, or bacteria. In each case, microorganisms (or pathogens) invade the plant and disrupt or interfere with its normal, healthy growth. Sometimes the symptoms of infection are minor and can be easily treated— or even ignored—and the plant recovers. But in severe cases a plant may be so badly weakened by disease that it dies.

(top to bottom) **Clean tools** carefully after use. Use a disinfectant solution or spray to kill any bacteria, and dry blades carefully to prevent rust.
When spraying products straight onto the leaves of affected plants, always measure quantities accurately and make up only as much as you need.

How diseases spread

Most fungal infections are spread by spores blown from one plant to another by the wind or transmitted by the splashing of water from a watering can or hose. Bacteria spread in the same way, although insects and animals can also carry them. Viruses are often transmitted by sap-feeding insects, especially aphids, although they can also be passed on via infected seeds or cuttings.

Preventing disease

Plants are most at risk when they are damaged or have just been pruned. It's often through open wounds that infections enter in the first place. They are also vulnerable in damp, humid, stagnant conditions, where diseases thrive and reproduce.
■ DON'T OVERCROWD plants. Give them enough space for light to get to them and for air to circulate freely.
■ WEED, water, and fertilize them, and give them the right growing conditions. The healthier your plants, the more resistant to infection they will be.
■ DISINFECT TOOLS before and after use—especially when pruning.
■ CLEAR AWAY all windfalls, fallen leaves, and offcuts from pruning. Burn, instead of composting, any material that you suspect might be infected.

Treating diseased plants

Some fungal diseases can be treated with fungicides, which kill off the fungal spores. However, in recent years, many once commonly used fungicides have been withdrawn. Traditional Bordeaux mixture and other copper-based compounds are no longer for sale to home growers, and very few synthetic fungicides available to home gardeners are permitted for use on food crops.

Viruses are rarely treatable. Dig up and destroy affected plants. Bacterial diseases are best combated with swift action. As soon as you see any telltale signs, remove all infected material and hope that the disease does not spread.

Common fruit diseases

1 Brown rot
The spores of this fungus usually enter fruit whose skins have split or that have been damaged by birds or insects. Brown rot can spread very rapidly (see p.326).

2 Canker
A fungal disease, apple and pear canker (see p.324) enters the wood via cracks in the bark or via pruning cuts. Bacterial canker (see p.324) spreads in the same way, affecting buds, shoots, and leaves, as well as stems and branches.

3 Dieback
When new growth wilts, withers, and dies off, a variety of different infections can be to blame. Two common types are Botrytis (see p.326) and Eutypa (see p.327).

4 Leaf spots
Irregular spots, blotches, patches, and discolorations can be hard to diagnose. One of the fungal infections known as fungal leaf spot (see p.327) may be the cause, or these may be a symptom of bacterial canker (see p.324).

5 Mildews
Powdery mildew (see p.329) is very common and affects a wide range of fruit. It's rarely fatal, but it can stunt growth, and it's important to prevent it from spreading. Downy mildew (see p.327) is restricted to grapes and melons.

6 Molds
Gray mold is the type you're most likely to encounter. It is caused by the fungus Botrytis (see p.326), and is worse in damp, humid conditions where air cannot circulate freely. Soft fruit tend to be badly affected.

7 Scab
Typically, the symptoms of scab are brown or black fungal growths that appear as patches on leaves and on the skins of fruit (see p.330). Badly infected apples, pears, and plums tend to be stunted and misshapen, and cracked or split.

8 Viruses
Viruses are notoriously difficult to diagnose. Symptoms may include distorted, stunted, or oddly colored leaves, but often growth is simply poor and crops are disappointing. Particularly susceptible fruits are raspberries, strawberries blueberries (shown here), and black currants.

A–Z of diseases and disorders

Listed here are the diseases that most commonly affect fruit trees, bushes, and other plants. Almost all are caused by fungi, viruses, or bacteria. Some are treatable, others are not. In all cases, good hygiene and the right growing conditions will help keep plants healthy, and swift action will prevent infections from spreading. In addition to the conditions listed here, plants may sometimes suffer from disorders that look much like diseases but are actually caused by a lack of essential minerals in the soil (see pp.320–21).

American gooseberry mildew

This disorder is caused by a fungus that thrives in still air. It tends to be worse on plants fed with high-nitrogen fertilizer, which stimulates new growth that is particularly vulnerable.

■ **Crops affected** Gooseberries, black currants.

■ **Symptoms** Powdery white patches appear on shoots and leaves, then on the fruit themselves. New shoots may become misshapen and fail to grow properly. Fruit skin may turn brown and feltlike or leathery. Although the mildew can be removed and the fruit eaten, they are not very appetizing.

■ **Treatment** Cut out and destroy all affected areas, taking care not to leave any diseased foliage or fruit on the ground. Space bushes well apart and prune them to open up their centers and to allow air to circulate freely. If necessary, spray with a fungicide in spring. In the future, grow resistant varieties and avoid nitrogen-rich fertilizer.

Anthracnose
■ See **Fungal leaf spot** (p.328).

Apple and pear canker

Cankers may be either bacterial or fungal. Several types of fungi can cause cankers on apples and pears. Spores enter via pruning cuts, cracks in the bark, and the small scars left when leaves fall. **Scab** makes a tree more prone to attack, too (see p.330). **Fire blight** (a bacterial disease) can also cause **cankers** (see p.324). Canker can be very destructive if not treated.

■ **Crops affected** Apples, pears.

■ **Symptoms** Areas of bark discolor, hollow, and split or crack in concentric, flaky rings. The infected site swells up, and growth ceases around it. Fungal growths may appear—creamy white in spring and summer, and red in fall and winter. Whole branches may die off.

■ **Treatment** Prune out and destroy infected wood, removing whole branches if necessary. Copper-based fungicides, such as Bordeaux mixture, are no longer available.

Apple scab
■ See **Scab** (p.330).

Arabis mosaic
■ See **Strawberry virus** (p.331).

Bacterial canker

This is a serious disease that needs prompt action to prevent it from spreading and killing the tree. The bacteria usually enters in the fall, via cracks in the tree's bark, wounds, or pruning cuts, although it can also attack new shoots and foliage in spring. Young trees are most at risk—especially if the weather is damp and windy.

■ **Crops affected** Apricots, cherries, nectarines, plums, peaches.

■ **Symptoms** Bacterial canker causes small dark spots in leaves that turn into round holes. The leaves subsequently yellow, wither, and die. Buds do not open, branches die back, and areas of infected bark become sunken and may ooze orange resin or gum.

■ **Treatment** Immediately prune out and destroy all infected wood, removing whole branches if necessary and treating cuts with special wound paint. Sterilize any tools you've used. Home growers may no longer use traditional copper-based fungicides, such as Bordeaux mixture.

Bacterial leaf spot
This disease can be particularly problematic in the Southeast.

■ **Crops affected** Apricots, cherries, nectarines, plums, peaches.
■ **Symptoms** Water-soaked, angular spots appear on leaves. The spots may later fall out, creating a shot-hole effect, and leaves may fall prematurely. Fruits develop dark, sunken spots or cracks. Cankers on twigs leak bacterial ooze in the spring, spreading the disease.
■ **Treatment** Prune and care for trees to keep them healthy. Spraying copper after harvest may stop the disease from spreading.

Bacterial wilt
When seemingly healthy melon plants mysteriously collapse, suspect bacterial wilt.
■ **Crops affected** Melons.
■ **Symptoms** Infected vines wilt quickly, then dry out. Sticky white strands appear inside stems.
■ **Treatment** There is no treatment; pull and destroy infected plants. Choose resistant cultivars, and control cucumber beetles, which transmit bacteria.

Bitter pit
This is a calcium-deficiency disorder. It occurs when apple trees are unable to absorb sufficient calcium from the soil. As a result, fruit cells die and rot. The deficiency is often caused by the roots being too dry.
■ **Crops affected** Apples.
■ **Symptoms** Small, round, dark spots or sunken pits appear on the skin of apples, and sometimes in the flesh, too. Fruit may be bitter.
■ **Treatment** Mulch around trees and water if necessary to keep soil moist. Use general rather than nitrogen-rich fertilizer.

Blackberry leaf spot
This fungal disease has symptoms similar to that of **raspberry leaf spot** (see p.330).
■ **Symptoms** Round purple or brown spots appear on leaves. The spots turn gray-white in the center but remain purple around the edges. On the canes they are more elliptical and may grow into blotches up to ½ in (1 cm) long. Tiny black specks of fungal growth may be visible in the white centers. In the case of serious infections, leaves and canes may die.
■ **Crops affected** Blackberries and hybrid bramble fruits.
■ **Treatment** Carefully prune out or cut down all infected canes. Destroy the diseased material; do not compost it.

Black knot
This fungus stimulates abnormal cell development in the host planting, resulting in black galls and swellings on stems and roots.
■ **Symptoms** Twigs and branches develop black (or green) swellings. Branch tips die back. In severe cases, limbs may die and trees are stunted.
■ **Crops affected** Cherries, plums.
■ **Treatment** Prune off infected limbs several times a year, cutting well below the knots. Sterilize pruning tools between cuts. Destroy prunings as well as any wild cherry or plum trees in the area. Spray lime-sulfur once in spring before buds swell.

Black rot
Fruit that rots or is deformed is a symptom of this fungal disease. One type affects grapes; another infects apples.

■ **Symptoms** Grapes develop purple-brown spots, and infected grapes shrivel up and die. Reddish-brown spots may appear on leaves and shoots. On apples, the disease causes leaf lesions, cankers, and a dry rot of the fruit starting at the blossom end.
■ **Crops affected** Apples, grapes.
■ **Treatment** Pick and destroy rotting fruit and infected plant parts. For grapes, remove mulch or put down fresh mulch, and to prevent problems, apply a copper-based fungicide before and after bloom. Applying fungicides can help to control the problem on tree fruits.

Blossom blight
This disease is caused by the same fungus responsible for brown rot.
■ **Crops affected** Apples, apricots, cherries, plums, peaches, pears.
■ **Symptoms** New blossoms turn brown, wither, and die. Leaves may be affected too.
■ **Treatment** Remove and destroy infected blossoms before fungus spreads to leaves and stems.

Blueberry stem blight
A fungus that usually infects plants via wounds, perhaps caused by pruning cuts or insect damage.
■ **Crops affected** Blueberries.
■ **Symptoms** Clusters of leaves turn brown, wither, and die but do not fall immediately. Instead, they remain on the affected stem, rather like a brown "flag" in contrast with surrounding healthy green foliage. Eventually, they do drop, the stem dies back, and the infection can quickly spread.

■ **Treatment** Cut out and destroy all affected stems, removing stems back to a point several inches below where any brown patches are visible in the wood.

Blueberry virus

Blueberries can be afflicted by a number of different viruses, including mosaic and ringspot. They are not always easy to diagnose, and can be hard to eradicate.

■ **Crops affected** Blueberries.
■ **Symptoms** Yellow-green, red, or pink mottling or mosaic patterns appear on leaves, new shoots may die back, and plants grow and fruit poorly.
■ **Treatment** Symptoms can vary in severity from year to year. If plants are badly infected, remove and burn them. Always buy certified virus-free plants.

Botrytis

Also known as gray mold, *Botrytis cinerea* is a fungus. The spores are spread in the air or by rain or water splash, and usually get into plants through wounds or damaged areas. Infections are worse in wet summers.

■ **Crops affected** Worst affected fruits include apples, strawberries, blackberries, grapes, raspberries, gooseberries, and figs.
■ **Symptoms** As its common name suggests, fluffy gray, off-white, or gray-brown mold appears on the stems of plants, on leaves, on fruit, and on flowers. Plants with badly infected stems may yellow, wilt, and die (see **Gooseberry dieback** p.328).
■ **Treatment** Remove and destroy any affected parts of

the plant. Don't leave any infected plant material lying around, since the spores will survive if they transfer to the soil. Make sure surviving plants have space for air to circulate freely around them.

Brown rot

This particular form of rot is caused by a fungus. The spores often find their way under the skin of fruit via damaged areas left where birds and insects have been feeding, though they can also be spread by rainwater.

■ **Crops affected** Apples, pears, apricots, cherries, plums, peaches.
■ **Symptoms** Initially, the fruit develops soft, brown, rotten patches. As these spread, white, crusty spots or pustules appear, often in circular patterns. Eventually the fruit shrivels up and either falls off or remains on the tree in a desiccated state.
■ **Treatment** Pick off and destroy all infected fruit, including windfalls. Prune out any stems or branches that have also become infected, as the fungus is able to overwinter and survive from one year to the next.

Cane blight

■ See **Raspberry cane blight** (p.330).

Canker

■ See **Apple and pear canker** (p.324), **Bacterial canker** (p.324), **Mulberry canker** (p.328).

Cedar apple rust

This fungus spends part of its life cycle in apple trees and part in junipers, especially Eastern red cedar. It causes galls on junipers.

■ **Crops affected** Apples, pears.
■ **Symptoms** Leaves develop small yellow spots that grow bigger and turn orange. Fruit is deformed. Leaves and fruit may drop off the tree.
■ **Treatment** There is no treatment for infected leaves and fruit. To prevent future problems, try spraying trees with sulfur when leaves are first emerging.

Cherry leaf spot

■ See **Fungal leaf spot** (p.328).

Chlorosis, lime-induced

■ See **Iron deficiency** (p.320).

Cluster cup rust

■ See **Gooseberry rust** (p.328).

Cercospora leaf spot

■ See **Shot-hole disease** (p.330).

Crown rot

A soil-inhabiting fungus, *Phytophthora*, causes the crowns of strawberry plants to rot and the leaves to wilt. Badly infected plants die. The problem is worse in warm weather and with strawberries grown under cover.

■ **Crops affected** Strawberries.
■ **Symptoms** Young leaves in the middle of the plant wilt and may turn yellow. Lifting affected plants and cutting through the crown will show it to be brown and rotten.
■ **Treatment** There is no cure. Dig up and destroy diseased plants, and do not replant strawberries on the site. If possible, choose resistant varieties in the future. In California and some other areas, soil solarization can kill the fungus in the soil.

Cucumber mosaic virus

This is a serious, widespread virus that can wipe out plants completely.

■ **Crops affected** Melons, cucumbers, and squash.

■ **Symptoms** Leaves become misshapen and stunted, and develop yellow mosaic patterning. Flowers may not appear. Any fruit that do form are small, hard, and inedible. Plants may die.

■ **Treatment** There is no cure. Dig up and destroy all affected plants.

Dieback

Dieback can be caused by a number of different infections. See also **Botrytis** (see p.326), **Eutypa** (see p.327), and **Gooseberry dieback** (p.328).

■ **Crops affected** Most tree and soft fruit.

■ **Symptoms** New shoots and leaves wilt, dry up, and turn brown. If the infection spreads, branches gradually die off and ultimately the whole plant may die.

■ **Treatment** Cut off and destroy infected foliage and branches. If necessary, spray with an appropriate fungicide. If the whole plant is affected, uproot it and destroy it.

Downy mildew

This type of mildew is caused by a range of different fungi that thrive in damp, humid conditions.

■ **Crops affected** Grapes, melons.

■ **Symptoms** Pale green, yellow, or brown patches develop on the upper surface of leaves, with off-white, fluffy mold on the underside. As the patches spread, the leaves die. Once the disease takes hold and the plant is weakened, **Botrytis** (see p.326) may follow.

■ **Treatment** Remove and destroy infected leaves. Discourage the onset of the disease by ensuring good air circulation and avoiding overwatering.

Eutypa

Dieback can be caused by a fungus called *Eutypa lata*. In the case of grape vines, the infection may take hold following pruning.

■ **Crops affected** Apricots, gooseberries, grapes, red currants.

■ **Symptoms** New shoots and leaf growth may be weak or stunted. Older leaves wither, dry up, turn yellow or brown, and fall off. Branches gradually die off completely. In the end, the whole plant may die.

■ **Treatment** Cut off and destroy infected foliage and branches. If necessary, spray with an appropriate fungicide. If the whole plant is affected, uproot it and destroy it.

Fire blight

This serious bacterial disease infects trees via their flowers. It is transmitted by rain splash and may be lethal over time.

■ **Crops affected** Apples, pears.

■ **Symptoms** Flowers turn brown, wither, and die. Then leaves do the same, and shoots bend over, creating a "shepherd's hook" appearance. As the disease spreads, stems and branches are affected too. Infected fruit may have dark lesions or be shriveled.

■ **Treatment** Prune out infested shoots early in the season. Avoid overfertilizing trees. Prune out and destroy all infected wood. Spray Bordeaux mixture when trees are dormant. Dig up and burn severely infected trees. Replant, avoiding susceptible varieties and rootstocks.

Foot and root rots

These rots are caused by a range of different fungi. They live in the soil and in standing water.

■ **Crops affected** Soft fruit, citrus, melons, and, in particular, container-grown plants.

■ **Symptoms** If the base of the plant stem is infected, it will darken and the tissues will start to shrink and die. Leaves and stems above will wilt, turn yellow or brown, and die. Infected roots may turn black or brown, and break up or rot.

■ **Treatment** Once the disease has taken hold, there is no remedy. Immediately remove and destroy infected plants—and the soil in which they are growing.

Fruit rots

A variety of fungi can cause fruit rots, especially during hot summer conditions. The same fungi can cause cankers (see **Apple and Pear canker**, p.324).

■ **Crops affected** Apples.

■ **Symptoms** Fruit develop brown, sometimes sunken, spots. Spots enlarge rapidly in hot conditions, developing concentric rings. Other fungi cause rot in the seed cavity of the fruit. Fruit may drop or shrivel and dry on the tree.

■ **Treatment** Prune and destroy cankered wood. Destroy all infected fruit. Fungicides may help control some types of fruit rot.

Fungal leaf spot

A range of different fungi attack the leaf tissues. Some target only specific plants. The disease is often worse in wet summers. See also **Bacterial canker** (p.324), **Blackberry leaf spot** (p.325).

■ **Crops affected** Apples, blackberries, currants, gooseberries, raspberries, strawberries. Two particular species can cause leaf spot in cherries and quinces, too.

■ **Symptoms** In May or June, leaves develop small brown or gray spots where tissue has died. The spots may spread and join, and leaves turn yellow before falling off. Young shoots, stems, and canes may be affected as well. Anthracnose fungi can also infect fruit. On raspberries, tiny pinprick-sized black or brown growths are the telltale sign that the disease is fungal rather than bacterial leaf spot.

■ **Treatment** If you catch it early, the disease is unlikely to be fatal. Remove and destroy infected leaves. Don't leave any lying around at the end of the year, or the spores may survive the winter.

Fusarium wilt

■ See **Verticillium wilt** (p.331).

Gooseberry dieback

Dieback is usually caused by a fungal infection, either **Botrytis** (gray mold; see p.326) or **Eutypa** (see p.327).

■ **Crops affected** Gooseberries, with similar problems on currants and raspberries.

■ **Symptoms** Leaves wither, dry up, turn brown, and fall off. The bark on stems may crack, and branches gradually die off. The whole plant may die.

■ **Treatment** Cut off and destroy infected foliage and branches. If necessary, spray with a suitable fungicide. If the whole plant is affected, uproot it and destroy it.

Gooseberry mildew

■ See **American gooseberry mildew** (p.324).

Gooseberry rust

A fungal growth also known as cluster cup rust. Serious infections often start after a dry spring, and then worsen during the summer, finally damaging the fruit themselves.

■ **Crops affected** Gooseberries, and less often currants.

■ **Symptoms** Dark orange or red blisters (or pustules) appear on leaves and may spread to fruit and to stems—where the telltale signs are tiny cup-shaped hollows with yellow outer rims.

■ **Treatment** Cut off and destroy infected foliage. If necessary, spray with a suitable fungicide. Don't grow gooseberries near sedges, which act as hosts to the fungal spores.

Gray mold

■ See **Botrytis** (p.326).

Honey fungus

The term covers a group of fungi that can attack all fruit trees and shrubs, and other plants too. It is also called shoestring root rot.

■ **Crops affected** All tree and bush fruit, and strawberries.

■ **Symptoms** A warning sign may be wilting leaves or poor foliage, but in some cases a plant may die surprisingly quickly and unexpectedly. Peel back the bark at the base of the trunk or stem, or inspect the roots, and you may find white fungus that smells like mushrooms. Sometimes, honey-colored toadstools grow around the base of infected trees.

■ **Treatment** Dig up and destroy infected plants, including their root systems.

Leaf spot

■ See **Bacterial canker** (p.324), **Fungal leaf spot** (p.328).

Lime-induced chlorosis

■ See **Iron deficiency** (p.320).

Mildew

See **American gooseberry mildew** (p.324), **Downy mildew** (p.327), **Powdery mildew** (p.329).

Mulberry canker

A fungal form of canker that attacks mulberries. It can be most troublesome after a wet spring.

■ **Crops affected** Mulberries.

■ **Symptoms** Young shoots wither and die back, as cankers encircle the stems. Spores may be visible on sunken or swollen bark.

■ **Treatment** Prune out and destroy all infected wood.

Mummy berry

This fungal disease is named for the appearance of infected berries.

■ **Crops affected** Blueberries

■ **Symptoms** Leaves and young shoots are blighted. Berries turn gray or cream-colored, shrivel up, and become firm and dry. Berries drop off plants early. Infected berries are a source of infection the following year.

■ **Treatment** Thoroughly rake the areas around plants in the fall and destroy all debris. Apply fresh mulch to cover up any remaining infected debris on the ground. Applying fungicides may help.

Orange rust

A difficult, systemic fungal disease that weakens and kills blackberries.
■ **Crops affected** Blackberries, black raspberries.
■ **Symptoms** Shoots are weak and spindly. Even healthy-looking canes fail to produce flowers. Leaves may be distorted, with orange blisters or pustules on the undersides.
■ **Treatment** Dig and destroy plants as soon as symptoms appear. Plant only healthy stock, and do not plant blackberries near patches of wild blackberries.

Peach leaf curl

This fungus is the bane of any gardener who grows peaches and nectarines. However, disastrous though it may appear, it is not usually fatal.
■ **Crops affected** Peaches, nectarines.
■ **Symptoms** Leaves curl, blister, and turn orange-red or even purple. If left in place, they develop an off-white, dusty mold, turn brown, and drop. New leaves that open subsequently are unaffected, though the tree may have been weakened by the initial loss of foliage.
■ **Treatment** Remove and destroy infected leaves at once. Traditional copper fungicides are no longer permitted so the best tactic is to cover wall-trained trees with a temporary rainproof sheet

to prevent spores from spreading the disease.

Peach rosette mosaic virus

Plants infected with this virus produce abnormal shoots with shortened internodes (spaces between nodes on the stems). Nematodes spread this virus.
■ **Crops affected** Blueberries, grapes, peaches, occasionally plums.
■ **Symptoms** Plants appear to produce rosettes of leaves instead of their usual plant form. Leaf discoloration sometimes occurs. Infected grape vines are weak; infected fruit trees usually decline and die quickly.
■ **Treatment** There is no treatment for infected plants; remove and destroy them. To prevent future problems, remove weeds and wild plum trees in the area where you want to plant, as these plants may act as asymptomatic hosts of the disease.

Pear scab

■ See **Scab** (p.330).

Plum pocket

A fungal infection that causes fruits to become distorted and hollow, and to drop early. They are inedible.
■ **Crops affected** Plums, gages, bullaces, and damsons.
■ **Symptoms** Young fruitlets become misshapen and elongated, like miniature, empty bananas. They shrivel like prunes, and do not contain stones. White spores may form on them before they eventually drop to the ground.
■ **Treatment** Remove and destroy all affected fruit to

prevent the fungus from overwintering.

Powdery mildew

This mildew is caused by a range of different fungi that thrive in dry soil. The spores spread in the air and via rain or water splashes.
■ **Crops affected** A wide range of fruit, including apples, cherries, plums, peaches, strawberries, raspberries, blackberries, currants, gooseberries, grapes, and melons.
■ **Symptoms** A white powdery coating of mildew appears on leaves—usually on the upper surface but sometimes on the underside as well. It may turn slightly purple. Leaves are yellow and fall off. Fruits such as grapes may split or burst open before rotting. The plant's growth is impaired, and it may even die.
■ **Treatment** Remove and destroy infected leaves. Spray with a fungicide, and try to prevent the onset of the disease by ensuring good air circulation and watering regularly.

Quince leaf blight

This disease is caused by a fungus similar to those responsible for other forms of **fungal leaf spot** (p.329). It is likely to be worse in wet weather.
■ **Crops affected** Quinces.
■ **Symptoms** Leaves develop small red or brown spots, which gradually spread and turn black. Leaves that have died fall early. Infected shoots may die back completely, and fruits may be spotted and misshapen.
■ **Treatment** Prune out affected areas, and clean up and destroy infected leaves and fruit.

Raspberry cane blight

Cane blight is caused by a soil-borne fungal infection that gets into the stems via wounds made by insects, pruning, or frost.
- **Crops affected** Raspberries.
- **Symptoms** Bark splits and peels just above soil level, and canes become brittle and may die.
- **Treatment** Cut down and destroy all infected canes.

Raspberry leaf spot

Cane spot is a fungus that targets many cane fruits. It is not uncommon.
- **Crops affected** Raspberries, blackberries, and hybrid berries.
- **Symptoms** Purple spots or elliptical patches with white centers appear on canes and leaves—also on flowers and sometimes fruit. There may be fewer berries than normal and some may be misshapen. In bad cases, leaves may fall, and canes may split and die. Blackberries and hybrid berries may be affected by this and also by the very similar **blackberry leaf spot** (p.325).
- **Treatment** Cut down and destroy all infected canes.

Raspberry spur blight

Like cane blight, raspberry spur blight is a fungal disease—but a less common and slightly less serious one. Damp weather increases the risk of spreading.
- **Crops affected** Raspberries, hybrid berries.
- **Symptoms** Leaves develop brown blotches and purple patches appear around new buds on new canes. Toward fall, they turn from purple to dark brown, then silvery-gray with visible black spores. Next year's crop will be poor, and new buds and shoots on infected canes may wither and die the following spring.
- **Treatment** Cut down and destroy all infected canes. Thin out any overcrowding.

Raspberry viruses

Many different viruses can attack raspberry canes. Once established, they are extremely difficult to eradicate.
- **Crops affected** Raspberries, blackberries, and hybrid bramble fruits.
- **Symptoms** Yellow-green mottling or mosaic patterns appear on leaves, which may also curl downward at the edges and become smaller than normal. Plants grow and fruit poorly.
- **Treatment** Remove and destroy infected plants. Do not grow cane fruit there again.

Red stele

A fungus that lives in the soil and attacks the roots of strawberries. It tends to be worse on heavy soils prone to waterlogging.
- **Crops affected** Strawberries.
- **Symptoms** Early signs usually become visible in late spring or early summer: stunted growth and discolored foliage—red-orange inner leaves and brown, dry outer ones. Berries are undersized and may ripen earlier than normal. Roots are dark-colored with a red rather than white central core.
- **Treatment** There is no cure. Moreover, the disease is easily spread and can persist in the soil for years. Dig up and destroy diseased plants, and do not replant strawberries on the infected site.

Rust

- See **Cedar-apple rust** (p.326), **Gooseberry rust** (p.328), **Orange rust** (p.329).

Scab

Scabs are fungal growths that can spread rapidly in humid conditions.
- **Crops affected** Apples, cherries, citrus, nectarines, peaches, pears, plums.
- **Symptoms** Dark-brown scabs appear on the skins of fruit and may spread to cover most of the surface. Badly infected apples and pears are small and distorted, and may crack and rot. Plums may split and ooze gum. Leaves and stems may be affected too.
- **Treatment** Cut out infected wood, remove infected fruit, and gather up and destroy fallen leaves. If necessary, spray with an appropriate fungicide. In winter, prune apple and pear trees to increase air circulation.

Shoestring root rot

- See **Honey fungus** (p.328).

Shot-hole disease

A disorder that can affect both leaves and fruit. It is usually the result of a fungal infection called *Cercospora* leaf spot, but can also be a symptom of **bacterial canker** (see p.324) or **bacterial leaf spot** (see p.324).
- **Crops affected** Apricots, cherries, nectarines, peaches, plums.
- **Symptoms** Small, red-brown leaf spots appear on foliage. The centers of the spots decay to leave holes in the leaves. Fruit may be covered with similar spots, which may be corky or slightly sunken, and may ooze gum.

■ **Treatment** If the disease is fungal and you catch it early, it is unlikely to be serious. Remove and destroy infected leaves, stems, and fruit. Otherwise, treat as for bacterial canker.

Silver leaf
This is a serious fungal disease that takes its name from a silvery sheen that develops on affected leaves. The fungus attacks via fresh wounds in the bark and pruning cuts.
■ **Crops affected** Cherries, peaches, nectarines, plums, and less often apples and pears.
■ **Symptoms** Infected leaf tissues have a silvery sheen, and leaves may turn brown at the edges. Sure signs of silver leaf are that infected wood is stained brown inside and that branches and stems die back progressively. Purple, white, or brown fungus may appear through the bark on dead wood.
■ **Treatment** Remove and burn badly infected trees. Otherwise, prune out all affected (stained) wood. In the future, prune only in June, July or August, when the fungus is less likely to attack, and always sterilize tools.

Sooty mold
■ See **Aphids** (p.334).

Stony pit virus
This virus infects pear fruit, making them inedible. It is more likely to affect older trees, but it is contagious and should be dealt with before it spreads.
■ **Crops affected** Pears, primarily in the Pacific Northwest.
■ **Symptoms** Pears become misshapen, pitted, and lumpy, with surface dimples. Inside, they may be hard and woody.
■ **Treatment** There is no cure for the virus. Dig out and burn badly infected trees.

Strawberry virus
Numerous different viruses affect strawberries, including strawberry mottle virus and yellow-edge virus. They are spread by insects, particularly aphids, but also by whiteflies and nematodes.
■ **Crops affected** Strawberries.
■ **Symptoms** Some or all of the following symptoms may be present: stunted growth, leaves distorted, crumpled, or crinkled, yellow edges, yellow spots and blotches, yellow streaks or mosaic patterning.
■ **Treatment** There is no cure. Remove and burn badly infected plants. Renew strawberries regularly. Depending on the variety, grow them afresh each year or for no longer than four years at the most. Rotate the position of crops as you would with vegetables.

Verticillium wilt
A fungus that persists in the soil as well as in dead plant matter and weeds. A *Fusarium* fungus causes a wilt disease with similar symptoms in melons.
■ **Crops affected** Apricots, cherries, melons, nectarines, peaches, plums, strawberries.
■ **Symptoms** Usually in summer, plants wilt, older leaves turn red or brown, and young leaves turn yellow. There may be black streaks on leaf stems. On fruit trees, branches on one side only may wilt and die. When branches are split open, discolored heartwood is seen. In severe cases, plants may die.
■ **Treatment** There is no cure. Remove and burn young infected fruit trees or badly infected strawberry and melon plants. For strawberries, replant new, certified disease-free plants elsewhere—but not on a site where potatoes or tomatoes have been grown previously. With fruit trees, if planting in an area where the disease was present, solarize the soil or grow cover crops for several years before planting.

Virus
■ See **Blueberry virus** (p.326), **Peach rosette mosaic virus** (p.329), **Raspberry viruses** (p.330), **Strawberry virus** (p.331).

Waterberry
This is a disorder that affects grapes, and one that may be caused by poor soil or too much or too little water.
■ **Crops affected** Grapes.
■ **Symptoms** Not all the grapes in a bunch ripen properly. And they take on odd colors: black grapes may be red, and green grapes may be translucent. Stalks shrivel, and grapes wither and taste watery, sour, and unpleasant.
■ **Treatment** Remove affected fruit. Reduce fruiting for a couple of years by removing more flower trusses than usual. Fertilize and water regularly, and if necessary topdress and mulch the soil.

Pests and parasites

All gardeners have a love/hate relationship with insects, birds, and animals. Some are easy to love: for example, bees and other pollinating insects, without which flowers would not be fertilized and fruit would not set. Others are harder to feel affection for: birds that strip buds and ripe fruit, animals that damage the bark of young trees, or grubs and larvae that tunnel into developing fruit, spoiling the crop and rendering it inedible.

(top to bottom) **Hang pheromone traps** in trees, in May for apples, and in June and July for plums. The female pheromone in the traps attracts male moths, which then get stuck to an adhesive sheet inside, preventing them from breeding. With luck, the result of this enforced birth control will be fewer codling moth and oriental fruit moth caterpillars. **Sticky tree bands** prevent female winter moths, who are unable to fly, from climbing tree trunks and laying their eggs during winter. Put them on tree stakes as well, so moths can't cross over via tree ties.

How to deter pests

Birds are a notorious problem. In winter they eat fruit buds, and in summer they eat the fruit itself. They are particularly fond of raspberries, strawberries, and currants, but few types of fruit are entirely safe. Let's be honest: scare devices don't really work, however ingenious they are. Birds get accustomed to them very quickly. The only guaranteed solution is to use nets or build a fruit cage.

Animals—primarily rabbits, deer, and groundhogs—both damage plants and eat the fruit. Only fences provide sure protection, provided they are sufficiently strong and tall, or sunk deep enough underground.

You can combat insect pests in a number of ways. Physical barriers such as sticky tree bands prevent them from invading and laying their eggs, and sticky traps will catch them, hopefully before they are able to mate. Regular inspection may allow you to remove and destroy them by hand. And keeping your yard clean and free of weeds, fallen leaves, and other plant debris offers them fewer places in which to set up home.

Using insecticides

The sale of insecticides to home gardeners is tightly controlled. In recent years, many well known, widely used products have been withdrawn, and more look likely to be banned in the future.

Insecticides are classified as either organic or synthetic. The ingredients of organic insecticides are derived wholly from plant or animal sources, and include fatty acids, insecticidal soaps, dormant sprays made from plant oils, and pyrethrum (which is derived from flowers). Synthetic insecticides are nonorganic; only very few are now permitted for use by home fruit growers.

If you decide to use an insecticide, follow these rules:
■ USE INSECTICIDES only on food crops for which they are explicitly stated to be appropriate, and follow the manufacturer's instructions.
■ WEAR GLOVES and, if necessary, a mask and goggles.
■ DON'T SPRAY when flowers are open or shortly before you harvest.
■ SPRAY EARLY in the morning or late in the evening, when bees and other beneficial insects are less likely to be harmed.
■ DON'T SPRAY when it is windy.

Common fruit pests

1 Birds
Birds will eat most soft fruit unless they are protected by nets. They are partial to tree fruit, too. Once they have punctured the skins, insects will join in as well, and rot soon sets in on anything they leave behind.

2 Aphids
There are hundreds of different species of aphids, most of which target specific crops.

3 Moth caterpillars
Winter moth caterpillars hatch in spring from eggs laid earlier in winter, and immediately start feeding on young shoots and leaves. They can cause severe defoliation. Codling moth and oriental fruit moth caterpillars tunnel into fruit.

4 Grubs and larvae
The larvae of various species of sawflies feed on apples (on which they leave ribbonlike scars), gooseberries, and plums. The cherry and pear slug is a sawfly, too. Other grubs include those of raspberry beetles, leatherjackets, and pear midges.

5 Mites
So small they are often invisible to the naked eye, mites usually live and feed inside buds, leaf tissue, or fruitlets, preventing them from developing properly. Different species infest blackberries (shown here), black currants, pears, strawberries, and grape vines.

6 Spider mites
Greenhouse or hoophouse infestations of spider mites can be very destructive. Foliage becomes discolored and wilts, and may be covered with silk webbing. In hot summers, spider mites colonize outdoor plants, too.

7 Scale insects and mealybugs
These flat, shell-like insects, sometimes covered in sticky white wax, are usually found on plant stems and on the ribs of leaves. They feed on sap and are widespread on plants grown in greenhouses.

8 Wasps
In mid- to late summer, when many fruit crops are ripening, wasps may make holes in soft-skinned fruit and feed on harder-skinned fruit that have already been damaged by birds.

A–Z of pests and parasites

Fruit trees and bushes spend much of their lives under attack from insect, bird, and animal predators, particularly as fruit ripens and become increasingly irresistible. But knowledge is power. If you recognize what you're dealing with, you'll be a lot more effective at combating it. It pays to know as much as possible about the life cycle, feeding habits, and behavior of all potential pests and parasites, from aphids to wireworms.

Aphids

There are hundreds of species of these tiny, sap-sucking insects, which multiply at an incredible rate: when they are just a week old, young aphids are themselves ready to breed.

■ **See Currant aphid** (p.335), **Leaf curl plum aphid** (p.337), **Mealy plum aphid** (p.337), and **Rosy apple aphid** (p.339).

■ **Crops affected** A wide range, many of which are targeted by aphid species specific to particular plant types, such as cherries, plums, currants, and gooseberries.

■ **Damage** A heavy infestation causes leaves to curl and distort, and can stunt growth. The sticky honeydew that aphids excrete fosters black sooty mold.

■ **Treatment** Organic controls include insecticidal soap or neem sprays, and for trees and bushes, a plant-oil-based dormant spray. Ladybugs, lacewings, and other insects can act as natural predators.

Apple leafminer

Small moths lay their eggs underneath young leaves in spring. Tiny caterpillars hatch and feed inside the leaves, leaving long, winding trails that become gradually wider until they exit.

■ **Crops affected** Apples, pears, cherries.

■ **Damage** The tracks are unsightly but the damage is not usually serious.

■ **Treatment** Not normally necessary.

Apple maggot

Small flies make small punctures in skin of young fruits and lay their eggs there. The maggots tunnel through the fruit, which often drop off the tree.

■ **Crops affected** Apples, apricots, blueberries, cherries, pears, plums.

■ **Damage** Unsightly brown tunnels in flesh; damage can lead to rot.

■ **Treatment** Gather up and destroy fallen fruit daily during the summer, then two times a month in the fall. To prevent the flies from laying their eggs, place apple maggot traps (red balls coated with a sticky substance) in trees in early summer to catch the flies. Clean off trapped flies every few days and add new a sticky coating. Cover young fruit with individual nylon, paper, or plastic bags to act as a barrier.

Appletree borers

Flat-headed apple tree borers and round-headed apple tree borers are two of several species of borers that can attack fruit trees. Adults are beetles that feed on foliage and fruit, but the serious damage is done by the larvae, which burrow into the inner bark and heartwood to feed.

■ **Crops affected** Apples, cherries, peaches, pears, plums, quinces.

■ **Damage** Trees become weak, and sawdust is present on trunks near the soil surface. Gummy sap appears on bark.

■ **Treatment** Take good care of trees; healthy trees are resistant to borer injury. Keep areas around tree trunks free of weeds. Secure paper or hardware cloth barriers around the base of trunks in spring, and leave them in place until the beetles cease laying eggs in early fall. Insert a piece of stiff wire into borer holes to kill borers inside.

Birds

A variety of songbirds, as well as crows, jays, and blackbirds, like to feed on fruit.

■ **Crops affected** All stone and soft fruit.

■ **Damage** Birds can strip trees and bushes of young buds, and may eat ripening fruits.
■ **Treatment** Bird-scarers of all kinds are always worth trying, but birds are smart and will soon ignore them. Nets and fruit cages are the only guaranteed solution.

Black cherry aphid
■ See **Aphids** (p.334).

Black currant sawfly
■ See **Imported currantworm** (p.336).

Blueberry maggot
This pest is closely related to the **apple maggot** (see p.334). Adult flies lay eggs under the skin of blueberries. Maggots feed inside the berries.
■ **Crops affected** Blueberries.
■ **Damage** Berries turn mushy and unappealing.
■ **Treatment** Hang red sticky balls in bushes, as for apple maggots. Pick berries frequently and destroy all infested fruit. Avoid planting blueberry bushes near wild blueberry plants.

Borers
■ See **Appletree borers** (p.334), **Peachtree borer** (p.338), **Raspberry cane borer** (p.339), and **Raspberry crown borer** (p.339).

Caterpillars
■ See **Cherry fruitworm** (p.335), **Codling moth** (p.335), **Grape berry moth** (p.336), **Oriental fruit moth** (p.338), **Tortrix moth** (p.341), and **Winter moth** (p.341).

Cherry fruit fly
Two species attack cherries, and they are closely related to apple maggots. The flies lay eggs on young fruit, and the maggots tunnel inside the fruit.
■ **Crops affected** Cherries.
■ **Damage** Fruit appears normal at first, but then the flesh turns brown and the cherries may rot.
■ **Treatment** Hang yellow sticky traps to monitor the presence of cherry fruit flies. Spraying with spinosad, a bioinsecticide, can prevent damage. Or to prevent damage, hang red balls coated with a sticky substance in trees to trap adult flies before they lay eggs. Clean off traps every few days and renew the sticky coating.

Cherry fruitworm
This pest is a caterpillar that feeds on fruit. Adults are moths that lay eggs on the berries in the spring. The caterpillars also produce webbing to provide protection as they feed. Cranberry fruitworm is a closely related pest.
■ **Crops affected** Cherries, blueberries, cranberries.
■ **Damage** Infested cherries and berries sometimes shrivel up, but other times appear normal. The webbing is inconspicuous.
■ **Treatment** Pick cherries and berries often, and destroy infested fruit. Rake up dropped fruit. *Bacillus thuringiensis* var. *kurstaki* can be effective if timed properly.

Cherry slug
■ See **Pear slug** (p.338).

Codling moth
The small female codling moths lay their eggs on fruit in spring

and early summer. On hatching, the larvae tunnel into the fruit, all the way to the core, eating as they go. After about a month, they depart, leaving an exit hole. Similar holes are created by European apple sawfly grubs, though they are likely to attack young fruitlets earlier in the summer.
■ **Crops affected** Apples, apricots, cherries, peaches, pears, plums.
■ **Damage** Fruit are riddled with tunnels and inedible. They may fall early from the tree.
■ **Treatment** In late spring, hang pheromone traps to attract and trap male moths, preventing them from mating (see p.332). Spray trees with kaolin clay just as petals start to fall and reapply as needed. Cover fruitlets with nylon or paper bags. Trap larvae in tree bands and destroy them.

Cranberry fruitworm
■ See **Cherry fruitworm** (p.335).

Currant aphid
The pale yellow aphids hatch in spring and colonize the undersides of leaves, where they feed on the sap. They fly off in summer but return in fall to lay eggs.
■ **Crops affected** Black currants, red currants, white currants.
■ **Damage** Leaves are distorted and puckered, with raised, bubble-like blisters that are unsightly but rarely affect the crop.
■ **Treatment** In midwinter, spraying with a plant-oil-based dormant spray on a mild, dry, still day may prevent eggs from hatching. Otherwise, in spring before symptoms develop, treat

young foliage with an organic insecticide spray such as pyrethrum.

Deer and other animals

In rural and suburban areas, deer, rabbits, and groundhogs can cause much damage. See also **birds** (p.334).

■ **Crops affected** All tree and soft fruit.

■ **Damage** Young shoots are eaten and a ring of bark may be completely stripped from around immature trees. Later in the summer, ripening fruit becomes a target.

■ **Treatment** Tree trunks can be ringed with mesh guards made from metal or tough plastic (see p.38), but ultimately fences are the only real deterrent— electric fencing can be very effective. With conventional fencing, high fence is needed to keep out deer. For rabbits and groundhogs, fencing must extend underground as well as above.

European apple sawfly

White larvae hatch from eggs laid when trees are in blossom and then tunnel into young fruitlets to feed. On exiting, they leave a hole filled with frass (excrement) similar to that left by a codling moth larva. European sawfly larvae tend to attack earlier in the summer than codling moths.

■ **Crops affected** Apples, primarily in the Northeast and on Vancouver Island.

■ **Damage** Young fruitlets fall early. Apples that survive and ripen may have ribbonlike scars on their skins.

■ **Treatment** Destroy all affected fruit. Hang white sticky cards in trees to capture adults. Make a thorough application of kaolin clay as soon as petals start to fall to discourage sawflies from laying eggs on fruitlets.

Foliar nematodes

■ See **Nematodes** (p.337).

Greenhouse whiteflies

■ See **Whiteflies** (p.341).

Grape berry moth

This pest is mainly problematic in the eastern United States and Canada. Moths lay eggs on or near flower clusters, and the larvae feed on flowers as well as the flesh and seeds of developing grapes. Larvae produce webbing in the clusters, or may cut into leaves and roll themselves up inside.

■ **Crops affected** Grapes.

■ **Damage** Infested berries split open and rot, and the rot may spread through the cluster.

■ **Treatment** Hand-pick and destroy damaged berries. Spray *Bacillus thuringiensis* var. *kurstaki* to kill the larvae. In the fall, rake and up destroy or bury fallen leaves.

Grape phylloxera

Phylloxera are small insects, related to aphids, that feed on the sap of vines.

■ **Crops affected** Grapes.

■ **Damage** Visible signs on leaves and roots include rounded, protective galls or swellings that the insects create around themselves. American grapes can tolerate phylloxera attack, but European grapes cannot and usually die.

■ **Treatment** As long as you grow American grapes or European cultivars grafted onto American rootstocks, phylloxera should not require treatment.

Groundhogs

■ See **Deer and other animals** (p.336).

Imported currantworm

The larvae of this pest are the damaging stage. They hatch in spring and summer from small, green eggs laid on the leaves, often deep in the middle of the bush. As the larvae grow, their appetites increase and they quickly eat their way out along the stems, devouring new foliage as they go. They grow up to 3/4 in (20 mm) long and have pale green bodies with black spots and black heads.

■ **Crops affected** Gooseberries, black currants, red currants, white currants.

■ **Damage** Leaves may be stripped clean, leaving no more than a skeleton of ribs and veins. Fruit is not affected, but plant may be badly weakened.

■ **Treatment** From late spring onward, inspect plants regularly and carefully, especially deep in the center of bushes. Pick off and destroy eggs and larvae or spray several times with a strong spray of water. Neem is effective for killing larvae, or for severe infestations, use pyrethrin instead.

Japanese beetle

These beetles are striking in appearance with their metallic green and bronze bodies, but they can cause serious damage by feeding on foliage and fruit.

They are a problem throughout the eastern United States and Canada. The beetles feed during the summer and lay eggs in late summer in the soil. The larvae feed on the roots of lawn grasses and other plants.

■ **Crops affected** Blackberries, grapes, raspberries, strawberries, most types of tree fruit, and a wide range of other plants.

■ **Damage** Leaves are reduced to skeletons, and feeding damage to raspberries, plums, and other fruit creates openings for disease.

■ **Treatment** Hand-pick or shake beetles off plants into a can of soapy water to drown. Cover plants with floating row cover; apply *Heterorhabditis* nematodes to your lawn to kill larvae. As a last resort, spray with neem.

Leaf curl plum aphid

The aphids are small and yellow-green in color. They suck the sap from the plant tissue of new leaves. Eggs are laid in the fall and overwinter on the trees, hatching early in the year. Young aphids feed on buds as they burst and new leaves emerge. In late spring, the adults depart, leaving further growth undamaged.

■ **Crops affected** Plums, gages, bullaces, damsons.

■ **Damage** New, young leaves are tightly curled and distorted. Their growth will be stunted.

■ **Treatment** In midwinter, when trees are dormant, treat with a plant-oil-based dormant spray. Choose a mild, dry, still day. In spring, young foliage can be sprayed with an approved systemic insecticide—but not when the tree is in blossom.

Leafminer
■ See **Apple leaf miner** (p.334).

Lygus bugs
■ See **Plant bugs** (p.334).

Mealybugs

Female mealybugs are small, flat, pale-colored insects that cover themselves and their eggs in a fluffy, sticky, white wax. They feed on sap. Males don't eat—and don't live long either.

■ **Crops affected** Figs, melons, citrus, and other tender fruit when grown in greenhouses or indoors.

■ **Damage** Heavy infestations can weaken plants.

■ **Treatment** Wash plants with a strong spray of water; spray several times with insecticidal soap; release predatory mealybug destroyers (*Cryptolaemus montrouzieri*) in greenhouses.

Mealy plum aphid

These aphids hatch in spring from eggs that overwinter on plum trees. They form colonies on the undersides of leaves, where they secrete a white, mealy wax with which they cover themselves.

■ **Crops affected** Plums, gages, bullaces, damsons.

■ **Damage** Leaves become covered in sticky honeydew, on which gray or black sooty mold tends to grow. Heavy infestations can stunt growth and spoil fruit. However, most of the aphids leave to colonize other plants during June and July, only returning in the fall.

■ **Treatment** In midwinter, when trees are dormant, treat with a plant-oil-based dormant spray. Choose a mild, dry, still day. In spring, young foliage can be sprayed with pyrethrum or insecticidal soap.

Mites
■ See **Pear leaf blister mite** (p.338), **redberry mite** (p.339), **rust mites** (p.340), and **spider mites** (p.340).

Moths
■ See **Cherry fruitworm** (p.335), **Codling moth** (p.335), **Grape berry moth** (p.338), **Oriental fruit moth** (p.338), **Peachtree borer** (p.338), **Tortrix moth** (p.341), and **Winter moth** (p.341).

Nematodes

These are tiny, multicelled organisms, sometimes called eelworms, that use sharp-pointed mouthparts to feed on plant tissue. Nematodes live in the soil or in a film of water on plant surfaces. Both foliar nematodes and root-knot nematodes cause damage to strawberries; root-knot nematodes also feed on fruit tree roots.

■ **Crops affected** Strawberries; tree fruits.

■ **Damage** On strawberry leaves, angular yellow patches that turn brown or black are a symptom of foliar nematodes. Stalks may be unusually short and thick or uncharacteristically long and red in color. Growth is stunted. Plants infested by root-knot nematodes are often stunted with yellow foliage. Galls form on the roots.

■ **Treatment** Spraying strawberries with insecticidal soap may help control foliar nematodes. Clear debris and weeds regularly to reduce the risk of infestation.

Thin out strawberry plants so they will dry quickly. Remove and burn affected plants. There is no cure for infected fruit trees. Choose resistant rootstocks; solarize the soil where possible before planting.

Oriental fruit moth

These gray and brown moths lay eggs in twigs or on the undersides of leaves. The larvae hatch and burrow into the tips of shoots. Later in the growing season, larvae burrow into fruit, too.
■ **Crops affected** Apple, cherry, peach, pear, and other tree fruits in the eastern United States, the Pacific Northwest, and Ontario.
■ **Damage** Shoot tips wilt and turn brown. Infected fruit may look fine on the outside, but rots easily in storage.
■ **Treatment** In early spring, cultivate around trees to destroy larvae that overwintered in the soil. Spray plant-based summer oil to kill eggs and larvae. Apply pheromone patches to trees to disrupt mating.

Peachtree borer

The peachtree borer is the larval stage of a moth that resembles a wasp. In the summer, female moths lay eggs in and around the base of peach trees. When the larvae hatch, they tunnel into the inner bark. Sap appears on the trunk at injury sites.
■ **Crops affected** All stone fruits.
■ **Damage** Infested trees are weakened; young trees can be completely girdled, resulting in death of the tree.
■ **Treatment** Probe with a piece of wire or a knife into holes made by borers to kill them. Cultivate lightly around trees to kill eggs and borers in the soil. Care for trees properly to maintain good health overall.

Pear leaf blister mite

The mites are microscopic insects that live within the tissue of the tree's leaves, releasing a damaging toxin as they feed.
■ **Crops affected** Apples, pears.
■ **Damage** Initially, pink or yellow-green blisters appear on the leaves, on either side of the central rib. They turn darker as the summer progresses. Fruit, especially pears, may be deformed.
■ **Treatment** Pick off and destroy affected leaves.

Pear leaf-curling midge

These tiny grubs hatch from eggs laid by flies on the edges of young leaves and, as they begin feeding, prevent the leaves from opening properly.
■ **Crops affected** Pears.
■ **Damage** Leaves remain tightly curled. They turn red, then black, and die off. Similar symptoms may be caused by the **tortrix moth** (see p.341).
■ **Treatment** Spraying is not normally effective. Pick off infected leaves and destroy them.

Pear psylla

Tiny, cicadalike insects that suck on plant juices; their feeding can transmit plant viruses.
■ **Crops affected** Pears, quinces.
■ **Damage** Infested leaves turn yellow; sooty mold grows on honeydew secreted by the pests. Plants may become infected with virus diseases.
■ **Treatment** In the spring, spray trees thoroughly with kaolin clay and repated as needed all season long; also in spring, spray trees with a plant-based summer oil; or, spray with insecticidal soap.

Pear slug

This pest is not a slug at all, but a sawfly larva. It gets its name from its coating of slimy black mucus. Cherry slug is a very similar pest.
■ **Crops affected** Apricots, cherries, pears, plums.
■ **Damage** The larvae usually feed on the upper surfaces of leaves, eating away the tissue and leaving brown, skeletonlike patches of exposed veins.
■ **Treatment** Sprinkling wood ashes on leaves can kill these pests, but don't overdo it. Spray small trees with a strong spray of water to wash off the slugs. For severe infestations, spray with insecticidal soap, spinosad, or neem.

Plant bugs

These are small flying insects that feed on the sap in leaves, shoot tips, flower buds, and fruit. Their saliva infects and kills plant tissue, and this causes a type of distortion in fruit called "catfacing." Adult females lay eggs in the fall, which hatch in spring, causing maximum damage from late spring into summer. Some species are very small and are hard to spot, so you may not realize that plants are infested until you see damage. Two common types that attack fruit trees and strawberries are lygus bugs and tarnished plant bugs.
■ **Crops affected** Apples, currants, gooseberries, peaches, raspberries, strawberries.

■ **Damage** New leaves and shoots are deformed; established leaves have red-brown spots and small brown-edged holes, and may appear tattered. Fruit can be irregularly shaped.

■ **Treatment** Apply *Beauveria bassiana* to control nymphs. Apply insecticidal soap or pyrethrum if plant bugs are a repeated problem.

Plum curculio
These pests are small hard-shelled beetles with a long snout, found throughout the U.S. and Canada, east of the Rockies. They cut a small flap in the skin of fruit to lay eggs. Larvae feed on fruit flesh.

■ **Crops affected** Plums, apples, apricots, cherries, nectarines, peaches, pears, quinces.

■ **Damage** Feeding can result in cuts in skin of fruit, deformed fruit, damaged flesh that may rot, and fruit that drop early.

■ **Treatment** Twice daily during the growing season, shake trees so that curculios fall out onto a drop-cloth; collect and destroy them. Spray kaolin clay as petals begin to fall and reapply weekly for up to 2 months. For severe problems, spray pyrethrin when damage appears and repeat one week later.

Rabbits
■ See **Deer and other animals** (p.338).

Raspberry cane borer
Adults are small black beetles that lay eggs a few inches below the tips of new canes. The larvae burrow down through the canes, eventually reaching soil level.

■ **Crops affected** Raspberries, blackberries, hybrid bramble fruits.

■ **Damage** At first, the tips of canes wilt. As the borers move downward, whole canes may die back.

■ **Treatment** Look for small punctures a few inches below cane tips, a sign of egg-laying. Prune off canes a few inches below these punctures or below tunnels inside the canes. To prevent future attacks, apply pyrethrin just before plants bloom.

Raspberry crown borer
When these grubs feed on raspberry crowns and roots, it can ruin the plants. They are the larvae of a moth that resembles a yellowjacket.

■ **Crops affected** Raspberries, blackberries, hybrid bramble fruits.

■ **Damage** Leaves wilt and dry out. The base of a plant may be hollowed out.

■ **Treatment** There is no treatment for this pest. Remove infested plants that are in decline. Provide good care for remaining plants, because vigorous plants can withstand some borer damage and still produce a crop.

Raspberry fruitworm
Adult beetles eat foliage and lay their eggs on flowers in summer. On hatching, the pale creamy-brown grubs feed on the ripening berries, burrowing inside.

■ **Crops affected** Raspberries, blackberries, hybrid berries.

■ **Damage** Leaves may have holes, but foliar damage is usually not serious. Berries may be small and have dried, shriveled patches around the stalk. Grubs (fruitworms) are present inside the fruit. Berries may drop early.

■ **Treatment** Cultivate soil around plant in early fall to expose pupae. Try to hand-pick the adult beetles.

Redberry mite
These are microscopically small mites that overwinter on plants, and emerge in the spring to feed on blossoms and young fruitlets. As they do so, they release a chemical that stops the fruit from ripening properly.

■ **Crops affected** Blackberries and hybrid bramble fruits.

■ **Damage** Fruit fail to ripen fully. While some parts of an affected berry turn black as normal, other parts remain red and hard. The problem increases in hot weather and is worse toward the end of the season.

■ **Treatment** Try cutting out and burning affected canes in an attempt to prevent the mites from overwintering and thus break their life cycle. Sprays of plant-based summer oils applied after green fruit or first pink fruit stage can be effective, but timing is important. Oils may cause foliar damage.

Root-knot nematodes
■ See **Nematodes** (p.337).

Rosy apple aphid
This aphid introduce from Europe more than 100 years ago has become a major pest in all apple-growing areas.

■ **Crops affected** Apples.

■ **Damage** Leaves are curled and distorted, sometimes turning yellow or red. Fruit may be small and misshapen. Growth of sooty

mold in honeydew secreted by the aphids can blemish the fruit.
■ **Treatment** Organic controls include pyrethrum, insecticidal soap sprays, and natural predators such as ladybugs.

Rust mites
These pests can damage the appearance of apples and pears, but since these mites are a good food source for predatory mites, it may be best to tolerate some damage.
■ **Crops affected** Apples, pears.
■ **Damage** Leaves develop a silvery or russeted sheen. Leaves may curl and turn brown. Fruit also looks russeted or bronzed.
■ **Treatment** If an infestation is severe, apply sulfur. Otherwise, no treatment is needed for these mites.

San Jose scale
See **Scale insects** (p.340).

Sawfly
■ See **European apple sawfly** (p.334), **Imported currantworm** (p.336), and **Pear slug** (p.338).

Scale insects
All scale insects have distinctive, shell-like coverings. Some secrete a white, waxy substance. Scale insects colonize trunks and branches of trees and stems of bushes. Of the numerous types of scale insects, those most often affecting fruit are San Jose scale, black scale, and cottony cushion scale.
■ **Crops affected** Tree fruit, citrus, vines, and soft fruit bushes, both outdoors and in greenhouses.

■ **Damage** The white, fluffy, waxy secretion and sticky honeydew that some scales produce can host gray sooty molds. Feeding by armored scales such as San Jose scale can cause yellowing of foliage and even result in death of entire tree limbs. Feeding on apples can cause red spots on fruit.
■ **Treatment** In midwinter, when outdoor, deciduous plants are dormant, treat with a plant-oil-based dormant spray. During the growing season, summer oil sprays may be effective, but not when adult scales are protected by waxy coatings. Prune off and destroy infested branches. Keep in mind that many predatory insects help to control scales as long as no sprays are used. Do not spray scales unless an infestation is severe.

Slugs and snails
The telltale trail of slime and the sight of decimated, spoiled plants are the bane of the gardener's life.
■ **Crops affected** Strawberries are particularly at risk, but sometimes black currants, raspberries, hybrid bramble fruits, and melons may be attacked too.
■ **Damage** Slugs may start feeding on tender new shoots of strawberry plants, though they will reserve their biggest onslaught for the ripe fruit.
■ **Treatment** Employ baits (overturned grapefruit halves, beer traps) and barriers (sharp gravel, crushed eggshells, copper bands). Keep down weeds to minimize hiding places. Apply iron phosphate baits around plants and renew as needed.

Spider mites
Spider mites can be a problem in both outdoor and greenhouse plantings. The mites live and lay eggs on the undersides of leaves, and feed on sap. They have eight legs, like true spiders, and are tiny—less than $1/25$ in (1 mm) long.
■ **Crops affected** A wide range of tree fruits and soft fruits.
■ **Damage** Leaves become dull and mottled, turn silvery-bronze or yellow-white, and may wilt, turn brittle, and fall. Plants may eventually be covered with fine, white silk webbing.
■ **Treatment** Indoors, spray with water regularly to increase humidity. Release purchased predatory mites as a biological control. If necessary, spray with insecticidal soap or neem. Outdoors, spray trees with a plant-oil-based dormant spray in early spring before buds swell.

Strawberry root weevil
Adult weevils are black beetles up to $1/4$ in (6 mm) long. They don't fly but are agile climbers. They usually hide during the day, and come out to feed on foliage only at night. More destructive are their white, brown-headed grubs, which feed on plant roots.
■ **Crops affected** Strawberries, grapes, raspberries, apples, peaches.
■ **Damage** Leaf edges are notched where adults have fed on them. Larvae feed on roots and crowns of plants.
■ **Treatment** Cover plants with floating row cover to keep adults away. Search out, pick off, and destroy adult weevils—at night, by flashlight, if necessary. As a

biological control, try introducing *Steinernema* nematodes to control larvae in soil.

Tarnished plant bug
■ See **Plant bugs** (p.338).

Thrips
These are small, slender insects that eat into the surfaces of leaves and feed on the sap. They can damage flower petals, too.
■ **Crops affected** Citrus fruit, as well as a wide variety of other plants, indoors and outdoors.
■ **Damage** Leaves may display yellow streaks or silvery patches, and tiny specks of black excrement may be visible.
■ **Treatment** Trees can withstand a fair amount of foliar damage without loss of fruit quality, so don't be too quick to spray. If necessary, spray citrus with spinosad to control thrips.

Tortrix moth
There are several species of these moths, which are native to Europe. The fruit tree tortrix moth spins silk in order to curl young leaves around itself.
■ **Crops affected** Apples, black currants, cherries, pears, plums, raspberries, strawberries.
■ **Damage** Leaves are stunted and growing shoots are sometimes damaged. Fruit may be spoiled.
■ **Treatment** Remove affected leaves by hand. If necessary, spray with an approved insecticide before leaves become curled.

Wasps
Wasps tend to be a pest only in mid- to late summer. Earlier in the year, young wasps are likely to act as beneficial predators, feeding on caterpillars and other grubs.
■ **Crops affected** Most ripe fruit crops.
■ **Damage** Wasps create holes in fruit as they feed on the flesh.
■ **Treatment** Don't interfere with wasps if you can avoid it. Nests should be dealt with by professionals. The best deterrent is perhaps to set up a bait of sweet, rotting fruit or a pot of jam or sugary liquid to lure them away from your most valued crops.

Whiteflies
Greenhouse whiteflies are tiny, mothlike flies with wedge-shaped, white wings that colonize the undersides of leaves, where they also lay their eggs. In some areas on the West Coast and in Florida and the Gulf Coast, whiteflies can also be an outdoor pest.
■ **Crops affected** Most types of fruit grown in greenhouses; outdoor citrus.
■ **Damage** The young suck sap from leaves, causing them to turn yellow and stunting plant growth. They secrete honeydew, which fosters black sooty mold.
■ **Treatment** If necessary, spray with insecticidal soap or pyrethrum. In greenhouses, use yellow sticky traps or release the parasitic wasp *Encarsia formosa*.

Winter moth
This is a pest native to Europe that has become a problem in British Columbia and some areas of New England and eastern Canada. Voracious caterpillars do the damage. They hatch early in spring from eggs laid by the moths on branches the previous fall. The caterpillars begin feeding on new leaves, flowers, and young fruitlets. Unchecked, they are capable of stripping leaves. The caterpillars are pale green with yellow stripes, and can grow to 1 in (2.5 cm).
■ **Crops affected** Apples, blueberries, cherries, pears, plums.
■ **Damage** Leaves may be stripped clean, leaving no more than a skeleton of ribs and veins. Severe attacks may produce malformed fruit and seriously weaken the tree.
■ **Treatment** During the winter, apply a plant-oil-based dormant spray to smother overwintering eggs. In spring, inspect small trees carefully and remove caterpillars by hand. Kill young caterpillars by applying *Bacillus thuringiensis* var. *kurstaki* or spinosad.

Wireworms
These are the soil-dwelling larvae of click beetles. The worms are orange-brown and up to 1 in (2.5 cm) long.
■ **Crops affected** Raspberries, strawberries.
■ **Damage** The stems of young plants may be severed, and roots may be eaten into.
■ **Treatment** Search the soil around damaged crops and destroy any wireworms you find. Apply *Heterorhabditis* nematodes to wireworm-infested soil.

Index

Page numbers in *italics* indicate an illustration. Page numbers in **bold** refer to a main section or entry.

Acknowledgments

Author's acknowledgments

Thanks to the following: Anna Kruger and Alison Gardner, who have brought their customary skill, professionalism, and patience to the production of what's now our third book together; Jo Whittingham for her eagle eye and valuable suggestions; Alison Donovan, Helen Fewster, Esther Ripley, and the team at Dorling Kindersley; Barbara Wood, my plot neighbor at The Royal Paddocks Allotments, Hampton Wick, who has been as helpful, wise, and generous as ever; a host of friends who have allowed the unforgiving eye of my camera lens free rein of their gardens and orchards— Charles and Annabel Rathbone, Mic and Julia Cady, Fiona MacIntyre and Nigel Waters, Christopher and Linda Davis, and Janice and Nick Maris; the staff at RHS Wisley, RHS Rosemoor, and the National Fruit Collection at Brogdale Farm in Kent; members of the RHS Fruit Group; and finally Jim Buckland and Sarah Wain of West Dean Gardens in Sussex, who have restored and run one of the most beautiful kitchen gardens in the country. If you've never visited, do so at once. It's an inspiration. www.westdean.org.uk

Index Michèle Clark

Picture credits

Dorling Kindersley would like to thank **Alan Buckingham** for new photography:

(Key: a-above; b-below/bottom; c-center; f-far; l-left; r-right; t-top)

1, 4tl, 4tr, 5tl, 5tc, 8br, 9, 13cl, 13c, 13cr, 13bc, 13br, 15cl, 15cr, 15bl, 15bc, 15br, 16tl, 16tr, 21cr, 24bl, 24bc, 25tl, 25bc, 25br, 27tl, 27tr, 27bc, 27br, 30bl, 32tl, 32tr, 34bc, 35, 36t, 36c, 36b, 37t, 37c, 37bl, 37bcl, 37bcr, 37br, 38tl, 38tcl, 38tc, 38tcr, 38tr, 39bl, 39bc, 39br, 40, 42tl, 42cl, 42tr, 42b, 43t, 43ctl, 43bl, 43br, 43cr, 44t, 44bl, 45t, 45ctl, 45ctr, 45cbl, 45cbr, 46tr, 46b, 47t, 47c, 47b, 48t, 48ctl, 48cbr, 48br, 49tl, 49tr, 49c, 49b, 50, 51t, 54tr, 54cr, 54cl, 54bl, 54bc, 54br, 55l, 55c, 55r, 61t, 63c, 64l, 64c, 64r, 65l, 65c, 65r, 66, 67bl, 67br, 68, 69tl, 69tc, 69tr, 69br, 70, 71bl, 72t, 74/5, 75tr, 76tc, 76tr, 76bc, 76br, 77tl, 77bl, 77bc, 77r, 78tl, 78tcl, 78tcr, 78bl, 78br, 79tr, 80, 82tl, 82cl, 82b, 83t, 83bl, 83br, 84t, 84cr, 84bl, 84br, 85t, 85b, 87br, 88tl, 88ccl, 88cr, 89, 90/1, 92t, 93t, 93b, 95, 96br, 97b, 98, 99ct, 99b, 100tl, 100tc, 100bl, 100bc, 100br, 101tc, 101bc, 101br, 102, 104tl, 104cl, 104cr, 104b, 105cr, 106cl, 106bl, 106br, 107t, 107ct, 107cb, 107b, 108, 109tr, 109cl, 109clc, 109bcr, 109bl, 109bcl, 110, 113tl, 113tc, 113tr, 115cr, 115br, 116bl, 116br, 118tc, 118bc, 118br, 119tl, 119bl, 119bc, 120, 122tl, 122tr, 122b, 123t, 123c, 123br, 125cl, 125c, 125cr, 129bl, 130tl, 130tcl, 130tcr, 130tr, 131cl, 131cr, 133tr, 134bl, 134bcl, 134bcr, 134br, 135tl, 135bl, 135br, 138tr, 138b, 139, 141t, 141c, 141b, 143tl, 143tr, 143c, 143b, 146b, 147t, 149tr, 151t, 151ct, 157t, 157ctl, 157ctr, 157cb, 158l, 158r, 159, 160bl, 160bc, 160br, 161, 162l, 162r, 164t, 164b, 166, 168tc, 170r, 172br, 173tl, 173tc, 173tr, 175tl, 175tr, 177tl, 177bl, 177tr, 177bcr, 179, 181tr, 181br, 182, 184t, 184bl, 185ct, 186tr, 188, 189br, 192tl, 193tl, 193tc, 194br, 195bl, 195br, 196, 198ctr, 198bl, 199bl, 200, 201bl, 201bc, 201br, 202t, 203tl, 203tcl, 203tcr, 204, 205r, 206ctl, 207c, 207cb, 207b, 208, 210cl, 210bl, 210br, 211tr, 211b, 212, 214br, 215tr, 215ct, 215cb, 215b, 216cr, 217tl, 217tc, 217bl, 217bc, 217r, 218, 220cl, 220b, 223tl, 224bl, 225tl, 225tc, 225br, 227cl, 227br, 228bl, 228tr, 228bc, 228br, 229bl, 229bc, 230, 232tl, 232ctl, 232cbr, 232br, 234tl, 234tc, 234tr, 235tl, 235bl, 236tr, 237tl, 237tc, 237bc, 237br, 240tl, 242bl, 242bc, 243tl, 243tc, 243tr, 243br, 245t, 245ct, 245cbl, 245cbr, 245b, 248cl, 248cr, 248bl, 249tl, 249tr, 249ct, 250, 254tl, 254tc, 254tr, 257tc, 257tr, 258, 260tl, 260tr, 265, 266br, 267c, 267b, 268, 274tl, 274tc, 277bl, 280tl, 280tc, 280bl, 280bc, 280br, 281br, 283, 284, 286tr, 286bl, 287t, 287cl, 293br, 293bl, 294, 297tl, 297tr, 297bl, 297br, 298tl, 298cl, 298cr, 298bl, 298br, 303tr, 303br, 304, 305, 306bl, 306br, 307tl, 307tr, 307br, 308bc, 309br, 310br, 315, 317bl, 320br, 321bl, 323tl, 323tr, 323ctl, 323ctr, 323cbl, 323cbr, 323br, 333tl, 333tr, 333ctl, 333cbl, 333cbr, 333br

Alan Buckingham © **Dorling Kindersley**

5tr, 8bl, 13tl, 13tr, 15c, 27bl, 43cbl, 44br, 45b, 46c, 48ctr, 48bl, 53tr, 54tl, 54c, 78bc, 79tc, 79bl, 79bc, 79br, 82tr, , 83c, 88ccr, 93ct, 93cb, 101bl, 105t, 105br, 109crc, 118bl, 119br, 124, 128, 134tl, 172bl, 173br, 184cl, 184br, 193tr, 198br, 203tr, 207t, 207ct, 210cr, 211c, 220t, 224tr, 225tr, 229br, 232tr, 232bl, 240bl, 320bl, 321br, 323bl, 332tl, 333ctr,

Dorling Kindersley would like to thank **Peter Anderson** for new photography:

2/3, 6/7, 11, 13bl, 15tl, 15tr, 17bl, 18, 20, 21t, 21b, 25tr, 25bl, 26c, 26bc, 26br, 39tl, 39tc, 39tr, 44cl, 61bl, 62, 72bl, 73, 78cr, 87tl, 92bl, 92r, 96t, 96bl, 97tc, 97tr, 105cbl, 106t, 111, 112tl, 112tc, 116tc, 116tr, 117br, 126, 132, 133c, 133ca, 132t, 132cb, 133b, 144, 146car, 147cb, 150, 151cb, 151b, 152, 154, 157b, 170l, 176, 180, 185bc, 198cl, 199t, 211tl, 220cra, 221bl, 223tr, 235bcr, 235br, 238, 240ca, 240tr, 240br, 246, 248t, 249bl, 255, 272, 273bl, 275, 299, 300bl, 300br.

The publisher would like to thank the following for their kind permission to reproduce their photographs:

4 **Blackmoor Nurseries**: (tc). 13 **Blackmoor Nurseries**: (tc). 15 **Corbis**: Ed Young/AgStock Images (tc). 17 **The Garden Collection**: Torie Chugg/Sue Hitchens, RHS Hampton Court 05. 19 **Alamy Images**: Wildscape/Jason Smalley. 22 **Dorling Kindersley**: Alison Gardner (bl). 23 **Dorling Kindersley**: Alison Gardner (t). **The Garden Collection**: Liz Eddison/Prieure Notre-Dame d'Orsan, France (bl). 29 **Photolibrary**: Mayer/Le Scanff/Garden Picture Library. 46 **R.V. Roger Ltd.**: (tc). 53 **Blackmoor Nurseries**: (bl). 56 **Dorling Kindersley**: Alison Gardner. 71 **Photolibrary**: Claire Higgins/Garden Picture Library (br). 77 **Dorling Kindersley**: Alison Gardner (cb). 91 **Sarah Wain, West Dean Gardens**: (tl) (tc) (tr). 101 **FLPA**: Nigel Cattlin (clb). 112 **Reads Nursery**: (br). 122 **Garden World Images**: Trevor Sims (cr). 123 **Victoriana Nursery Gardens**: Stephen Shirley (bl). 136 **Getty Images**: Inga Spence. 138 **Blackmoor Nurseries**: (ca) (cb). Ron Ludekens: (cr). 146 **Blackmoor Nurseries**: (tr). **GAP Photos**: (ca). 147 **Photolibrary**: Paroli Galperti/Cuboimages (cla). 155 **Sarah Wain, West Dean Gardens**. 168 **Alamy Images**: John Glover (tr). **Photoshot**: Michael Warren (tl). **Ron Ludekens**: (c). **Science Photo Library**: (cr). 169 **Photolibrary**: Martin Page/Garden Picture Library (br). 177 **Dorling Kindersley**: Alison Gardner (cl). 184 **Photoshot**: Photos Horticultural (cr). 185 **GAP Photos**: (clb). **Photoshot**: Michael Warren (tl). 191 **Dorling Kindersley**: Alison Gardner (tl). 194 **FLPA**: Nigel Cattlin (bl). 198 **Alamy Images**: Greg Wright (crb). **Photoshot**: Photos Horticultural/Michael Warren (tr). 199 **Photoshot**: Photos Horticultural/Michael Warren (cla). **Scottish Crop Research Institute**: (clb). 210 **Photoshot**: Flowerphotos/Jonathan Buckley (tr). 221 **GAP Photos**: Dave Bevan (tl); J S Sira (bc). **R.V. Roger Ltd.**: (cl) (cb). 240 **Blackmoor Nurseries**: (crb). 242 **Corbis**: Image Source (br). 248 **Tadeusz Kusibab**: (br). 249 **Tadeusz Kusibab**: (cb). **Thompson & Morgan**: (bc). 252 **Dorling Kindersley**: Alison Gardner. 253 **Garden World Images**: John Swithinbank (r). 257 **Dorling Kindersley**: Alison Gardner (cla) (tl). 259 **R.V. Roger Ltd.**: (cr) (br). 261 **Garden World Images**: Trevor Sims. 262 **Corbis**: Mark Bolton (c). **Photolibrary**: Garden Picture Library/Michel Viard (br). **Thompson & Morgan**: (tr). 263 **Alamy Images**: John Glover (cl). Corbis: Gallo Images/Martin Harvey (bl); Tania Midgley (tl). **Photoshot**: JTB (c). 266 **Alamy Images**: Hendrik Holler/Bon Appetit (tr). **Corbis**: Ed Young/AgStock Images (bc) (cr). **GAP Photos**: Richard Bloom (tc). **Garden World Images**: Trevor Sims (c). 267 **Blackmoor Nurseries**: (tl). 281 **Dorling Kindersley**: Alison Gardner (clb). 286 **Corbis**: Ed Young/AgStock Images (br). **The Garden Collection**: Derek Harris (ca). **Photolibrary**: Garden Picture Library/David Cavagnaro (tc). 287 **Corbis**: AgStock Images (bl); Bill Barksdale/AgStock Images (cb). 288 **Photolibrary**: Garden Picture Library/Friedrich Strauss. 290 **Photolibrary**: Garden Picture Library/Michele Lamontagne. 293 **Dorling Kindersley**: Alison Gardner (cl). 296 **Corbis**: Bill Barksdale/AgStock Images (tc). 302 **Corbis**: AgStock Images (t). **Getty Images**: Visuals Unlimited/Inga Spence (crb). 308 **Corbis**: Bill Ross/Surf (bl). **Garden World Images**: Liz Cole (br). 309 **Corbis**: Douglas Peebles/Encyclopedia (bl). 310 **Corbis**: Melinda Holden/Comet (bc); Douglas Peebles/Encyclopedia (bl). 311 **Corbis**: Jose Fuste Raga/Encyclopedia (br); David Samuel Robbins/Documentary (bc). **Garden World Images**: Trevor Sims (bl). 312 **Garden World Images**: Flora Toskana (bl). 313 **Corbis**: Stefano Amantini/Atlantide Phototravel/Latitude (bl); DK Limited/Encyclopedia (bc); Michelle Garrett/Documentary Value (br). 316 **Garden World Images**: (bl). 333 **Dorling Kindersley**: Alison Gardner (bc)

Jacket images: Front and spine: **Photolibrary**: Foodfolio. Back: **Dorling Kindersley**: Peter Anderson tr; **GAP Photos**: Pernilla Bergdahl cr; Geoff Kidd bl; Zara Napier fcr; S&O fcl; Friedrich Strauss cl.

All other images © Dorling Kindersley For further information, see www.dkimages.com

Fruit nurseries and suppliers

Adams County Nursery
Fruit trees
26 Nursery Road
PO Box 108
Aspers, PA 17304
Phone: (717) 677-8105
www.acnursery.com

Almost Eden Plants
Tropical and unusual fruits
1240 Smith Road
Merryville, LA 70653
Phone: (337) 375-2114
www.almostedenplants.com

Big Horse Creek Farm
Heirloom apple trees
PO Box 70
Lansing, NC 28643
www.bighorsecreekfarm.com

Burnt Ridge Nursery & Orchards
Fruit trees, vines, and bushes
432 Burnt Ridge Road
Onalaska, WA 98570
Phone: (360) 985-2873
www.burntridgenursery.com

Cummins Nursery
Fruit trees
1408 Trumansburg Road
Ithaca, NY 14456
Phone: (607) 227-6147
www.cumminsnursery.com

Edible Landscaping Online
Fruit trees, vines, and bushes
361 Spirit Ridge Lane
Afton, VA 22920
Phone: (434) 361-9134
http://ediblelandscaping.com

Fedco Trees
Fruit trees and berries
PO Box 520
Waterville, ME 04903
(207) 426-9900
www.fedcoseeds.com/trees.htm

Forestfarm
Fruit trees and plants
990 Tetherow Road
Williams, OR 97544
Phone: (541) 846-7269
www.forestfarm.com

Hidden Springs Nursery
Organically grown fruit trees
170 Hidden Springs Lane
Cookeville, TN 38501
Phone: (931) 268-2592
www.hiddenspringsnursery.com

Logee's Greenhouses
Tropical fruit trees and vines
141 North Street
Danielson, CT 06239
Phone: (888) 330-8038
www.logees.com

Miller Nurseries
Fruit trees and vines
P.O. Box 1800
Louisiana, MO 63353
Phone: (800) 325-4180
http://www.starkbros.com/

Nourse Farms
Berry bushes
41 River Road
South Deerfield, MA 01373
Phone: (413) 665-2658
www.noursefarms.com

Pense Nursery
Berries and grapevines
2318 Highway 71 NE
Mountainburg, AR 72946
Phone: (479) 369-2494
www.alcasoft.com/pense

Raintree Nursery
Fruit trees and unusual fruits
391 Butts Road
Morton, WA 98356
Phone: (360) 496-6400
www.raintreenursery.com

The Strawberry Store
Alpine and heirloom strawberries
107 Wellington Way
Middletown, DE 19709
Phone: (302) 250-3195
www.thestrawberrystore.com

Trees of Antiquity
Heirloom fruit trees
20 Wellsona Road
Paso Robles, CA 93446
Phone: (805) 467-9909
www.treesofantiquity.com

Whitman Farms
Berry bushes
3995 Gibson Road NW
Salem, OR 97304
Phone: (503) 585-8728
www.whitmanfarms.com

Wyntour Gardens
Fruit for northern gardens
8026 Airport Road
Redding, CA 96002
Phone: (530) 365-2256
http://www.wyntourgardens.com/